HOW TO
MAKE YOUR OWN
WEDDING GOWN

Also by Claudia Ein

HOW TO DESIGN YOUR OWN CLOTHES
AND MAKE YOUR OWN PATTERNS

CLAUDIA EIN

How to
Make Your Own
Wedding Gown

Illustrations by the Author
Technical Illustrations by Susan Frye
Photography by Conrad Ein

1978
DOUBLEDAY & COMPANY, INC. · GARDEN CITY, NEW YORK

Library of Congress Cataloging in Publication Data

Ein, Claudia, 1943–
How to make your own wedding gown.

Includes index.
1. Dressmaking.   2. Wedding costume.   I. Title.
TT560.E36   646.4'7
ISBN 0-385-11105-3
Library of Congress Catalog Card Number 77–74299

To my father

ACKNOWLEDGMENTS

I would like to thank the following firms for their assistance: Swiss Bernina, Inc.; Artvale, Inc.; Scovill-Dritz, Evelyn Forsythe Creations, Inc.; Emil Katz and Co., Inc.; Roth Import Co.; Stern & Stern Textiles, Inc.; June Tailor, Inc.; J. Wiss & Sons Co.

Fabric Conversion Chart courtesy of Cooperative Extension Service, Rutgers University, The State University of New Jersey.

CONTENTS

4
MAKING AND FITTING YOUR GOWN IN MUSLIN

5
SEWING SPECIAL FABRICS

6
LACE

7
TRIMMINGS

8
DESIGNER FINISHING TECHNIQUES

9
BRIDAL HEADWEAR

10
SEWING THE ATTENDANTS' OUTFITS AND BRIDAL ACCESSORIES

INTRODUCTION

Have you ever dreamed of making your own wedding gown but felt discouraged because you thought it was too complicated? Well, take heart—it is not as difficult as you might think. If you enjoy sewing and know how to sew well enough to set in a sleeve, then you should be able to make your own wedding gown. All you need besides that is time to do a nice job and a little patience.

By making your own gown, you will have a dress like no one else's, one that you created yourself and will be proud to wear on your special day. And you can save a lot of money. By far the largest part of the cost of a ready-made wedding dress is labor. Since you can provide your own loving labor, you can make a dress equivalent to one costing well over $500 for less than $100.

I am a professional designer. In this book I will tell you all about bridal fabrics and how to handle them, and about the professional way of using laces and trimmings (known only to designers). You will learn how to pick a style that is right for your figure and type of wedding, how to design your own gown, how to make your own headpiece and veil, and much more. There are step-by-step directions for cutting, fitting, and sewing your gown. Following the method used by professional designers, the gown is first made in muslin, and all the adjustments and fittings are done on the muslin before the gown is cut in fabric. Then the muslin is taken apart and used as the pattern for the gown. With the confidence of having a perfectly fitted pattern, you can enjoy making your gown and not worry that it may not turn out well.

If you are wondering where you can get the right fabrics and trimmings, more and more fabric stores are opening bridal boutiques, selling exactly the same laces and fabrics used by wedding gown designers. There are also bridal fabrics available by mail. At the back of this book is a Shopping Guide that tells you where to write for catalogues or to find out where bridal fabrics are available at a store near you.

I hope that your wedding is beautiful.

Claudia Ein

HOW TO
MAKE YOUR OWN
WEDDING GOWN

1

Making Your Own Wedding Gown

USING THE DESIGNER METHOD

By following the system used by designers in the garment industry you will be able to make your own wedding gown, which will look as professional as those you see in bridal salons and brides' magazines. With this method you can make a very formal beaded lace gown that would cost hundreds or even thousands of dollars to buy ready-made, or you can make any of the simpler, less formal styles. The secret of most wedding gowns is the way the lace is used. Working with lace the designer's way is not difficult but is almost unknown to home sewers. The methods and techniques are explained in detail in Chapter 6. All you have to do is be willing to spend some time. Making a wedding gown should be thought of as an exciting and enjoyable project that will be worked on over a period of time. It is not a "make it tonight, wear it tomorrow" proposition.

Besides learning how to use lace, the other important part of making your gown is making a test model first in muslin. This is the only way to achieve a professional result. It gives you the chance to make changes and alterations before they become costly mistakes. A professional designer works this way, refining the muslin dress until the fit and style are perfect. Only then is the gown cut in expensive fabric. No trimmings or finishing details are used in the muslin, just the basic pattern pieces. Step-by-step instructions for making and fitting your gown in muslin are given in Chapter 4. Once your muslin is correct, it is taken apart and used as the pattern to cut your gown. The muslin dress is like a rehearsal. Just as you wouldn't have your wedding ceremony without a rehearsal, you shouldn't make your gown without one, either.

By making your own gown you can save a tremendous amount of money. To give you an idea of how much you can save, here is the cost breakdown of a hypothetical factory-made wedding gown costing $900, shown in *Figure 1*. Be aware that the figures given here are the wholesale costs that the manufacturer would pay for fabrics and trimmings. You would have to pay retail price, which would be about twice as much. But even if you paid $150 for your materials, you would still be saving 83 per cent of the cost of a $900 ready-made gown.

French Alençon Lace
    36" Galloon for bodice, sleeves, and appliqués
        1⅞ yards @ $20.00 a yard   37.50
    14" Galloon for skirt hem (cut apart)
        2 yards @ $9.75 a yard   19.50
    2" Scallop edge for neck and waistline
        1¼ yards @ $1.75 a yard   2.18

Fabrics
    Imported silk-blend organza for skirt and train, 45" width
        6 yards @ $1.65 a yard   9.90
    Taffeta for skirt lining, 45" width
        3⅜ yards @ $1.40 a yard   4.69
    Tulle for lining and underskirt, 108" width
        3 yards @ $.55 a yard   1.65

Trimmings
    Crystal beads in bulk   .55
    Pearls in bulk   .75

Notions
    Zipper   .28
    Thread   .08
    Horsehair braid   .20
    Button loops   .40
    Covered buttons   .85

                                            TOTAL $78.53

Astonishing, right? Somebody is getting very rich? Wrong! If the materials for a $900 dress cost $78.53, then where did all that other money go? In the cost of the dress, the manufacturer has to figure his expenses, which include labor and salaries, fringe benefits, rent, insurance, utilities, taxes, and advertising, as well as profit.

FIGURE 1

The manufacturer sells the $900 dress to the retailer for about $450. In the retailer's price of $900 he must include his own expenses, which again include salaries, fringe benefits, taxes, advertising, and so on, plus services such as delivery, credit cards, and a luxuriously outfitted bridal salon, in addition to his profit. By making your own gown you are paying only for your materials, not for labor and overhead, which are by far the greatest part of the cost of a purchased gown.

You may long for a beautiful, expensive-looking gown but feel that such a dress is far too complicated to make. In fact, most wedding gowns are not difficult to make. There are admittedly quite a few more steps in making a gown than in making a regular dress, but the steps themselves are not usually complicated. The $900 gown is actually just a fancy version of a basic Empire dress. If you are an average sewer you already know most of the steps involved. Working with lace and applying beads and pearls are probably the only techniques you haven't used before. You can make a plain gathered skirt and a plain A-line skirt, right? For the dress in *Figure 1* you would make a gathered skirt of organza, a gathered underskirt of tulle (for body and fullness), and an A-line lining skirt of taffeta (for shape and opacity). Each skirt is simple in itself. Each is made separately, and then all three are attached at the waistline before being joined to the bodice. Wedding gowns do not require the type of sewing that most people consider most difficult, such as intricate seaming or shaping, welt pockets, shirt plackets, and so on. Because the trimmings of a wedding gown are what make the dress, the simplest pattern styles are usually the best. Many dresses that at first look hopelessly complicated are actually simple silhouettes lavishly embellished with lace and other trimmings. Lace is very forgiving—because of the texture, most small mistakes won't even show. Once you become familiar with the professional ways of using lace and trimmings, you will be able to look at a gown, figure out how the special effects were created, and duplicate them yourself, or create your own.

SELECTING YOUR GOWN PATTERN

If you haven't already done so, you should first decide what type of a wedding you want: very formal, formal, semiformal, or informal. The formality of the wedding will to a large extent influence the style of your gown and your choice of fabrics and trimmings. Read about wedding types in Chapter 2.

To get some idea of the style you would like, first look through the bridal magazines, *Bride's* and *Modern Bride*. Tear out pages that show any ideas that you like such as silhouettes, necklines, laces, and use of trimmings, and keep them together in a folder. You should also go to a bridal shop or department and try on some gowns to see what silhouettes and fabrics look well on you and to look at the way the dresses are made. (Don't worry about high-pressure salesladies who might try to talk you into buying a dress. Just say that you need time to think about it, or that you have to come back and look some more with your mother or brides-maids.) Try to look at the pattern catalogues from the four major pattern com-panies before you make your final decision. You are not restricted only to the wed-ding gown section of the pattern book—another long dress may be just the style you want. Look for the basic silhouette that you have in mind, such as an Empire with a gathered skirt, A-line, natural waist with a full skirt, or whatever. A train can be added to the pattern if necessary. If you can't find a pattern for just the style you want, you can arrive at a new style by combining parts from different pat-terns, and by making changes and redesigning the pattern. Don't let this scare you. Because you will be making your gown first in muslin, you will be able to test any changes to be sure that everything is correct. A description of gown styles with rec-ommendations for different figure types is found in Chapter 2. Information on cre-ating your own gown style is found in Chapter 3.

Once you select your pattern, be sure that you buy the right size. As obvious as this seems, many people spend needless time on fitting and alterations because they have not bought the correct size pattern to start with. Body measurements and figure type should be considered. Junior-size patterns are designed for a shorter figure that has a smaller bust and hip measurement in proportion to the waist. Misses-size patterns are designed for someone a little taller and with a more devel-oped figure. Many young women continue to buy Junior sizes out of habit, even though their figures have become more suited to the measurements of a Misses pattern. The pattern size charts give actual body measurements. When you take your measurements, you should wear the kind of underwear or foundations that you normally wear. Pull the tape measure fairly snug but not tight, and don't cheat. There seems to be some confusion about what is called the hip measure-ment in the pattern charts. This measurement actually refers to the fullest part of the buttocks and has nothing to do with the area around the hip bone. It is usually about nine inches below the waist in Junior and Misses sizes and seven inches below the natural waist for Junior Petite and Misses Petite sizes. Very few people are the same measurements as the standard sizes listed in the pattern catalogues. Choose the size of your pattern by the bust measurement, since the hip and waist areas are easier to alter.

When designers sketch their ideas they use a figure called a croquis (pro-nounced *kro*-kee). Tracing paper is placed on top of the croquis and then a design is drawn. I've included a croquis here (*Figure 2*), which you can use to sketch your own ideas.

SELECTING FABRIC AND TRIMMING

Read Chapter 5 on fabrics, Chapter 6 on lace, and Chapter 7 on trimmings to de-cide what you like and to see which ones you would enjoy working with. At the

FIGURE 2

end of this book is a Shopping Guide, which lists a number of mail order sources for bridal fabrics and trimmings. It would be a good idea to send for a swatched catalogue to help you become more familiar with bridal fabrics.

You may have been wondering where to start—with fabric or with the pattern. Designers work both ways. Sometimes they have a fabric they love and design a dress to make the most of it. Other times they have a style in mind and will look for a fabric to make up that design. You can work either way, buying your fabric before or after you decide on your style. There are advantages and disadvantages to working both ways. If you buy your fabric first, you should have a general idea of the kind of style you want—long sleeves or short, gathered skirt or flared—to know the type of fabric that would be best and also to figure the amount of fabric you will need. By purchasing fabric first, you will be able to adapt your dress pattern to the particular fabric. When working with lace, you can plan your dress to make the most of the design of the lace and to use the various widths and forms that the lace may come in. The disadvantage is that by not having made your muslin first, you may not be able to figure the exact amount of yardage you will need.

The style and the fabric should be right for each other. If you are making a gathered style, the fabric should be soft and drapable so it will fall softly. For an A-line style, the material should have enough body to hold its shape. The same type of fabric can vary tremendously depending on the way it is finished. For example, satin can be extremely soft and drapey or quite heavy and stiff, so don't go simply by the name. It's best to take the bolt of fabric to a mirror and drape some of it over yourself. If you're not sure whether the fabric you are thinking about will be right for what you want to do with it, buy a small piece to try out at home. Experiment with gathering, pressing, easing, and so on to see how it handles.

One of the most important considerations in selecting a fabric or trimming is quality. Quality does not necessarily mean buying what is most expensive; it means getting the best value you can for the money that you have to spend. Shop around —prices can sometimes vary considerably from store to store. It is better to buy a smaller quantity of good lace than to spend the same amount of money on miles of cheap lace. See Chapter 6 for how to judge the quality of lace and ways to use lace on a budget.

Fabric consumption can vary enormously from one style to another. An A-line gown will obviously use less yardage than one that has a tremendous gathered skirt, but using a small amount of an expensive fabric may turn out to take less money than using a large amount of low-cost fabric. Some of the most expensive bridal gowns are the simplest shapes, beautifully made, but requiring only a small amount of costly fabric.

Things you do yourself will also give you better value for your money than buying things ready-made. For example, lace bought with beads already applied may cost twice as much as the plain version of the same lace. For very little money, you can buy the same beads and apply them yourself (see instructions in Chapter 7). Buying a small amount of lace and cutting your own appliqués will cost less than buying the lace appliqués individually (see instructions in Chapter 6).

You will also want to give some thought to the color of your gown. Most brides select white or off-white, but there are quite a few different shades. Pure white can be warm or cool, and off-whites include ivory and candlelight. Ivory is a delicate, pale, creamy color, and candlelight has a slight pinkish cast to it, although the two words are often used interchangeably. Pure white is more often used for summer weddings and worn by those whose skin or hair coloring is fair or light. Ivory and candlelight are used more for fall and winter weddings and are usually more flattering to darker-haired or darker-complexioned young women. Candlelight will warm up a sallow complexion, while ivory will tone down a rosy one. White tends to add to the figure visually, so would not be the best choice for a full figure. The best way to judge is to take a bolt of fabric in each color and drape one over each shoulder in front of a mirror. Try to do this in natural window light rather than fluorescent.

The shades of the various fabrics and trims you will be using together on your gown should harmonize. They don't have to be exactly the same but should blend. Pure white and off-white usually don't work well together, although this combination is occasionally used. White lace can be dyed ivory (see Chapter 6).

When choosing your fabrics, keep in mind the season when your wedding will take place. Fabrics used year round include all types of lace, organza, chiffon, satapeau, crepe, taffeta, lightweight satin, and jersey. Those used primarily in spring include voile, piqué, leno, and organdy. Fabrics used mainly in winter include velvet and velveteen, brocade, and heavy satin.

When selecting your fabric, check for crease resistance. Squeeze a corner of the fabric tightly in your hand and then let go. If it springs back with only faint lines, then it should not wrinkle too much. When there are deep creases the fabric will wrinkle easily.

SPECIAL-OCCASION DRESSES

A special-occasion dress is definitely a worthwhile sewing project. If you want to look fabulous for an important event but can't bear to spend hundreds of dollars on a dress to wear a few times, the answer is to make one. As in sewing a wedding gown, the more expensive the type of dress you make, the more money you can save, since in most high-priced dresses much of the extra cost is in the labor. If you have the patience to add designer details (embroidery, beading, lining, and such), it is possible to make a dress that would cost $300 to buy for $50 in materials—a savings of 85 per cent. Almost all of the fabrics used for bridal wear are also used, in colors, white, and black, for special-occasion dresses. In addition to the fabrics already mentioned for brides, metallic and beaded fabrics are used for evening wear.

The procedure for making a special-occasion dress is the same as for making a wedding gown. If you want to create your own style by modifying or combining pattern pieces, see Chapter 3. The dress should first be made in muslin to test the fit and style, and to make alterations. If you're just not up to making the dress in muslin, try making it first in an inexpensive fabric so you can also wear your test dress. Then refer to Chapter 5 for specific instructions for cutting and sewing your special fabrics.

EQUIPMENT AND SUPPLIES

Don't underestimate the importance of good equipment. Even if you have fantastic sewing skills, poor-quality or badly maintained equipment will make it impossible for you to achieve professional results. In a designer's sample room (work room), scissors are sharpened every week, machines are kept oiled and repaired, and the best-quality equipment is used. The equipment is good but basic—there are very few gadgets. For the home sewer, a carload of gadgets is not needed, but what you have should be the best that you can afford. Good quality costs less in the long run. Bargains are really not bargains—inexpensive scissors don't cut well, low-cost thread will break. A few of the items shown here may be unfamiliar to you. They are used in designers' sample rooms but are not generally known to the home sewer. Some equipment is used for the majority of sewing projects; other things are needed for certain fabrics or more specialized sewing. The numbers in parentheses refer to the items shown in *Plate 1*.

Cutting and Marking

SHEARS AND SCISSORS Eight- or nine-inch-long dressmaker's shears are needed for cutting fabric—do not use them for cutting anything else or they will get dull. Embroidery scissors, four or five inches long, are used when working with lace. The small scissors are also handy for cutting threads, for doing hand work, and for opening buttonholes. Other shears are useful for specific fabrics, such as lingerie scissors for sheer fabrics and serrated-knife-edge shears for synthetics. When buying shears, be sure that the blades are held together by a screw and not a rivet, otherwise they cannot be taken apart to be sharpened. Your scissors should be clean, sharp, and free of rust. Occasionally add a small drop of oil at the pivot. Many shears and scissors are too tight. The screw may be loosened slightly to make the scissors more comfortable. Pinking shears should never be used to cut out a garment. This is totally unprofessional. If your garment is cut out with pinking shears, it will be impossible to judge the seam allowance accurately, the neckline and curved areas will stretch, and you will have a lot of trouble when making alterations. Pinking shears should be used only to neaten seams after the garment has been constructed and fitted.

THREAD CLIPPERS are handy to keep by the machine for cutting threads.

A TAPE MEASURE made of fiberglass is the best. Don't use an old wrinkly cloth one.

A CLEAR RULER (1) 2 inches by 18 inches, called C-Thru, is used by professional designers and pattern makers. This ruler, as well as the French curve and drafting triangle, can be found in art supply stores. This ruler is very much faster and more accurate for making changes or alterations on patterns and for measuring and marking hem allowances.

A FRENCH CURVE (2) is an important tool for accurate pattern alterations. The shape of the neckline and armhole are included in the curve.

A FASHION RULER (3) is also used for pattern alterations. It can substitute for the French curve. It includes the shape of the French curve as well as a longer hip curve.

A DRAFTING TRIANGLE (4) is used to check the straight grain and to locate true

PLATE 1
Measuring and Marking Tools

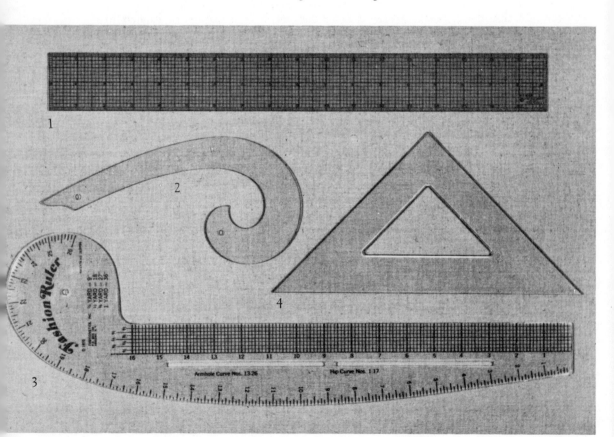

bias. It should be 8 or 10 inches long. Be sure to get a 45-by-45-by-90-degree triangle. Do not use a 30-by-60-by-90-degree triangle.

A YARDSTICK made of aluminum is the best kind, but wood is the most commonly available.

DRESSMAKER'S CARBON PAPER AND TRACING WHEEL should be used to mark muslin and lining fabric only. Do not use them to mark your good fabric.

TAILOR'S CHALK should also be used only on muslin or lining in most cases. Buy the clay type, which is dry and chalky. The waxy type can stain fabric or disappear when the muslin is ironed.

SKIRT MARKER The only way to mark most hems accurately so they will hang evenly is by measuring up from the floor. The pin type of marker is more accurate and is preferable to the powder type. (Floor-length wedding gowns are not marked this way.)

Miscellaneous Supplies

MUSLIN For making your test dress use ordinary, all-cotton, unbleached muslin—the kind used by all designers. Do not use permanent-press or fancy muslin. Select a heavyweight muslin if your gown will be made of heavy fabric, a lightweight muslin if your gown will be made of light fabric. Do not under any circumstances make your fitting dress using that lightweight nylon pattern-tracing fabric which is claimed to be good for making test garments.

WHITE TISSUE PAPER When stitching lace and sheer fabrics, strips of tissue are placed underneath to prevent tangling or stretching. Sheets of tissue paper are needed to wrap cut parts of the gown to keep them clean, and crumpled tissue paper is used to pad out the gown on a hanger.

A SEAM RIPPER should be used with care, as it can rip into the fabric quite easily. For buttonholes and intricate ripping, embroidery scissors are better.

A LOOP TURNER is necessary to turn thin bias tubing, which is used for button loops.

A BODKIN is used to draw ribbon through lace beading and to insert drawstrings and elastic into casings.

A SNAG FIXER is used on knits to pull a snag through to the wrong side.

BEESWAX is used when hand-sewing to strengthen the thread and keep it from tangling. Draw the thread through one of the slots in the holder.

Pressing Equipment

See *Plate 2.*

STEAM IRON The "Shot of Steam" type is the closest to a professional iron. The sole plate should be kept clean and smooth.

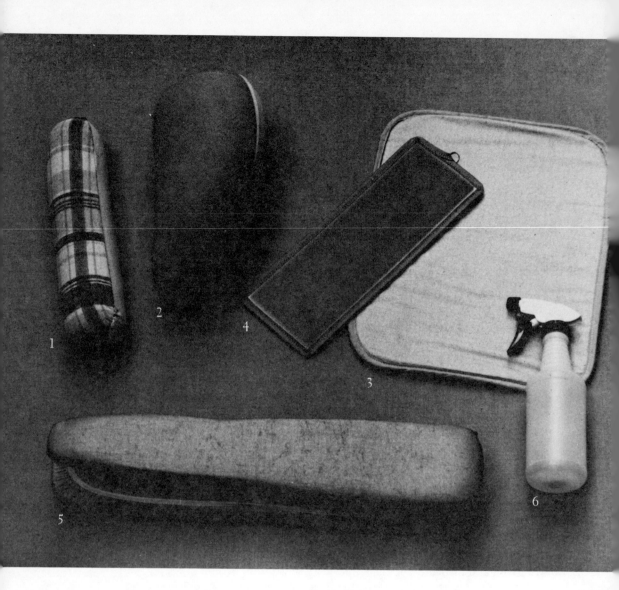

PLATE 2
Pressing Equipment

A SLEEVE BOARD (5) is necessary for pressing sleeves so they have no crease along the length of the arm, and for pressing other small areas. The end of the board can be used to shape the sleeve cap.

The TAILOR'S HAM (2) is an important piece of equipment. It allows you, when pressing, to shape garment areas to body contours, such as bust or hips.

A SEAM ROLL (1) should be used to press seams open because it prevents the impression of the seam allowance from showing on the right side of the fabric. The end of a seam roll can also be used to shape the sleeve cap.

A NEEDLE BOARD (4) (also called a velvet board) is used for pressing pile fabrics. It looks something like a carpet made of fine wires. The fabric is placed face down on the needles so the pile is not flattened during pressing. The needle board is flexible and can be placed over a seam roll. As a substitute, you can sometimes use a thick towel or another piece of velvet face up.

A PRESSING PAD (3) is a soft pad used when pressing areas that have raised trim, such as appliqués, re-embroidered lace, or beads. The fabric is placed face down on the pad so the raised areas sink in, which prevents flattening or puckering. A folded towel can be substituted, or you can make your own, using quilt batting covered in muslin.

PRESSING CLOTHS are important when working with special fabrics because many such fabrics will react badly if an iron is placed directly on them. There are many different types of pressing cloths available for use with specific fabrics. A transparent pressing cloth made of organdy is best for pressing lace.

A SPRAY MIST BOTTLE (6), sold for house plant misting, is used to dampen fabrics that are wrinkled, to help remove the center crease, and when straightening the grain. It will dampen a pressing cloth evenly and with just the right amount of moisture.

2

Choosing Your Wedding Type and Gown Style

Before you decide on the style of your dress, you should first decide what type of wedding you want. This will make the other decisions much easier because the style of your gown and veil, as well as the outfits your groom and attendants wear, is determined to a large extent by the formality of the wedding. In addition to the style of dress, factors that establish the formality of the wedding include the time of day, the number of guests, the number of attendants, and the lavishness of the reception. Six o'clock is the hour separating daytime and evening.

WEDDING TYPES

The four main types of weddings are very formal, formal, semiformal, and informal.

VERY FORMAL This is the largest and most elaborate wedding. It can be held at high noon or in late afternoon or evening for two hundred or more guests. There is a lavish reception with a sit-down dinner and an orchestra for dancing. The bride wears a stately, elegant dress with a cathedral train. Her arms are covered by long sleeves, or by long gloves if the sleeves are short. The veil is long, with a train, or, if shorter, very full with many layers and an elaborate headpiece. There are from six to twelve bridesmaids, who wear long dresses and short veils or other headwear. A flower girl and page boy are often included. The groom, male attendants, and fathers wear white tie and tails in the evening or a cutaway coat with striped trousers in the afternoon. The men may also be in contemporary formal wear, usually in black. Mothers wear floor-length dresses with hats and gloves.

FORMAL A formal wedding is held in the morning, afternoon, or evening, usually for a hundred or more guests. The reception may include a sit-down dinner or a dinner or luncheon buffet, often with dancing. The bride wears a long dress with a chapel train. Headwear can be a long, fingertip, or elbow-length veil or mantilla. There are two to six bridesmaids, who wear long dresses and hats or headpieces. The groom, male attendants, and fathers are in formal wear: tuxedo or dinner jacket for an evening wedding, Oxford gray stroller (formal daytime jacket) with striped trousers for a daytime wedding. The men may also wear contemporary formal wear in colors. The mothers wear elegant dresses, long in the evening, long or short in the daytime. Hats and gloves are optional.

SEMIFORMAL This type of wedding is held in the morning, afternoon, or evening, usually for fewer than a hundred guests. The reception is fairly simple, such as a buffet, wedding breakfast, or cocktail party. The bride wears a long dress with a short train or no train. The veil is elbow-length or shorter, with a simple headpiece. There are one or two bridesmaids, who wear long or short dresses, with or without a hat or headpiece. The groom, male attendants, and fathers wear business suits or daytime formal wear before six o'clock. After six they can wear dinner jackets, tuxedos, or contemporary formal wear. Mothers wear long or daytime-length dresses.

INFORMAL This is a small wedding ceremony, usually held in the daytime in the clergyman's study or judge's chambers, for family and a few close friends. The reception can be a simple champagne toast. The bride wears a short dress or suit with a hat, simple headpiece, or shoulder-length veil. The only attendant is a maid of honor, who wears a short dress or suit, as do the mothers. The groom, best man, and fathers wear business suits.

These are only general guidelines—do not feel bound by rigid rules. Many lovely weddings combine formal and less formal elements.

The biggest change in wedding wear has been for men. Instead of conservative black, gray, or white, now colors and patterns are used in profusion and men's wear is as well styled as that of the bride and her attendants. Ruffled shirts, patterned vests, cummerbunds and bow ties, contrasting-color jacket and pants, even patterned jackets with velvet and satin trims are worn. With all these choices of men's wear, as well as those for the other attendants, care must be taken in planning the colors and styles so that everything harmonizes. The outfits of the men attendants and the bridesmaids should have the same degree of formality, and the colors should complement each other. By having your attendants make their own gowns you have a much better opportunity to choose co-ordinating fabrics. Before you decide on your maids' outfits or their colors, it might be a good idea to visit the formal-wear department of the store where you will be renting the men's attire. You can reserve formal wear well in advance, and knowing the colors and styles available for the men can help you decide on the maids' outfits.

You can also make something for the groom and the other men of the wedding party to wear to co-ordinate with your gown or your bridesmaids'. For more about this, see Chapter 10.

WEDDING THEMES

Having a theme for your wedding will help you in planning colors, attendants' outfits, flowers, and so on. Following are some themes for different times of the year. Most can be adapted to very formal, formal, or semiformal weddings.

GARDEN PARTY WEDDING This is a beautiful, romantic spring or summer wedding, indoors or out. The bride wears a dress of a gossamer floating fabric such as chiffon, organza, or voile trimmed with lace or embroidery, or an all-lace dress. On her head she could wear a veil with real flowers for the headpiece, a lace cap, or a picture hat wrapped in chiffon with long streamers drifting down the back. Maids wear romantic dresses of sheer fabric in solid pastels or water-color prints. A waistline sash and picture hat with ribbons and flowers are pretty touches. The maids might also wear white dresses with pastel trim and carry pastel bouquets or baskets of flowers decorated with ribbon and lace. A flower girl and page boy are often included at this wedding. The page boy could wear a pastel linen Eton suit and the flower girl a long white or pastel dress. The men wear white or pastel formal wear.

RAINBOW WEDDING This is a pretty look for spring and summer, suitable for even the most formal weddings. The bride wears a simple or elaborate gown. Each maid wears the same style dress in a different pastel color. (If you have a large number of maids, each pair of maids can wear a different pastel.) Select three, four, or five pastels from the following: maize, pink, aqua, mint, lilac, pale blue, melon, lime. The men can wear white or pastel formal wear to match the maids'.

ALL-WHITE WEDDING This is a beautiful and dramatic wedding for spring and summer. For a very formal wedding, the bride could wear a pure white lace dress with a long train and veil and carry a white bouquet. All members of the wedding party dress completely in white. As a variation, you could use a touch of color for the attendants. Maids can wear white dresses with pastel sashes or embroidery, or white hats trimmed in color. Men might wear pastel shirts, or colored bow ties and cumberbunds, with white formal suits. This could also be done as an all-ivory wedding if the bride's gown is ivory.

MONOCHROMATIC COLOR THEME In this wedding, the bride wears white or ivory and the maids and other attendants dress in shades of one color. For instance, the maids might wear various shades of blue from pastel to deep roval, the men wear deep royal tuxedos with blue shirts, and flower girl and page boy wear pastel blue. This idea will work with other colors such as red, from palest pink to burgundy; yellow, from maize to deep gold; green, from mint to deep forest; or brown, from ivory to chocolate. You can use this theme at any time of the year.

JEWEL-TONE WEDDING This is a richly colored wedding suitable for the winter months, especially around the holidays. The bride wears white or ivory and the maids wear deep jewel tones such as emerald, ruby, sapphire, topaz, or amethyst. Men's formal wear matches the color of the maids' dresses. Velvet and velveteen look especially rich in jewel tones. Parts of the maids' dresses such as collars, sleeves, or trimming can be white or ivory to match the bride's dress. For a wedding at Christmastime, you could choose ruby and emerald.

AUTUMN HUES For a fall wedding, you can use the colors of autumn as your theme. The bride wears ivory and the maids colors such as gold, terracotta, bittersweet, rust, cinnamon, burnt orange, olive, or deep brown. The maids can all wear the same color, or, for a fall version of the rainbow wedding, each maid can wear a different color. Men can wear gold, brown, or deep olive formal suits.

COUNTRY WEDDING This is a less formal wedding suitable for any season, depending on the colors and fabrics. For a fall wedding, the bride might wear a dress of natural-color muslin, leno, or voile, trimmed in matching Cluny or Venise lace. The maids can wear dresses of patchwork made of dark-color prints, or calico accented with Cluny lace. For a spring or summer wedding a dress of white eyelet, dimity, or dotted swiss could be worn by the bride. The maids might wear flower-printed chintz dresses trimmed in Cluny lace, or gingham checks with eyelet. The maids and flower girl could wear bonnets or kerchiefs instead of the usual headwear.

CHOOSING YOUR GOWN STYLE

Once you have decided on the type of wedding you want, the next thing is to choose the pattern style, fabric, and trimmings for your gown. The bride's gown is decided on first, then the headpiece and veil. After that, attendants' attire is selected to complement the bride's. (If, however, you have a treasured heirloom veil or mantilla that you are planning to wear, then the dress would be chosen to complement the headwear.) When you think about the dress you want, remember that you are not limited to the patterns in the pattern catalogues. It is easy to create a new style by making minor alterations in a pattern, and by switching about parts from two or more patterns. Making a neckline lower, adding a train, or using a different sleeve can all be done quite simply. This is explained in detail in Chapter 3.

There are two basic considerations in deciding on the design of your wedding gown. The first is the silhouette of the basic gown, and the second is the fabric and the trimming. The basic gown pattern is referred to in the trade as the "gown body." There are only a limited number of gown bodies, but a great many dress styles are made from them by varying the fabric and trimming.

An illustrated list follows of the various components of the gown body, to help you decide what you like.

Gown Silhouettes

The most popular silhouettes for wedding gowns are shown in *Figure 3*.

EMPIRE-WAISTLINE STYLES The waistline seam of an Empire dress ranges from two or three inches above the natural waistline to just under the bust. The skirt can be A-line, gathered, flared, or smooth in front with gathers in the back only. The Empire style with an A-line skirt takes the least amount of yardage, so it would be a good choice when using a very expensive lace or fabric. This is a popular shape and is used for many elaborately trimmed gowns.

PRINCESS STYLES Princess-line dresses have seams for shaping, instead of darts. The seams most often originate at the shoulder or the armhole and end at the hem. With the A-line princess, the bodice is fitted at the bust, then the skirt flares

FIGURE 3

Natural Waistline

Fitted Princess

Gathered Empire

A-Line Empire

A-Line Princess

from under the bust. With the waistline fitted princess style, the bodice fits closely and the skirt flares out from the waistline.

NATURAL-WAISTLINE STYLES The most popular skirt for a waistline dress is gathered or circular gathered. A circular gathered skirt looks very pretty because it has a generous sweep at the hem but only a small amount of gathers at the waistline, so there is less bulk. A natural-waistline dress with a very full gathered skirt is called a bouffant.

Trains

See *Figure 4*. Trains can be attached or detachable. Most attached trains are simply an extension of the skirt itself. A panel train can be joined to the dress at the back waistline seam or attached to the dress with hooks or snaps, so it can be removed at the reception. A Watteau train refers to one that originates high on the back bodice or at the shoulders. It can be attached or detachable.

The longer the train, the more formal it is considered. The most popular train length is chapel, which extends beyond the dress 30 to 54 inches (1½ yards). The

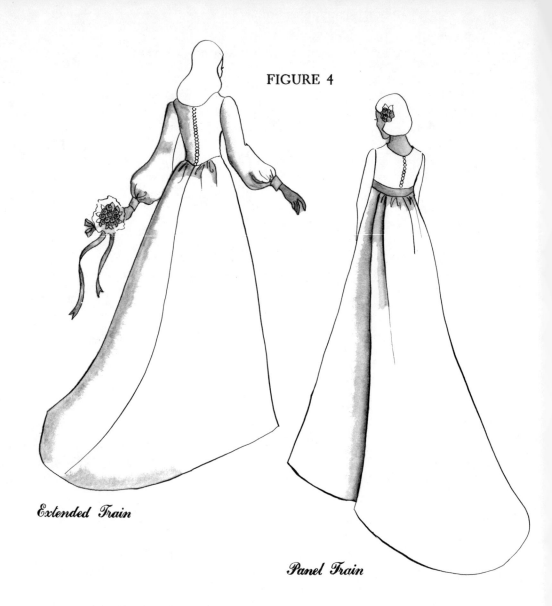

FIGURE 4

Extended Train

Panel Train

cathedral train is used at very formal weddings. It extends as much as 2½ yards beyond the gown and is wider than the chapel train. (The train length measurements do not include the skirt length from waist to floor.)

Necklines and Collars

See *Figure 5.*

A JEWEL NECKLINE is the basic round neck that fits closely at the base of the
neck. It is most often used with a collar or neckband.

LOW NECKLINES can be scoop, square, or V. They can be cut just a few inches
below the base of the neck or quite low. On a wedding gown, a lower-cut neckline
is usually covered with an overlayer of sheer fabric or English net.

FIGURE 5

Jewel   *V-shaped*   *Scoop*   *Square*

Sweetheart   *Cowl*   *Victorian Neckband*   *Bias Neckband*

The SWEETHEART NECKLINE is named for its heart shape. It can be quite high and narrow or low and wide.

A COWL NECKLINE is a draped neckline cut on the bias. It is very elegant and sophisticated and should be made of soft lightweight fabrics such as chiffon or crepe.

The VICTORIAN COLLAR has quite a few variations. The neckband can be wide or narrow, made of lace or of fabric. It is often trimmed with lace appliqué or a ruffle. The trimming treatment used on the Victorian collar is often repeated on the sleeve.

BIAS NECKBANDS can fit close to the neck or stand away. A bias band that stands away from the neck is sometimes referred to as a "wedding band" collar. It may stand up like a Victorian collar or fold over like a turtleneck.

Bibs and Yokes

See *Figure 6.*

BIBS can be square, V, or rounded. A bib is frequently combined with some type of Victorian collar. The bib seam is often trimmed with lace or a ruffle, with the same trim repeated on the Victorian collar.

YOKES may be straight or curved and, like bibs, are often trimmed with lace or a ruffle. The yoke is sometimes made of lace or a different fabric from the gown.

FIGURE 6

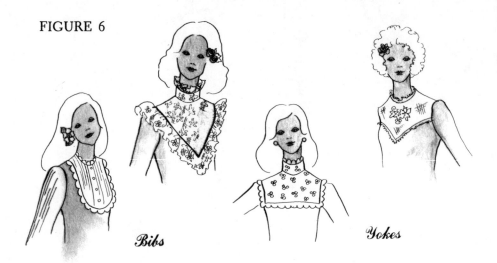

Bibs   *Yokes*

Sleeves

There are a great many different sleeve possibilities for wedding gowns (see *Figure 7*). When using an elaborate sleeve, choose a simple gown body so the whole effect won't be overdone. For summer use a short cap or puffed sleeve or shoulder ruffle.

A PUFFED SLEEVE is a very pretty sleeve for a summer wedding for bride and bridesmaids.

A MELON SLEEVE is an elbow-length version of the puffed sleeve.

A JULIETTE SLEEVE is made in two parts—the top is a puffed sleeve and the lower part fitted.

The SHEPHERDESS SLEEVE is the opposite of the Juliette—it is fitted at the top and puffed below. The short upper sleeve is often made from a wide lace edge so the end is scalloped.

A VICTORIAN SLEEVE consists of a melon sleeve extending just below the elbow, and joined to a long fitted cuff. The cuff is usually closed by a row of tiny covered buttons.

A LONG FITTED SLEEVE is one of the basic wedding gown sleeves. It should have a zipper or buttons at the wrist to fit properly. An extended wrist, pointed or curved, looks very pretty with this sleeve.

A CAP SLEEVE is a very short fitted sleeve.

A SHIRT SLEEVE is gathered into a cuff at the wrist.

A BISHOP SLEEVE is a full version of the shirt sleeve. It may or may not have gathers at the cap.

A WEDDING BELL SLEEVE is flared and can be long, short, or in-between.

A BUTTERFLY SLEEVE is circular and has more fullness than the wedding bell sleeve. It is sometimes called a cape sleeve.

A TRUMPET SLEEVE is fitted to the elbow, then flares out.

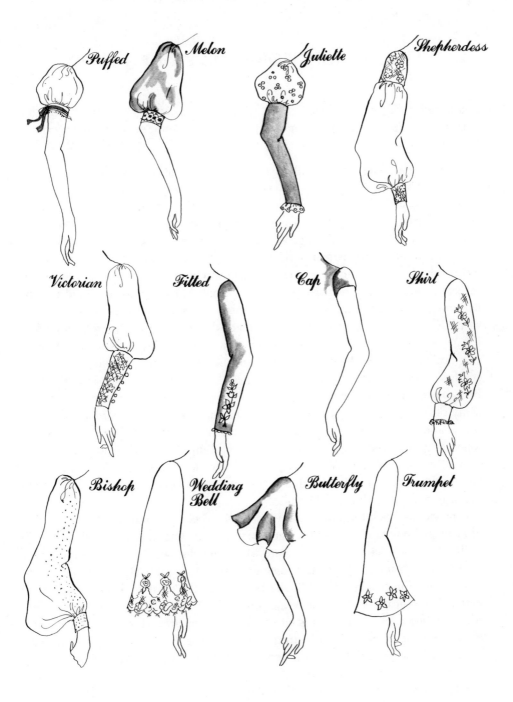

FIGURE 7

STYLE SUGGESTIONS FOR FIGURE TYPES

Before you decide on the style of your gown, keep in mind that certain styles are more suitable to some figures than to others. Here are some suggestions for various figure types.

PETITE Keep things in a small to medium scale, but not overly tiny or cute. Avoid huge billowy sleeves, very full skirts and large ruffles. Do not use strong horizontal lines, such as bands of horizontal trimming, or seams that will cut your height. Vertical lines visually add height, so princess seams, long fitted sleeves, or vertical rows of lace would be good ideas. If you are using lace appliqués, place them in a vertical, rather than horizontal, arrangement. An Empire waist with an A-line skirt is a good silhouette. A chapel train would be preferable to a tremendous cathedral train. A modified scoop neck or a small Victorian collar would also be flattering. If you are thin, avoid clingy fabrics because they will make you look wispy. Keep your headpiece relatively small and don't make the veil extremely full.

TALL You can wear an opulent, elegant gown that would overwhelm a smaller girl. Scale is important—avoid overly dainty or tiny details. If you want to de-emphasize your height, avoid strong vertical lines and a solid expanse of dress. Break up the lines of the gown with trimming such as lace, ruffles, or beading. A floaty skirt or sleeves or a low neck would be good. A bib, yoke, or waistline sash would also be flattering. Avoid very high neckbands, long fitted sleeves, and slim A-line or princess styles. Do not choose very limp fabrics that would hang in straight vertical folds. Be sure that your veil and headpiece are in proportion and have enough drama not to look doll-size. Choose a headpiece style that fits close to the head to avoid adding height.

FULL FIGURE Look for a pattern with smooth, sleek lines and select a fabric that has enough body to glide over the figure rather than cling. A matte-finish ivory fabric is a better choice than a shiny pure white one that would make things appear larger. Avoid bouffant shapes and fussy details, such as puffy sleeves or full ruffles. If you want ruffles, place them at the hemline or the wrist. A lightweight lace is better than a heavy Venise. An A-line princess style with long fitted sleeves and a slightly scoop neck would be a good silhouette. Your dress should fit closely without being tight. Many girls with larger figures fit their dresses too loosely, which actually makes them look bigger. Choose a veil that is fairly smooth without a lot of gathers or layers, or wear a mantilla.

SMALL BOSOM Select a style with some sort of bodice interest such as ruffles, beading, lace appliqués, tucks, or shirring. Softly gathered sleeves or an Empire style with gathers or a sash under the bust would also be a good choice. Avoid a plain bodice or severe, tight sleeves.

LARGE BOSOM Select a dress style with a smooth, simple bodice and place your trimmings on the skirt. Choose a modified scoop neckline and fitted sleeves. Avoid high neckbands, shoulder ruffles, and short fluffy sleeves. The best silhouettes would be a princess line or a natural waistline with a moderately gathered skirt. Do not wear an Empire style. Your veil should be elbow-length or longer.

LARGE HIPS Avoid shiny or extremely clingy fabrics. Keep the upper part of the skirt fairly plain and place the trim near the hem and on the bodice. Vertical bands of trim, a princess line, or a flared skirt would be good choices.

THE SOPHISTICATED BRIDE

If you are in your mid-twenties or older, or have been married before, you may not prefer a traditional wedding gown. By sewing your own gown you have a chance to create a style especially suited to your taste, one that would be very difficult to find ready-made. For the most elegant and sophisticated designs, look in the Vogue pattern catalogue in the "After Five" and "Designer" sections. These dresses were not designed as wedding gowns, but by choosing the right fabrics and trimmings, many can be made appropriate for a wedding. As you look at the sketches and photographs, try to picture the styles made up in white or ivory, rather than the colors or prints illustrated.

Dresses made of two parts can look more sophisticated than a one-piece dress. You might consider a lace jacket or tunic, or sheer floor-length coat over a long dress. A long shirtwaist dress in chiffon or georgette with tucks and tiny pearl buttons can be worn over a slip dress. Knits such as Qiana, maracaine, and matte jersey are good possibilities or, for a winter wedding, think about luxurious sweater knits, such as mohair, angora, or cashmere. Other soft, drapey fabrics include crepe de chine, silk, and satin-back crepe. For trimming, consider real fur, marabou or ostrich feathers, crystal beads, or pearls. Ivory and candlelight shades tend to look more sophisticated than pure white. For headwear, your dress or jacket might have a hood attached, or you might wear a picture hat, turban, cloche, or mantilla.

3

Creating Your Own Gown Style

By restyling a pattern or combining parts from several patterns, you can create just the style you want. Such things as changing the shape of a neckline, adding a train, or varying a sleeve can be done easily and will give you many new design possibilities.

If you are especially interested in designing your own patterns, you can find detailed information on this subject in my book *How to Design Your Own Clothes and Make Your Own Patterns,* published by Doubleday.

For some pattern restyling, you will have to cut into the pattern. If you want to keep the original pattern intact, trace it onto a new piece of paper, then use the traced pattern to make your variations. Large-size tracing paper is available on rolls at art supply stores.

COMBINING PARTS FROM DIFFERENT PATTERNS

By following a few guidelines, you can combine pattern pieces from two or more different patterns such as the sleeve of one style with the bodice of another. This will usually work best if you use patterns from the same company. Each manufacturer has its own master patterns from which all other patterns are made, so although styles vary they should be the same in basic measurements, such as neckline, center front and center back length, and basic armhole size. Since your gown will be made in muslin first (see Chapter 4), you don't have to worry about making drastic mistakes and can feel free to try different pattern combinations.

Sleeves

If you are using a regular set-in sleeve armhole, most gathered cap sleeves such as puffed, bishop, or leg-of-mutton will work because the sleeve gathers can be adjusted to fit the new armhole. If you are using a sleeve with a fitted cap, you must compare the armhole shapes of the two patterns (see *Figure* 8). To do this, place the front tissue pattern that goes with the sleeve on top of the front pattern that you want to use, aligning the shoulders of both patterns at the armhole. Compare the back armhole patterns the same way. If the armholes are exactly or almost the same size and shape, the sleeve will fit into your pattern. If the armhole is slightly larger or smaller, you can add that amount to or subtract it from the underarm seam of the sleeve, up to ¼ inch on each side, as you see in the illustration. If there is more than a ½ inch total difference between the two armholes, however, you should not use the sleeve.

FIGURE 8

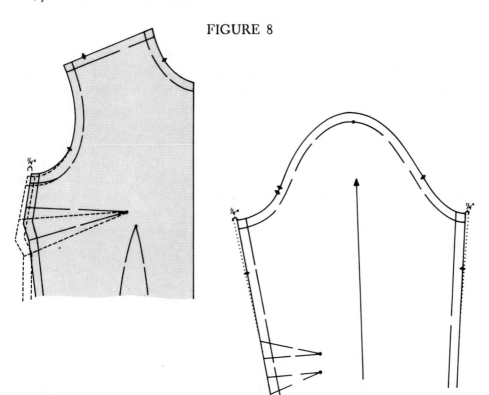

FIGURE 9

Combination Sleeves

Many wedding gowns feature sleeve designs created by combining two or more sleeves, as you see in *Figure 9*. Often a long sleeve is combined with a short full sleeve, such as a butterfly. You can use the sleeve included with your pattern and add a sleeve from another view of the pattern, or from a different pattern. The two sleeves can be of the same fabric, or each of a different fabric. A combination of one sleeve of lace and the other of fabric is also effective. The sleeve in *Figure 9A* shows a long fitted sleeve of velvet with a butterfly sleeve of lace. *Figure 9B* shows a bishop sleeve of organza with a pinafore sleeve and cuff of tucked organza. Another combination sleeve is made using two or more of the same sleeve varied in length. *Figure 9C* shows a sleeve made of four layers of chiffon, each 1 inch longer than the next. Many sleeve variations can be made using different combinations of trimming, lace, and fabric.

Combining Bodice and Skirt Patterns

You can usually combine the bodice of one pattern with the skirt of another as long as both patterns are the same basic style and fit. For example, the waistline seam of a dress may be at the natural waist or raised several inches. In order to combine the skirt of one with the bodice of another, both patterns must have the waistline seam in the same position. A gathered-skirt pattern can be switched easily, because the gathers can be adjusted to fit the waistline. With an A-line skirt, some easing at the waist or alteration at the side seams may be needed. As you see in *Figure 10*, the gathered skirt of pattern A has been added to the bodice of pattern B to create style C. Because the waistline seam is in the same place and is the same shape, it will work with no trouble. The skirt of pattern D, however, will not work because of the unusual shape of the waistline seam.

FIGURE 10

RESTYLING SLEEVES

Gathered-sleeve Variations

A pattern for a sleeve that is gathered at the bottom, such as the puffed or bishop, will give you a completely different sleeve style if the bottom is left ungathered. A puffed sleeve that is not gathered becomes a flutter sleeve (see *Figure 11A*). A very full bishop sleeve with a gathered cap becomes an angel sleeve (*Figure 11B*), while a bishop sleeve with no gathers at the cap becomes a wedding bell sleeve (*Figure 11C*). The only change needed in the pattern may be a modification of the shape of the bottom. A bishop sleeve pattern curves down on one side and up on the other. If this curve is an exaggerated dip, as you see in *Figure 11D*, it should be smoothed to resemble *Figure 11E*. A puffed sleeve pattern also curves down at the bottom. If the curve is very deep, as in *Figure 11F*, redraw the shape to resemble *Figure 11G*. A French curve is best for doing this. If the bottom of the sleeve looks wavy when you try on your muslin gown, have someone trim the edge of the sleeve while you wear the dress.

If you are using a bishop sleeve pattern that was originally designed with a cuff, you will need to add the width of the cuff to the sleeve pattern so the sleeve won't be too short. (For example, if the sleeve had a 2-inch cuff, add 2 inches to the bottom of the sleeve pattern.)

FIGURE 11

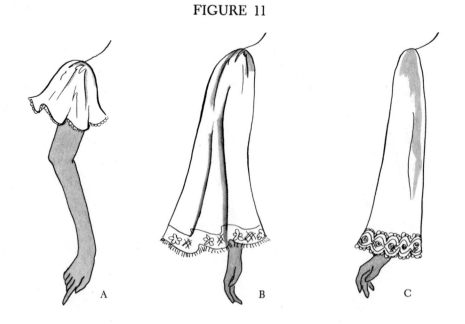

A   B   C

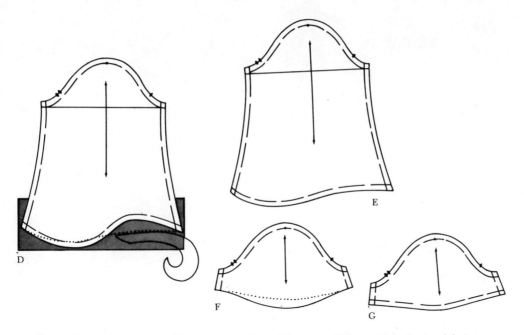

These sleeves are especially pretty made of lace or lightweight floaty fabrics. The end of the sleeve can be finished with a lace edge, narrow bias facing, hand-rolled hem, or one of the narrow hems in Chapter 8 (see index).

Another variation of the bishop sleeve pattern can be made by gathering the upper part of the sleeve, as you see in *Figure 12A*. Use a pattern with a gathered cap for a puffier look. The sleeve can be gathered using a drawstring and casing, by stretching narrow elastic and zigzag-stitching it across the sleeve, or by applying lace beading and using a ribbon drawstring. Notice that the line across the sleeve is not straight but dips between 1 and 2 inches at the center of the sleeve (*Figure 12B*). The line can be marked on your fabric with thread tracing.

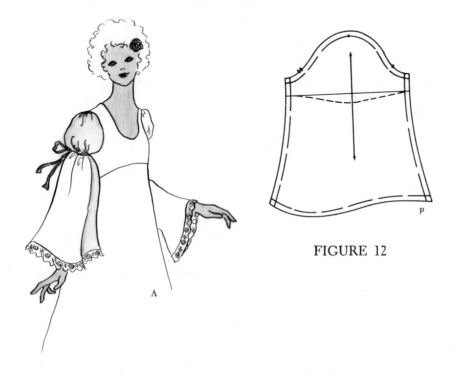

FIGURE 12

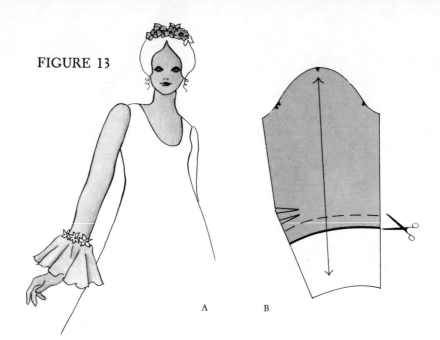

FIGURE 13

A   B

Fitted Three-quarter Sleeve

Figure 13A. This is a shortened version of a long fitted sleeve (see *Figure 13B*).

1. With your ruler measure up from the bottom of the sleeve about 4 inches and mark in several places.
2. Connect the marks, preferably with a French curve. The new line should follow the same shape as the original bottom line of the sleeve.
3. To make a pattern for a shaped facing to finish the end of the sleeve, measure up 2½ inches from the new line and mark a facing line, following the same method used to mark the first line. See dotted line in drawing.
4. Cut sleeve pattern along new line (*not* along facing line).

Full Three-quarter Sleeve

Figure 13C. Follow the steps for the fitted three-quarter sleeve, referring to *Figure 13D*.

Cap Sleeve

Figure 14A. This tiny sleeve is good for summer weddings. It is a shortened version of the short fitted sleeve.

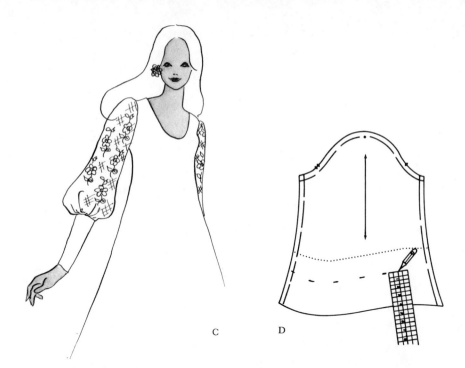

C   D

1. At the center of the sleeve, measure up from the bottom 2 to 3 inches.

2. Draw a line as you see in *Figure 14B*. Notice that the line is not straight, but arches up. Leave a minimum of 1¾ inches at the underarm seam so you will have enough seam allowance.

3. Cut your pattern along the new line.

4. Fold the pattern in half lengthwise so that the underarm seams meet. Check to see that the shape of the bottom of the sleeve is the same on both sides, and that both the underarm seams are the same length.

To finish the bottom of the sleeve, a sleeve is cut of lining fabric and used as a facing. The cap of the sleeve and the facing sleeve are attached at the armhole.

FIGURE 14

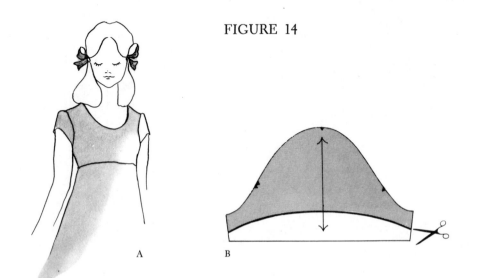

A   B

Extended-wrist Sleeve

Figure 15A. A long fitted sleeve with an extended wrist is very traditional and is usually found on more formal styles. The extension may be round or pointed. The edge of the sleeve can be trimmed with a row of seed pearls or picot-edge lace, or you might add a small lace appliqué near the point. Begin with a long fitted sleeve pattern. To modify your pattern:

1. Tape tracing paper to the wrist, as you see in *Figure* 15B.
2. Fold the sleeve in half at the wrist line and crease to indicate the center of the wrist.
3. From the center crease, draw a line down 1½ to 2½ inches long, as shown.
4. Draw a line from the original wrist line at the seam to the lowered line, as you see in the illustration. (Be sure you draw from the cutting line, not the stitching line.) You can make your line curved or pointed.
5. Measure up 2 inches from the original wrist line and mark a facing line, as shown.
6. Cut out your pattern on the new line.
7. Fold the pattern in half again to be sure that both sides of the wrist are the same. Trim away any unevenness.

Check the final shape of the wrist when you try on your muslin dress.

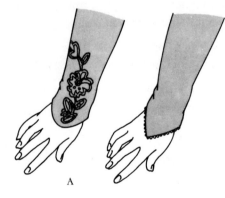

A

FIGURE 15

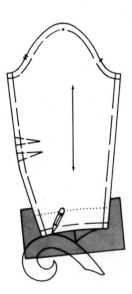

B

RESTYLING THE NECKLINE

Scoop-neck Pattern

Figure 16 shows how to change a pattern with a jewel neckline to a scoop neckline. The basic principle can be applied to other necklines as well. A French curve should be used to draw the new neckline shape. When drawing a new neckline, it is better to make it too high than too low. You can easily lower the neckline on your muslin gown, but it is more trouble to raise it.

1. Refer to *Figure 16B*. Using a colored pencil, mark the new neckline where you want it. You can draw the neckline freehand, then use your French curve to make the line smooth and even. Use the bust dart lines as a reference for how low to cut the neck.

2. Use your ruler and black pencil to add ⅝ inch seam allowance.

3. You will also need a facing line so that you will know where to cut the facing for your new neckline. At the center front, measure 3 inches down from the cutting line of the neckline and mark. The side of the facing follows the shape of the armhole (see *Figure 16C*). When you sew your dress, stitch the side of the facing to the seam allowance of the armhole and it will not stick out of the neckline. The facing must not extend below the bust dart. If you have a very low neckline, the facing will be narrower than 3 inches, to avoid the bust dart.

FIGURE 16

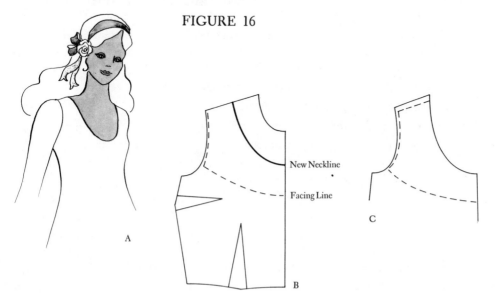

New Neckline

Facing Line

A

B

C

FIGURE 16

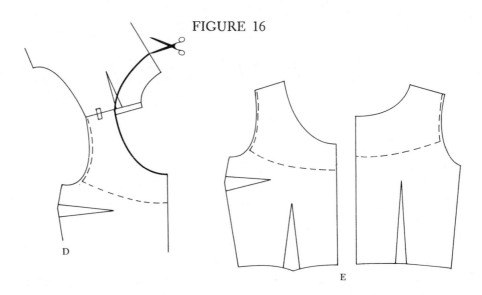

4. Cut out your front pattern. Be sure to cut on the cutting line (not the stitching line) of the new neckline.

5. When you make the back neckline pattern, the front and back patterns must be joined at the shoulder seam so that the neckline can be blended in one continuous line. You can ignore the back shoulder dart for this step. Crease along the stitching line of the front shoulder seam and fold the seam allowance under. Place the front pattern so that the stitching line (edge of the fold) on the front shoulder is lined up against the stitching line of the back shoulder, as you see in *Figure 16D*. Tape together.

6. Now you can continue the front neckline onto the back pattern. Keep the line from the front to the back neckline flowing smoothly over the shoulder seam. Blend the line with your French curve. When the neckline is shaped so that it eliminates more than half of the shoulder dart, you may leave out the shoulder dart entirely. If the neckline is only slightly larger than the original neckline, then the shoulder dart should remain.

7. Separate the front and back by cutting the tape.

8. Mark the facing line as you did on the front pattern. If your pattern has shoulder darts, your facing should also have them. When you make your dress, press the dart on the facing toward the armhole and the dart on the dress toward the center back.

9. The necklines of your finished front and back patterns should look like *Figure 16E*. When you cut your facing in muslin, cut around the pattern at the neckline, shoulder, armhole, and top part of the side seam to the facing line. Slip a piece of dressmaker's carbon paper face down between the pattern and the fabric. Mark the facing line with your tracing wheel. Remove the pattern and cut on the traced line. The neckline facing patterns will be used when

you cut your gown in fabric. You don't need the facings for the fitting muslin. Remember that if you alter the shape of the neckline on the muslin dress, you will have to alter the shape of the facing neckline to match.

Other Neckline Shapes

Figure 17 shows V-shaped, sweetheart, and square neckline patterns. To make any of these necklines, follow the steps given for the scoop neckline, but draw the neckline shape as shown.

FIGURE 17

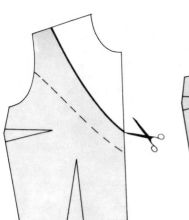
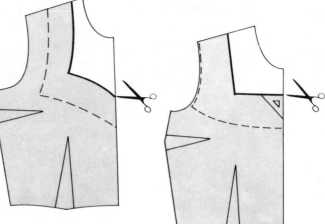

ADDING A TRAIN

If you are using a pattern without a train, you can add one to the pattern yourself. There are two types of trains (see *Figure 4*). The extended train is created simply by making the skirt pattern longer at the back. The panel train is a separate piece attached at the back waist. When you make a pattern for the train, don't worry about the shape or length being absolutely perfect—they can be adjusted when your dress is made up in muslin. When in doubt, make it longer and wider because you can easily trim away excess from the muslin.

Extended Train

This can be added to an A-line, gathered, or flared skirt. If your pattern has princess seams, you will have to join the side and center skirt pieces before adding the train to the pattern (see below, "Joining Princess Seams"). Lengthen or shorten the pattern, if necessary, before adding the train.

1. Place the front and back skirt together, matching the stitching lines (*not the cutting lines*) of the side seams (see *Figure 18*). The seam allowances will overlap. The hemline of the front and back must coincide, not be higher or lower on one side. The side seams of the upper part of the skirt will probably curve away. The important thing is that they be matched at the hemline. Tape the front and back skirts together where the side seams meet.

2. Tape a large sheet of paper to the hem. With a yardstick, extend the center back line by an amount equal to the length you want your train. (For example, to make a 2½-foot-long train, extend the center back line 2½ feet.)

3. Beginning at the center back, lightly sketch in a curved shape, as you see in the drawing. Notice that the line is at a right angle at the center back and curves gradually up to the side seams. Do not curve the line in too abruptly or the train will look skimpy.

4. On the front skirt just beyond the side seam, continue the line into the *finished* hemline, not into the cutting line of the hem. This is done because the hem will have a facing, not be turned under.

5. Using your ruler, add ⅝ inch seam allowance to the outside hem edge (see the dotted line in the drawing).

6. Cut out your pattern on the dotted line and along the center back line. Clip the tape to separate the front and back skirt.

You can use a shaped or a bias facing (see index under *Hem facings*) to finish the hem of your skirt.

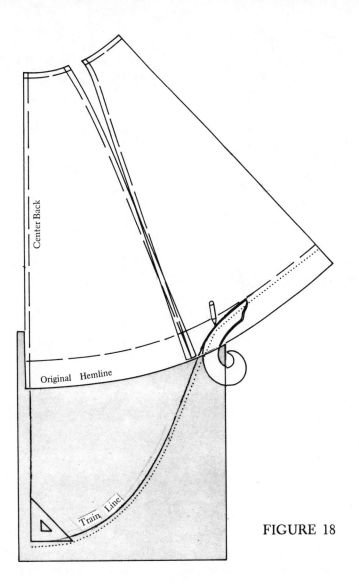

Center Back

Original   Hemline

Train   Line

FIGURE 18

Panel Train

A panel train can be made as a separate detachable train or it can be joined to the dress at the waistline seam. If it is attached, it must have at the center back a slash with a placket and snaps the same length as the zipper of the underdress. A detachable train can be joined to a band that snaps or hooks to the back of the dress (white fabric-covered snaps are best) or to a sash that ties around the waist (*Figure* 19A). The sash could be made of matching dress fabric, ribbon, or lace. A panel train can be used on an Empire or natural waistline dress, with an A-line or gathered skirt. To make this pattern, you will need a very large sheet of paper 5 to 6 feet long.

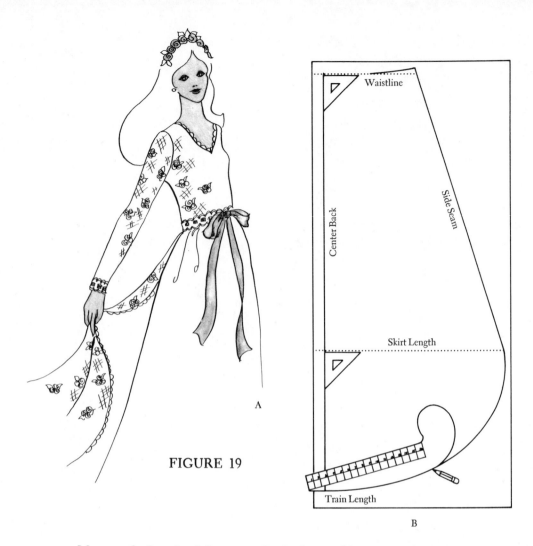

A

B

FIGURE 19

1. Measure the length of the center back of your skirt pattern from the waist to the finished hemline. Measure from the Empire waist if you are using an Empire waist pattern.

2. Using your yardstick, draw a line down the left side of the paper (see *Figure 19B*). The top of the line indicates the waistline. Mark the length of the skirt on the line, as you see in the drawing. Extend the line down by an amount equal to the length you want your train. For example, if you want a 2-foot train, then extend the line 2 feet below the skirt-length mark. Mark this line CENTER BACK—PLACE ON FOLD.

3. To mark the waistline, with your ruler draw a line across the top of the paper at a right angle to the center back at the waistline mark. This line should be about 11 inches long if your fabric is heavy, to 15 inches long for lightweight fabric (see dotted line).

4. Draw the waistline (solid line), as shown. Note that the line curves up ¾ inch from the straight line.

5. Mark the width of the train. At the skirt-length mark, draw a line at a right

angle to the center back line measuring 18 inches for heavy fabric to 23 inches for lightweight.

6. Connect the waistline and the hemline, forming the side seam.

7. To finish the pattern, draw the curved bottom shape of the train, as shown. Connect the length-of-train mark at the center back with the side seam. Notice that the line curves gradually from the center back up to the side seam.

8. Cut out your pattern.

When you make your train in fabric, the panel should be completely lined. Cut one panel of gown fabric and one of lightweight lining fabric. Pin right sides together and stitch around the outside edge, except the waistline. Clip, press, and turn right side out as you would a collar. Gather the top edge of the panel (the waistline) to measure between 9 and 11 inches wide.

Joining Princess Seams

In order to make an extended train pattern or hem facing when using a princess-seam style, the side front and center front, as well as the side back and center back pattern pieces, must be joined while the pattern is being constructed. To join the front skirt sections, place the side front and the center front patterns together, matching the stitching lines, *not the cutting lines,* as you see in *Figure 20*. The seam allowances will overlap. The hemline of the side and center sections must coincide. (It doesn't matter if the pieces curve away from each other farther up toward the waistline.) Attach with Scotch tape. Join the back pattern pieces the same way.

FIGURE 20

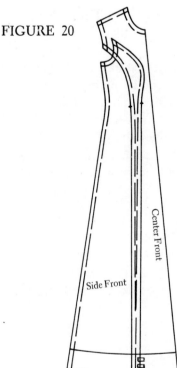

Center Front

Side Front

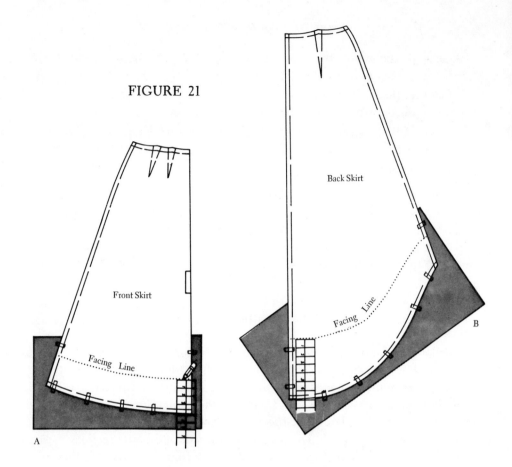

FIGURE 21

SHAPED HEM FACING

A shaped hem facing is used on skirts that have a pronounced curve, such as a hem with a train or a very flared skirt. The facing gives a smooth, professional-looking finish because there is no excess fullness to be eased in. If you are making a pattern for a hem facing using a skirt with princess seams, you must first join the center and side panels of the skirt, as explained above.

Make any necessary alterations in skirt length before making the hem facing. The procedure is the same whether the skirt has a train or not.

1. Trim the hem allowance to ⅝ inch, which will be the seam allowance for the facing.
2. Place a sheet of paper under the hem of the skirt and tape in place. *Figure 21*A shows the front skirt; *Figure 21*B shows the back skirt with a train.
3. Measure up from the edge of the pattern 3½ inches and mark along the hem, as shown in *Figure 21*A. Connect the marks freehand or preferably with a French curve.

4. On a skirt with a train, the facing is wider at the back of the train. Measure up 3½ inches at the side seam and 6½ inches at the center back, as you see in *Figure 21B*. For a skirt with no train, the facing is the same width front and back. Draw a line connecting the marks, as shown.

5. Using a tracing wheel (carbon paper is not needed), trace the facing line, hemline, and side seams of the facing. Remove the skirt pattern and mark the center front and the center back of each facing. PLACE ON FOLD. Cut out the facings on the traced line.

PATTERN ADJUSTMENTS FOR
SLEEVELESS DRESSES

A sleeveless dress is not just a dress with the sleeves taken out. The armhole of a dress with set-in sleeves is larger and the shoulder seam wider to allow for ease of movement with a sleeve. For a sleeveless dress, the armhole should be made smaller and the side seams fitted more closely to the body; otherwise the armhole will be too large and look very unattractive. I know you've seen the pattern companies show the same pattern with and without a sleeve, but this would never be done in the garment industry. The changes you need to make in the pattern are quite simple and worth the few extra minutes. If there isn't enough tissue at the armhole of your pattern, tape a small piece of paper to the armhole. Refer to *Figure 22*.

FIGURE 22

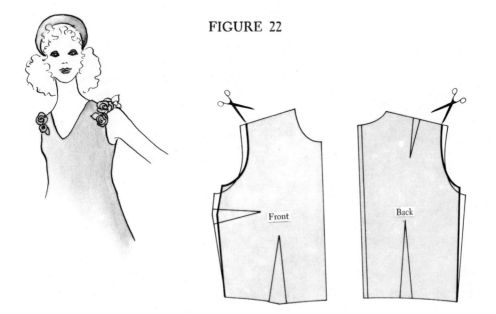

Front

Back

1. Measure in at the shoulder seam ½ inch and mark.
2. At the armhole, measure in from the side seam ½ inch and mark.
3. Extend the side seam up ½ inch from this mark, as shown.
4. Draw a new armhole with your French curve by connecting the raised side seam with the mark on the shoulder seam.
5. Draw a line from the original side seam line to the new armhole.
6. Cut out your pattern, following the new side seam and armhole.
7. Follow the same steps for the back pattern.

PATTERN ADJUSTMENTS FOR BUTTONS AND LOOP CLOSINGS

The best and most expensive wedding gowns have buttons and thread loops as a closing at the center back. (See index under *Thread loops* for directions on making the loops.) A pattern designed for regular buttonholes has an extension beyond the center back so there is a place to make the buttonholes and sew on the buttons. Because loops are added at the center back, no extension is needed on the top layer. An extension is required only on the underlayer where the buttons are sewn (see *Figure 23A*). The buttons are placed on the right side (as you wear the dress) and the loops on the left. A pattern designed for a zipper opening has no extension.

Adjustment with Zipper Opening

A pattern using a zipper opening has ⅝ inch seam allowance at the center back. For the right-side pattern, the seam allowance is used as the extension (see *Figure 23B*).

1. Cross out the words CUTTING LINE on your pattern and write FOLD LINE. Mark notches at the top and bottom of the fold line, as in the drawing.
2. Tape a strip of paper to your pattern at the center back.
3. With your ruler, draw a line parallel to the fold line 1½ inches to the left, as you see in *Figure 23B*.
4. Extend the neckline and waistline to meet this line.

When you make your garment, fold the right side on the fold line and the extra 1½ inches will become the facing. Sew the buttons on the center back line. On the left side of your garment (*Figure 23C*), the center back line is the fold line and the thread loops are made along the center back edge. If this is too confusing, you can make a separate pattern for the left and right side.

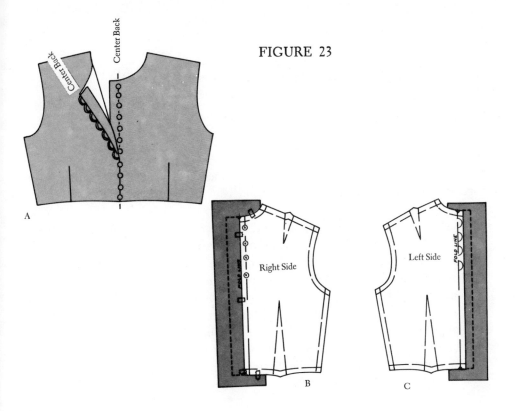

FIGURE 23

Adjustment with Button Opening

A pattern with a button extension can be used as it is for the right side. For the left side, use the center back line as the fold line instead of the fold line indicated on the pattern. (This eliminates the extension on the left side.)

Note: This will not work if your pattern has a one-piece combined neckline and front or back opening facing.

Adjustment for Fabric Loops

When you use fabric loops, adjust the right side of the pattern in the same way as for thread loops, explained above. The left side must have a facing along the center back opening since the fabric loops must be set into a seam. If you are using a pattern with a zipper opening, cut a strip of fabric 2⅝ inches wide and 3 inches longer than the opening to use as a facing on the left side. Stitch the facing along the center back line. If you are using a pattern with a buttonhole extension, add ⅝ inch seam allowance to the center back line (*not* the fold line) in red pencil. After you cut the right side of your garment, cut the left side on the red line. Cut a facing strip as for a zipper opening.

PATTERN ADJUSTMENT FOR RUFFLES AND EDGES

If you plan to add a ruffle or lace edge at the end of a sleeve or skirt, you must subtract the width of the trim from the pattern, otherwise your sleeve or skirt will be too long. For example, to add a ruffle 3 inches wide to a sleeve, the sleeve pattern would be shortened by 3 inches. See instructions for three-quarter sleeves on page 32. Shorten the sleeve by the width of your trim instead of by the measurement given.

When adding a ruffle or lace edge to the hem of a skirt, the skirt length should be correct because there will be no hem to let down or take up. You must subtract the hem allowance and also the width of the ruffle or edge. The skirt pattern in *Figure 24* has a 2½ inch hem allowance and will have a 6-inch ruffle. To adjust the pattern, you would subtract 8½ inches (hem allowance plus width of ruffle) from the bottom of the skirt. Measure up with a ruler and mark a line across the bottom of the skirt, as shown. This line is the stitching line. Measure down from the stitching line and add ⅝ inch seam allowance (dotted line). Cut the pattern on the seam allowance line, *not* on the stitching line.

FIGURE 24

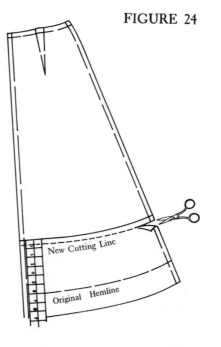

New Cutting Line

Original Hemline

ESTIMATING YARDAGE

Fabric Yardage

There are so many styling variables in making a wedding gown or formal dress that the yardage information on the pattern envelope may no longer apply. If you juggle pieces from several different patterns, add a train, or plan to cut parts of your dress from different fabrics (to name a few situations), you will need to estimate the yardage yourself. Keep in mind that the following will require consideration when estimating yardage:

NAP When using a nap or one-way-design fabric (see page 74), you will need more yardage than with an ordinary layout.

MATCHING You will need additional fabric for matching printed, woven, or lace designs.

BORDERS If you are cutting your dress on the cross grain to take advantage of a lace, embroidered, or printed border, you will need a new pattern layout if your pattern was not designed for borders.

BIAS You will also need a pattern layout if you are cutting any parts of your dress on the bias.

LAYERS Cutting sheer fabric in several layers will require extra fabric if your pattern yardage is given for only one layer. Multiply the amount of the yardage in your layout by the number of layers. For example, if your layout takes 3½ yards and your dress will use three layers of fabric, then you would need a total of 10½ yards (3 times 3½).

FABRIC WIDTH The width of bridal fabrics varies tremendously. Illusion can be 108 inches wide, other fabrics only 36 inches. Lace comes in a variety of unusual widths, such as 12 inches and 21 inches all the way up to 72 inches. Before you estimate yardage, know the width of the fabric you plan to use. If it is sold in more than one width, try a pattern layout several ways. You may be able to save quite a bit of yardage by using a wider fabric, or the wider fabric may simply be wasteful.

To figure the yardage yourself, collect all the pattern pieces you will be using. If they are going to be cut on the bias, cross grain, or one-way, have the lengthwise grain arrows pointing in the right direction (see pages 74 and 75). Use a piece of fabric or a sheet, folded to the same width as the fabric you plan to buy. If you are using two different fabrics, be sure that you make a separate layout with the correct pattern pieces for each of the materials. Spread your fabric on a large table or the floor so that you can work with all the pattern pieces at once. Refer to several of your pattern layout sheets to help you if you have trouble. Switch the pieces around until you get a tight layout. Grain line arrows *must* be kept on the grain. Remember to allow for as many parts as you need. As elementary as it sounds, it's very easy to forget that you need two sleeves, a left and right back, and so on.

The fabric conversion chart that follows shows the approximate equivalent amount of fabric needed in various widths. For example, reading across the top, if your layout requires 1¾ yards of 36-inch fabric you would need approximately 1⅜ yards of 45-inch fabric or 1 yard of 60-inch fabric for the same pattern. The figures can vary depending on the size and shape of your pattern pieces.

FABRIC CONVERSION CHART

Fabric Width	35"-36"	39"	41"	44"-45"	50"	52"-54"	58"-60"
	1¾	1½	1½	1⅜	1¼	1⅛	1
	2	1¾	1¾	1⅝	1½	1⅜	1¼
	2¼	2	2	1¾	1⅝	1½	1⅜
	2½	2¼	2¼	2⅛	1¾	1¾	1⅝
	2⅞	2½	2½	2¼	2	1⅞	1¾
Yardage	3⅛	2¾	2¾	2½	2¼	2	1⅞
	3⅜	3	2⅞	2¾	2⅜	2¼	2
	3¾	3¼	3⅛	2⅞	2⅝	2⅜	2¼
	4¼	3½	3⅜	3⅛	2¾	2⅝	2⅜
	4½	3¾	3⅝	3⅜	3	2¾	2⅝
	4¾	4	3⅞	3⅝	3¼	2⅞	2¾
	5	4¼	4⅛	3⅞	3⅜	3⅛	2⅞

Trimming Yardage

To figure the amount of yardage you need for a flat (ungathered) trim, pin seam binding to your muslin dress or pattern where you want your lace or trimming to be, and measure the length of the seam binding. Allow extra for turning corners, finishing ends, and so on. If you are using gathered trim, pin seam binding as mentioned, then turn to page 170 to figure the amount needed for lace or fabric ruffles.

4

Making and Fitting
Your Gown in Muslin

Be aware that the muslin is only utilitarian so you won't be disappointed when you find it doesn't look like the lovely gown you've pictured. The muslin gives you a chance to test the pattern and to make corrections before they become costly mistakes. Expect to make changes. There is nothing wrong with that, and it certainly doesn't mean you've failed in any way. This is how professional designers work, refining and changing a style many times—ripping out one sleeve and trying another, raising the waistline, lowering a neckline, and so on until everything looks just right. Only then is the design cut in expensive fabric.

The muslin also makes a far better pattern than tissue paper for cutting your gown. It will not wrinkle or tear and the muslin pattern will cling to the fabric.

Use all-cotton unbleached muslin. Select a heavy weight if your fabric is heavy, a light weight for lightweight materials. Purchase an extra yard or two for corrections. Press the muslin and straighten the grain (see index under *Fabric grain*). Cut only the main pattern pieces: bodice, sleeves, skirt, and so on. Facings, linings, bias strips, and such are not needed. Follow the sewing instructions included with your pattern, omitting any finishing details. You can sew a zipper in the muslin, or pin the back opening during the fitting. Construct the sleeves, but do not set them in until the bodice and skirt have been corrected. Use all-cotton thread (it is easier to rip) in a contrasting color, and set your machine for a long stitch. Separate parts such as a capelet or detachable train are fitted last, while the muslin gown is worn.

FITTING BASICS

When fitting the muslin dress, it is very important to wear the undergarments that you will actually wear with the gown. A different bra can change the shape of the bust considerably. Also, if your gown has a low neckline, you must be sure the neckline shape does not reveal any of the bra. With a dress made of soft, clinging fabric, such as knit or crepe, select a bra that has smooth seamless cups and a flat closing. Be sure that your slip and bra straps fall in the same place so there isn't a collection of straps showing under the gown.

If your gown has a full skirt, you will need either a net underskirt attached to the gown or a separate petticoat to hold out the skirt. A slip or petticoat should be made or purchased first because the underlayers affect the length of the finished gown. If your gown will have an attached net underskirt, it would be best to make the underskirt first so you can wear it when you mark the finished length of the muslin dress. Most wedding gowns do not have a typical hem that you can easily take up or let down. The hem is usually finished with a hem facing or a lace border, so there is no hem allowance for length adjustments after the gown is made. This is why it is important to have the length of the muslin gown be correct.

You will need someone to help you with part of the fitting since it is quite difficult to fit the back and shoulders yourself. Fit the muslin dress right side out on your own body, not on a dress form. To mark, you can use tailor's chalk, pins, or a combination of both. If you choose tailor's chalk, be sure it is the dry clay type, because markings made with the waxy kind will disappear when you press the muslin.

It is important not to fit the muslin too tightly. Every garment must have what is called "wearing ease," which is the difference between the measurement of the garment and the measurement of your body. For example, in a fitted style, the waist measurement of the garment is about an inch larger than your own waistline measurement so that the dress is comfortable and you have room to move. When fitting, remember that the facings and linings in the actual gown will take up some of the wearing ease. If you are using a lightweight fabric with give, such as knit or crepe, fit the muslin more closely than if you are using a heavy or stiff fabric, such as brocade or satin. After you've made a fitting change, move your arms and walk around a little to be sure you've left enough wearing ease.

Fabric, of course, is flat, while bodies are rounded and curved. The easiest way to make fabric curve around the body is with a dart. The more fabric that is taken into the dart, the more it will curve. This means that if your body is fuller than average in the bust or hips, you will need to take more into the dart; if it is flatter than average, you will need less fabric in the dart.

When a dress fits improperly, you will see wrinkles, whether the garment is too tight or too loose. As a general rule, if you see loose folds or wrinkles or breaks in the smooth flow of fabric, it means that either the garment is too large in that area or the dart near that area takes in too much fabric. If you see taut wrinkles with stress lines, either the garment is too tight in that area or the dart takes in too little fabric. When you see straining in the muslin, open the seam or dart in that area to release it. You will see where extra fabric is needed by observing the space where the seam opens. When an area is too loose, open the seam or dart and lightly smooth excess fabric into the seam or dart to mold the fabric to the body shape.

Unless you can see right away where something is wrong, fitting starts at the neck and shoulders and proceeds down the dress to the hem, which is done last. In the drawings, the fitting problems may be exaggerated to show what needs correcting. The actual appearance of the problem area of your gown could be much more subtle.

A dress that fits correctly will mold smoothly over your body contours and not have any pulls, puckers, wrinkles, or gaps. It will feel comfortable because there is no strain on the fabric and there is enough wearing ease.

NECKLINES

Jewel Neckline

A jewel neckline should conform to the base of the neck without binding or standing away from the neck. If the jewel neck comes too high up the neck, you will see bubbling on the chest above the bust line (*Figure 25A*). To relieve this, clip small notches into the neckline until the bubbling smooths out (*Figure 25B*). Re-mark the new neckline. If the neckline is too big or stands away at the back or front, this can often be alleviated by taking in the shoulder seams. When the neck is too low or wide, cut a bias strip and baste it around the neckline. Re-mark your new neckline on the bias strip (see *Figure 25C*).

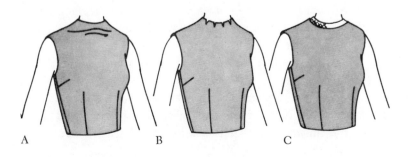

A   B   C

FIGURE 25

FIGURE 25

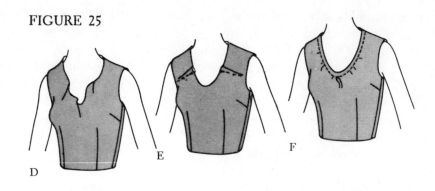

D   E   F

Low-cut Necklines

A low-cut neck should fit close to the body and not stand away or gap. A neckline can gap because the bust is too tight or the front pattern is too narrow. To check the bust fit, see below. If the neckline droops and ripples (*Figure 25D*), excess fabric should be removed. Take in at the shoulder seams or by pinning across the chest, as you see in *Figure 25E*. When the neckline is cut too low, baste a bias strip. If you are full-busted, you can fit the neckline better by running an easing stitch around the neck and pulling the thread to ease it in very slightly before applying the facing (see *Figure 25F*).

SHOULDER AND ARMHOLE

This part of the fitting is done before the sleeves are set in. The shoulder seam should be positioned along the top of your shoulder, not slant to the front or the back (unless that is part of the design). The shoulder dart should be at the center of the shoulder and point toward the shoulder blade. With set-in sleeves, the finished shoulder seam should end just beyond the shoulder bone, which you can feel as a small bumpy bone on your shoulder. If the shoulder of your muslin is too wide, mark where it should end with chalk or pins. When the shoulder is too narrow, you can baste a strip of muslin at the armhole to mark the correct position. If your shoulders are very square, the muslin will pull at the armhole and shoulders (see *Figure 26A*). Release the shoulder seams and repin so they fit properly. If your shoulders slope, you will see wrinkles or loose folds at the shoulders or chest, as in *Figure 26B*. Pin in the shoulder seams to take up the excess fabric. (The armhole may then need lowering.)

The stitching line of a set-in sleeve armhole should be about 1 inch below the armpit. If the armhole binds, redraw a lower armhole, using a French curve (*Figure 26C*). For an armhole that is too loose and baggy, take in at the side

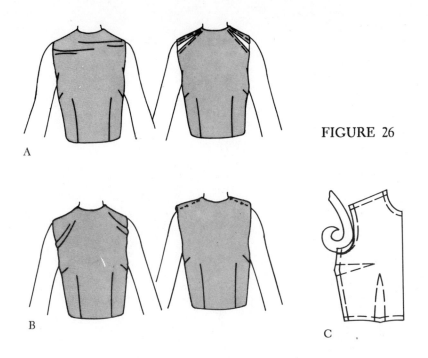

FIGURE 26

seams. When the armhole is too low, baste a strip of muslin to fill it in and redraw a higher armhole, using a French curve. A set-in sleeve armhole is not fitted snugly, to allow for wearing ease when the sleeve is set in. (A sleeveless armhole has a somewhat different shape than a regular armhole. See *Figure 22* for pattern adjustments for a sleeveless dress.)

FRONT BODICE AND BUST LINE

In fitting and in making patterns, the point of the bust is referred to as the apex. A dart should never come all the way to the apex because it would look pointy and unattractive. A properly fitted dart blends smoothly into the garment. The bust dart should line up with the fullest part of the bosom and point toward the apex. Depending on your figure and the length of your dart, the dart should end ½ inch to 1 inch from the apex.

Stand sideways and look in the mirror at the dart. If the dart is positioned above or below the fullest part of your bust line, it will be obvious and the result will be wrinkling on the front of the bodice. Mark the correct apex on the muslin with chalk. Open up the side seam of the bodice and the dart and press. With tracing wheel and carbon paper, trace the dart from the pattern onto the muslin in the new position, using the apex as a reference. Remember that you have marked the

FIGURE 27

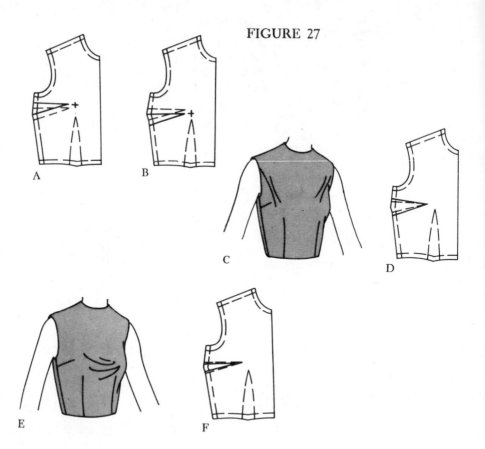

apex on your muslin, but the dart itself should not extend all the way to the apex. Refer to *Figure 27*A to raise the dart, and *Figure 27*B to lower the dart.

If you see a wrinkle or a fold forming from the bust line to the shoulder or armhole (*Figure 27*C), this means that the dart is too shallow and you need to take more fabric into the dart. To make a larger dart, use your ruler or French curve and redraw the dart, as in *Figure 27*D. If you see folds of excess fabric across the bust (*Figure 27*E), this indicates that the dart is too deep for your figure and should be made shallower to take in less fabric. Redraw the dart, as in *Figure 27*F.

The bodice front should fit smoothly with no pulling, wrinkling, or bubbling. Stress or pulling could mean that the front bodice is too narrow in width from side seam to side seam, that the back is too narrow, or both. Release the side seams and repin to achieve a better fit.

If the darts seem to be in the right place and the right size but the bodice still looks big or loose, it may simply need to be taken in at the side seams and possibly at the shoulder seams as well. When pinning in the side seams, you may find that you need to take in only the front side seams or only the back side seams, not front and back evenly. When adjustments are made, the side seams should remain along the side of your body, not slant toward the front or back.

BACK BODICE

The back should fit smoothly without wrinkling or pulling and allow enough room to move your arms and accommodate your shoulder blades comfortably. The back will look wrinkled if it is too wide. This can be corrected by taking in at the side seams, the center back, or both. A tight or narrow back can be corrected by letting out the side seams, the center back seam, or both. Back waistline darts should end below the shoulder blades. If the darts are too long, there will be stress marks across the back, as you see in *Figure 28A*. If they are too short, there will be bulges or ripples at the top of the dart, as in *Figure 28B*. Back waistline darts can also be taken in or let out to alter the back fit.

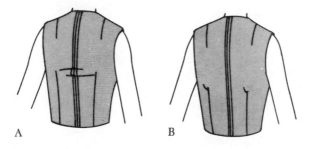

A   B

FIGURE 28

WAISTLINES

Empire Waistline

The waist seam of an Empire-style dress should be attractively positioned under the bust. If the seam rides up on the bosom, then the bodice is too short. Separate the bodice and skirt. Add a strip of muslin to the bodice waistline to extend the bodice. Repin the skirt in a lower position. (The best way is to wear the bodice and have someone else pin the skirt to it.) For a graceful appearance, the back waist is usually slightly lower than the front. There should be 1 inch of wearing ease at the Empire waist seam, or more if you will be using a bulky fabric.

Natural Waistline

A natural-waistline bodice should fit smoothly through the midriff. If there are taut stress lines or bubbling out in that area, release the waistline dart and repin for a better fit. When the bodice is too long, the waistline will ride up and cause a blousy looseness in the midriff. Tie a string snugly around your waist to locate your natural waistline accurately. If the waistline of the muslin dress is not correct, mark the location of the string on the muslin, using tailor's chalk. Remove the skirt from the bodice and rejoin on the new line. The back waistline is lower than the front waistline on most people.

SKIRTS

Empire A-line Skirt

An A-line skirt attached to an Empire-waistline style should fall smoothly with no breaks or ripples. It sometimes takes a little work to get this skirt to hang properly. Most of the corrections involve raising or lowering either the back or the front of the skirt at the waistline seam. When you do this, be sure to work with only the skirt waistline seam and not alter the shape of the bodice waistline seam. Stand sideways and look at the side seams in the mirror. They should hang straight and perpendicular to the floor, not swing to the front or the back (see *Figure 29A*). When the side seam swings toward the back or there are ripples across the upper part of the front skirt, it indicates that the skirt should be raised in the front. To do this, release the front waistline seam, pull the skirt up until it hangs correctly, and repin (see *Figure 29B*). When the side seam slants toward the front or there are ripples across the back skirt above the hips, raise the skirt at the back by opening the back waistline seam and repinning (see *Figure 29C*). There should be at least 3 inches of wearing ease at the hips. The skirt of the gown (not the muslin) should be underlined to hang smoothly.

Flared Skirt

A flared skirt joined to a natural or Empire waistline should hang in soft, even folds. The side and center back seams should be perpendicular to the floor. If the skirt does not hang attractively, try raising the front or back skirt at the waistline, as explained above.

Wrong

B

C

FIGURE 29

Gathered Skirt

A gathered skirt does not require much fitting. You may decide to change the amount of gathers, depending on your gown fabric. For sheer, lightweight fabric, you may want more fullness. If you are using a stiff or heavy fabric, you may need fewer gathers than the amount included in the pattern.

Do not mark the hem at this point. Once the bodice and skirt have been fitted, set in the sleeves and see information on fitting sleeves below.

PRINCESS-SEAM STYLES

Princess-seam styles can fit close to the body through the bodice or have a less fitted A-line shaping. Princess seams usually originate at the shoulder or armhole, but designers use other lines as well. The seams should follow the contours of your body. If there is stress, rippling, or looseness anywhere along the seam, release the seam and repin to achieve a smooth fit. Refitting the side seams may also help.

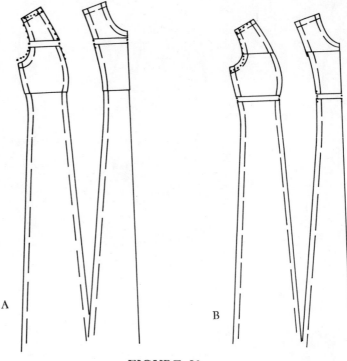

FIGURE 30

If the front bodice seams do not fit well, the bust shaping may be too high or too low for your figure. When the bust shaping is too high, the muslin will bubble on the chest above the bust. When the shaping is too low, there will be bubbling or ripples below the bust. To correct either of these problems, you will have to alter the paper pattern and recut the muslin bodice.

To adjust the pattern to lower the bust line, see *Figure* 30A. Slash both the center front and the side front patterns, above the bust line, as shown, and spread the pattern the amount the bust needs to be lowered. Fill in with tracing paper. A corresponding amount must be removed below the bust line by taking a tuck in the pattern. (If you spread the pattern 1 inch, then the tuck should take in 1 inch.) Using your French curve, raise the armhole and smooth any jogs in the princess seams, as shown.

To raise the bust line, see *Figure* 30B. (This procedure is the reverse of lowering the bust line.) Slash the pattern below the bust and spread the amount needed to raise the bust line. A corresponding amount should be removed above the bust line. Lower the armhole and smooth the seam lines, as shown.

If applicable to your pattern, check to see that front and back princess seams meet at the shoulder, and bodice and skirt princess seams meet at the waist.

Set in the sleeves once the bodice and skirt have been fitted.

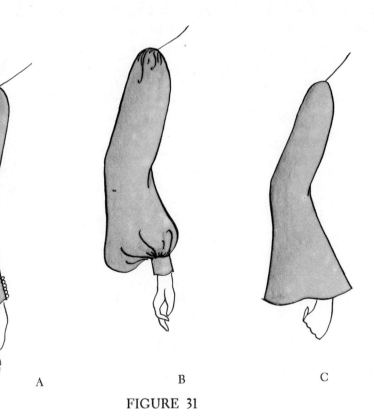

A   B   C

FIGURE 31

SLEEVES

There are two kinds of set-in sleeves: fitted cap (*Figure 31A*) and gathered cap (*Figure 31B*). A sleeve can have a fitted cap even if the lower part of the sleeve is flared or gathered (*Figure 31C*). A fitted cap should round smoothly over your shoulder and have no wrinkles or puckers. The underarm seam should be about 1 inch below the armpit. If the cap puckers or appears to have excess fabric, the height of the cap may need to be lowered. Take out the sleeve, and open the seam. Refer to *Figure 43A*. Once the adjustment is made, reset the sleeve to check the correction. At the shoulder, the armhole seam should be positioned just beyond the shoulder bone. If the sleeve is set too high on the shoulder, it will feel tight and look unattractive. If it is set too low, it will look droopy and there will probably be ripples in the sleeve just below the shoulder. While wearing the dress, release between the notches the stitching joining the sleeve to the armhole. Try not to break the easing thread. If the sleeve is set too high, it will move to the correct position by itself, once it is released. When the sleeve is set too low, pull up the cap and repin it in the right place on the shoulder.

A long fitted sleeve has one or two darts at the elbow. When there is one dart, it should be at the point of the elbow when you bend your arm. With two elbow darts, the point of your elbow should be centered between the darts. The correct finished length for a long fitted sleeve is at the wristbone. A 4- or 5-inch zipper or a button and loop closing will be needed at the wrist.

A sleeve with a gathered cap does not require much fitting at the cap. The gathers should be smooth and evenly distributed or the sleeve will not hang properly.

Cuffs should fit comfortably, not be too tight or too loose. A cuffed sleeve that is not the correct length can be adjusted either on the cuff or on the sleeve.

A long sleeve that will have a ruffle or lace edge at the end must be shortened to allow for the width of the trim (see page 46).

Once you have made a correction on the sleeve, move your arm and bend your elbow to be sure the sleeve feels comfortable.

HEMS

When marking the hem, wear shoes with heels the same height as those you will be wearing with your gown. Be sure to wear whatever petticoat or underskirt you will use with your finished gown. Stand up straight and have someone else pin up the hem. The gown should be ½ to 1 inch from the floor so your shoes do not show when you stand still and only the toe of a shoe is visible when you walk. A train that is too long can be shortened when the hem is pinned. To lengthen the train, machine-baste a large piece of muslin to the back skirt at the hem. Then, using the paper pattern, recut the curve of the train on the muslin extension. (If your skirt has a hem facing, you will have to alter the hem facing if you lengthen or shorten the train.)

Hem allowance can vary quite a lot depending on the fabric, the shape of the skirt, and the type of hem that will be used on the gown. Refer to Chapter 8 for detailed information on hems.

If your pattern has a shaped facing at the hem, the length adjustment must be made in the upper part of the skirt rather than at the hem edge, or the facing will no longer fit the hem. The original skirt pattern should have a crosswise line to indicate where to make it longer or shorter. To shorten the skirt, pin a tuck across the muslin skirt in the same location as the alteration line on the pattern. The muslin skirt should be ⅝ inch longer than the finished skirt to leave the seam allowance for the facing. To lengthen the skirt, slash across the muslin at the location of the alteration line and machine-baste a strip of muslin wide enough to add the required length.

MAKING A MUSLIN PATTERN

Once the gown has been fitted and corrected, the muslin is marked and then taken apart so it can be used as the pattern to cut your gown. The seams should be pressed open and darts well pressed so you can mark them properly. Use a soft-tip pen such as Flair or Bic Banana in a contrasting color from other marks on your muslin.

Tissue patterns are for only half a dress because usually the fabric is folded and cut in two layers. However, a number of special fabrics and laces should not be cut on the fold (see Chapters 5 and 6). If you have one of these fabrics, you will need a pattern for an entire dress since the fabric is cut in one layer. When making a complete dress pattern, mark both right and left sides of the muslin. Otherwise mark only the right side (as you wear it) of the muslin. Carefully draw the pen along all the seams and darts, pressing the point firmly into the seam, to be sure that the ink marks both sides of the seam. At the end of each dart point, make an X; where one seam joins another, make a cross mark (see *Figures 32A and B*). Be sure to mark the armhole, sleeve, waist seam, darts, shoulder seam, center back, and the edge of the hem. Write the name of each pattern piece on the muslin: BODICE FRONT, SKIRT BACK, and so on. If you are making a pattern for the entire dress, write LEFT FRONT, RIGHT FRONT, and so on for each piece. Once the muslin is marked, carefully take it apart, using a seam ripper or scissors. If you are using half a pattern, discard the left side. Open up the darts and press the muslin pieces flat.

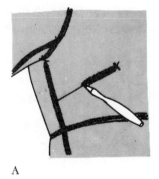

A

FIGURE 32

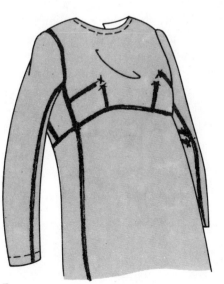

B

FIGURE 32

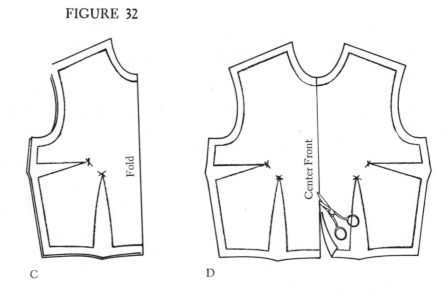

C   D

To make half a pattern from the complete front, fold the muslin in half, matching the shoulder seams, armholes, and side seams accurately. Smooth the muslin and crease along the fold with your fingernail (*Figure 32C*). Open up the muslin and cut along the crease (*Figure 32D*). Discard the left side. Mark the cut edge of the right side CENTER FRONT—PLACE ON FOLD.

If you are using a whole muslin pattern, fold the front in half to check the shape of the neckline. If the right and left sides are not identical, trim the neckline to make both sides the same. Also place the right and left back patterns together to compare the back neckline.

The last step is to correct the seam allowance. Since the muslin has been altered there is probably no longer ⅝ inch seam allowance in all places. Use your ruler to check the width of the seam allowance. If it is too wide, measure and mark ⅝ inch and trim away excess. Where the seam allowance is too narrow, attach a strip of muslin to the pattern, using Scotch Magic Tape. Mark the seam allowance on the strip and trim away excess. On better ready-made dresses, the seam allowance at the side and center back seams is sometimes 1 inch. This extra seam allowance is especially recommended for fabrics that are slippery (except sheers), bulky, or loosely woven, or that fray easily.

5

Sewing Special Fabrics

A finished dress is the result of a number of different steps, each often quite small in itself. Because so many are simple, it is often tempting to think that each one does not count for very much, and so not pay a great deal of attention. Actually one step done not too carefully multiplied by ten or twenty is what results in a homemade-looking dress. Think of a choir—one off-key voice may get lost, but a dozen off-key voices will ruin it no matter how beautiful the rest are. Taking care of such seemingly small things as selecting the exact color of thread, correct needle size and stitch length, straightening the fabric grain, carefully pressing each seam, steaming a sleeve cap, using interfacing, gathering evenly, or choosing the best type of hem for your dress style and fabric will add up to a truly professional dress that you will be proud of. Good fitting is just as important as good sewing. A beautifully sewn dress that droops or pulls on the body will not do you justice either. Read the information in this chapter and in Chapter 4 on making a fitting muslin dress before you begin sewing your special fabric.

LININGS, UNDERLININGS, AND INTERFACINGS

Don't neglect the inside of your dress—this is one of the areas that can make the difference between a homemade or professional result. If you look at expensive

ready-to-wear, you will see that it is the attention to details that separates it from ordinary clothes. By spending just a little extra time and money, you can more than double the equivalent retail value of your dress.

LINING A lining is assembled separately and then sewn into the garment with the raw edges of the lining toward the inside of the dress. All of the inside construction details, such as seams, darts, and hems, are hidden. This gives a smooth, luxurious feeling and a quality, custom-made look. A lining preserves the shape of the dress and adds body to soft fabrics. It also cuts down on wrinkling—an important consideration when you have to sit in a car on the way to your wedding ceremony or social event.

UNDERLINING Underlining differs from lining. The dress fabric and underlining fabric are basted together and the dress is constructed as if of one layer. Inside construction is not hidden. Underlining is used to give body to fabric that would not hold its shape and to prevent lace or sheer fabric from appearing too transparent. A dress that is underlined will look more attractive on the outside because the facings, interfacings, and hem can be anchored to the underlining only, so that no stitching will show on the right side of the dress. The underlining must be cut on the same grain as the dress to avoid stress or pulling. (If your dress has parts cut on the bias, then your underlining would also be cut on the bias.) Some very expensive dresses have both lining and underlining.

INTERFACING Interfacing is used in specific areas to give body and to maintain shape. In most gowns, collars and neckbands, necklines, front or back openings, and cuffs should be interfaced. Generally, regular interfacing (as opposed to fusible, iron-on type) is a better finish. If you do use fusible interfacing, never iron it to the gown itself—apply it only to hidden areas such as cuff backing, undercollar, or facing.

As a rule, any inner fabric should be lighter in weight than the dress fabric, except when using sheer fabrics or lace, which are underlined in an opaque fabric. Usually, interfacing should be lighter in weight than the dress fabric and less stiff. To help you choose the correct linings and interfacings for your fabric, see the following chart.

PLATE 3
Bridal and Special-occasion Fabrics:

1. Dull-face satin   2. Cotton jacquard   3. Moiré   4. Raschel knits
5. Printed dimity   6. Leno fabrics   7. Panne velvet   8. Lightweight satin   9. Sequined chiffon   10. Chiffon   11. Flocked organza   12. Satapeau   13. Ottoman   14. Lamé   15. Maracaine
16. Satin stripe   17. Brocades   18. Satin crepe   19. Embroidered satin

WOVEN FABRICS

DRESS FABRIC	INTERFACING
SHEERS chiffon georgette organdy organza satapeau voile	Not used unless dress is underlined in opaque fabric, then lightest-weight non-woven; also organdy or organza are used as interfacing
SOFT LIGHTWEIGHT crepe de chine silk	Soft featherweight to lightweight
CRISP LIGHTWEIGHT batiste dimity dotted swiss eyelet gingham lightweight cottons tissue taffeta	Woven or non-woven lightweight—crisp but not stiff
SOFT MEDIUM-WEIGHT crepe crepe-back satin panne velvet some satins	Soft light- to medium-weight woven or non-woven
CRISP MEDIUM-WEIGHT linen piqué some satins shantung taffeta	Crisp light- to medium-weight woven or non-woven
HEAVYWEIGHT brocade faille moiré bridal satin peau de soie velvet velveteen	Crisp medium to heavy woven or non-woven, or none if fabric is quite stiff

UNDERLINING	LINING
Chiffon and georgette are often underlined in self fabric or taffeta, also batiste for crisp sheers; also see lining fabrics	China silk or lightweight silk-like lining, lining crepe or taffeta; lining can be made as separate underdress
Not usually underlined; if used, see lining fabrics	China silk or lightweight, soft silk-like polyester or rayon lining fabric
Batiste or lightweight rayon lining fabric; patterned batiste underlining can be used for a special effect so the fabric design shows through	Batiste, lawn, or lightweight rayon lining fabric
No underlining for gathered and drapey styles; for more structured styles, see linings	Medium-weight rayon or polyester lining, lining crepe, or China silk
For extra body use light- to medium-weight (but not stiff) woven interfacing as underlining; also see linings	China silk, batiste, light- to medium-weight rayon or polyester lining fabric
Usually necessary for A-line and other structured styles—same fabrics as listed for crisp medium-weight, also taffeta	Same fabrics as listed for crisp medium-weight, also taffeta or acetate lining fabric, lightweight satin, or satin crepe

WOVEN FABRICS

DRESS FABRIC	INTERFACING
METALLIC FABRICS	Select by weight and softness of fabric as for non-metallic counterpart listed above
BEADED AND SEQUINED FABRICS	Not generally used on closely beaded fabrics; for sparsely beaded fabrics select interfacing by type of base fabric

KNITS

STABLE (NON-STRETCHY) KNITS double knits of wool, Qiana, polyester, etc.	Knit interfacing; also see soft medium-weight listing above
UNSTABLE (STRETCHY) KNITS interlocks jersey types knit panne maracaine	Knit interfacing; also featherweight non-woven bias

LACE

SHEER LACE Alençon Chantilly English net point d'esprit	Not used
HEAVY LACE Cluny Venise	Used only if lace is underlined with opaque fabric; crisp light- to medium-weight woven or non-woven

UNDERLINING

Select from fabrics listed above of appropriate weight

Select according to weight of base fabric from list of fabrics above

Seldom underlined

Seldom used; you can use a double layer of knit so second layer acts as underlining

For sheer effect, use organza, tulle, or net; for opacity, use taffeta

For sheer effect, use organza, organdy, or tulle; also batiste, crepe, rayon lining fabric, or taffeta in flesh tone for sheer effect, and in matching or contrasting color for opacity

LINING

Usually needed for comfort since beaded and metallic fabrics can be irritating against the skin; should be closely woven

May be left unlined—if lined, select fabric from soft medium-weight listing, or tricot

Not usually lined; skirt of dress may be lined with petticoat of taffeta or crepe attached at waist; also separate slip or petticoat can be made of lining fabric

May be made as separate underdress (underline lace in sheer); use China silk, lightweight silk-like crepe lining for soft styles, taffeta for crisp shaping. Skirt lining may be made of several layers of net or organza over silk or taffeta. Lining may be flesh tone, matching or contrasting color if underlining is sheer

FABRIC PREPARATION

Before you begin cutting, your fabric may require one or more of the following: preshrinking, straightening the grain, or removing the center crease.

Preshrinking

Preshrinking fabric is not necessary for a wedding gown because obviously you'll be wearing it only once. It is also not necessary to preshrink nylon or polyester. For other dresses, you should, besides the fabric, also preshrink all of the components including the lining, interfacing, zipper, seam binding, and trimmings. Some cotton laces and other trimmings shrink a tremendous amount. (If you have had a dress come back from the cleaner with a rippled zipper because the zipper tape shrank, or a puckered hem because the seam binding shrank, then you know how important preshrinking is.) Washable fabric may be preshrunk by dampening or by washing in the washing machine. You can put small items such as seam binding and zipper in one of those nylon mesh bags used for washing stockings. Dry-cleanable fabrics should be preshrunk by sending to a dry cleaner. Woolens can be preshrunk at home using a damp sheet, as follows.

Place a very damp sheet on a flat surface and lay the wool fabric on the top of the sheet. Carefully fold the wool and the sheet together, always keeping the sheet next to the wool. Place the folded fabric in a plastic bag and leave overnight. Unfold the fabric and smooth it into shape. Hang it over a shower rod until just slightly damp. Press, using a dry pressing cloth.

Fabric Grain

When fabric is woven, the crosswise threads, called the filling, are placed at a right angle to the lengthwise threads, called the warp (see *Figure* 33A). However, during the finishing processes the fabric can be pulled out of shape so that the warp and filling run at an off angle. When this occurs, fabric is said to be off grain. Because off-grain fabric does not hang smoothly and is difficult to fit, it is important to straighten the grain of the fabric before you cut.

To see if your fabric grain is straight, you must first straighten the cut ends of your fabric. The best way is to pull a thread (see *Figure* 33B). Clip into the selvage and, with a pin, pull out one crosswise thread. Gently pull on the thread so that the fabric puckers, then cut along the puckered line across the width of the fabric. This should be done at both ends. To straighten the ends of knit fabrics, see p. 110.

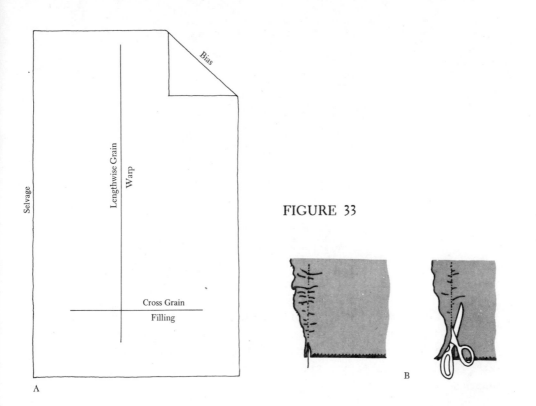

FIGURE 33

A

B

After the ends are straightened, the easiest way to see whether the fabric grain is straight is to place the fabric on a square or rectangular table, aligning the selvage with one side of the table. If the grain is straight, the cross grain will line up with the corner of the table (*Figure 33C*). If the grain is off, it will look like *Figure 33D*. You can also check the grain by placing an L square at the corner of your fabric. Another way to see if the grain is straight is to fold the fabric so the cut edges meet and pin the edges together. If the fabric is on the grain, it will fold flat and

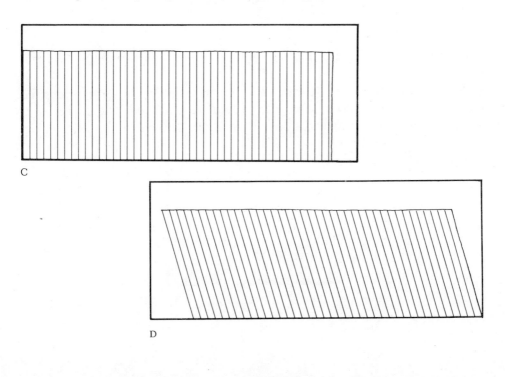

C

D

FIGURE 33

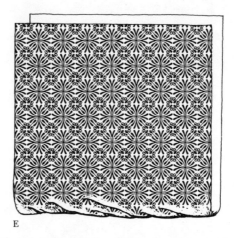

E

smooth. When the fabric is off grain it will ripple at the fold, as you see in *Figure 33E*. You can straighten the fabric by steam pressing or by pulling along the bias in the opposite direction from the way the fabric is off grain, as you see in *Figure 33F*. For stubborn fabric, you can use a combination of pulling and steam pressing.

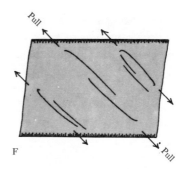

F

Laces and nets do not have a grain, so you do not have to straighten these fabrics.

When you lay out your pattern pieces, the grain line of the pattern must be placed along the lengthwise grain of the fabric. To check this, use a ruler or L square and measure accurately the distance from the grain line to the selvage (*Figure 33G*).

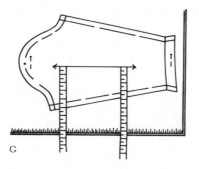

G

Straightening and Shrinking

If your fabric needs both straightening and preshrinking, these can sometimes be accomplished at the same time.

WASHABLE FABRICS Fold the fabric in half crosswise, matching the cut ends, as in *Figure 33E*. Baste the cut ends together. Fold the fabric a number of times into a small bundle. Place the fabric in tepid water and soak until thoroughly wet. Remove from the water and squeeze the water out, but do not wring or twist. Unfold the fabric and, leaving it basted, shape it so that the bubbles and ripples along the fold are eliminated. Allow to dry flat.

WOOL Fold and baste the fabric as described for washable fabrics, above. Then follow the directions for preshrinking wool using a dampened sheet. To dry, leave the basting in and spread the fabric flat or hang over a shower rod, smoothing the fabric so that there are no bubbles or puckers along the fold and the ends remain at right angles.

Removing the Center Crease

Fabrics that are sold doubled and rolled on bolts have a crease along the center. The crease in circular knits is permanent and cannot be removed, although it can be minimized. With circular knits, the center crease should never be used as the fold line when placing your pattern because this will result in a garment with a discolored line down the center front or center back. With woven fabrics, you may or may not be able to remove the crease completely. Place the fabric face down on the ironing board and press the fabric, using the appropriate method (see specific fabric headings in this chapter). If you can use moisture with your fabric, place a pressing cloth over the crease and spray the pressing cloth, using a spray mist bottle. With a simple washable fabric, such as cotton, you can spray the fabric itself and then press again. Turn the fabric face up, spray again, and press. If the crease is still there, try washing or dry cleaning. After this treatment, if the crease is still noticeable, it cannot be removed, and you should place your pattern pieces carefully to avoid having the crease in a conspicuous spot. This means that you will not be able to fold your fabric in half lengthwise the way the pattern layout may specify.

Even if your fabric did not require straightening, preshrinking, or removal of the crease, it should be pressed before you begin cutting.

NAP AND ONE-WAY-DESIGN FABRICS

Many special fabrics must be cut using a one-way or nap layout. This means that the tops of all pattern pieces go in the same direction, as you see in *Figure 34A*. A fabric mut be cut in one direction either because the way it reflects light causes the color to appear a different shade in each direction, or because it has a design running one way only. Some fabrics that must be cut this way are velvet, velveteen, velour, satin, sateen, brocade, and some laces, as well as some plaids, stripes, and prints. Velveteen and velvet should be cut with the pile running up toward

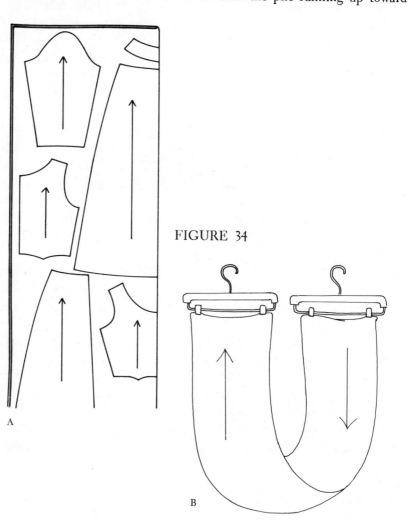

FIGURE 34

the face to give a rich color. Panne velvet is usually cut with the pile running down toward the floor. The direction that looks best may depend on the individual fabric. With a bright color pencil, circle the top of the grain line arrow on each pattern piece to remind you to place them in the same direction. If yardage for a nap layout is not given with your pattern, see index, *Estimating yardage*.

If you are not sure whether your fabric is one-way, or to see which way looks best, use the fabric direction test. To do this, take two skirt hangers and clip one on each of the cut ends of the fabric. (Do not clip onto the selvage.) Hang the hangers next to each other on a door, as you see in *Figure 34B*. One side of the fabric will be facing up and the other side will be facing down. In good light, preferably daylight, stand back and look at the fabric carefully. If one side appears different in color, shading, or design, the fabric is one-way. With prints, most patterns are either a two-way or tossed layout with some of the figures right side up and some upside down so the fabric will look the same in either direction. With a

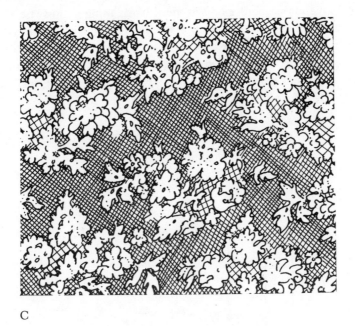

C

one-way print, when the fabric is hung the wrong way the figures will look distinctly upside down. With a one-way-design lace you will see that the texture or pattern of the lace looks different in each direction (*Figure 34C*). Study lace carefully, as this difference may not be immediately apparent. Decide which direction looks best and mark it with an arrow or pins along the selvage, pointing in the direction you want to place the pattern.

If you are looking at a fabric in the store and want to see if it is one-way, unwrap several yards from the bolt and drape the fabric so that one side runs up and one side runs down. If possible, take the fabric to the window so that you can see the color in natural light.

PATTERN PREPARATION

Your pattern, whether paper or muslin, should be pressed before you use it. With certain fabrics you may need to change the grain line on the pattern, or make duplicate or transparent pattern pieces before cutting.

Changing the Grain Line

The pattern grain line must be placed on the lengthwise grain of the fabric. Unless your pattern shows a border or bias view, when using a crosswise (border) or bias layout you must change the direction of the grain line arrows on your pattern pieces in order to lay them out correctly.

(A pattern that is to be placed on a border must have a straight line along the border edge. A pattern with a curved line, such as a flared skirt, will not work—see *Figure 35A*.)

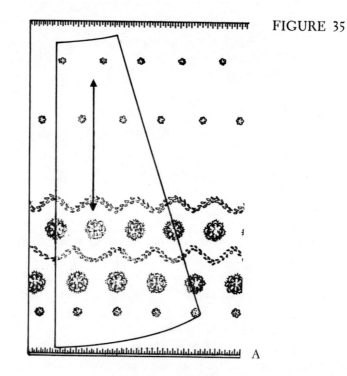

FIGURE 35

A

The easiest way to change the arrow direction is with a triangle (see equipment in Chapter 1). For a crosswise layout, place your triangle with one short side along

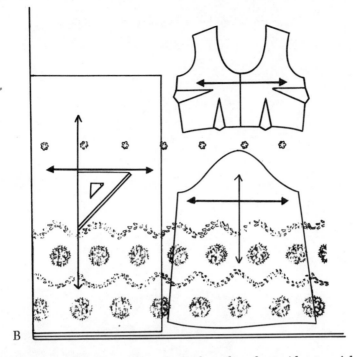

B

the lengthwise arrow and draw a line along the other short side at a right angle to the lengthwise arrow (*Figure 35B*). Use a yardstick or ruler to extend the line across your pattern. This line is now the lengthwise grain line. Mark each pattern piece the same way.

If you are changing your layout to bias, place the short side of your triangle on the lengthwise arrow of your pattern. Draw a line following the long side of your triangle (*Figure 35C*). Extend this line with a ruler or yardstick. This line is your new lengthwise grain line.

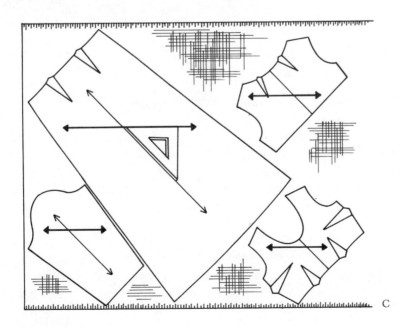

C

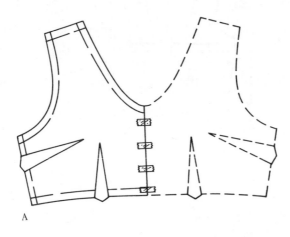

A

FIGURE 36

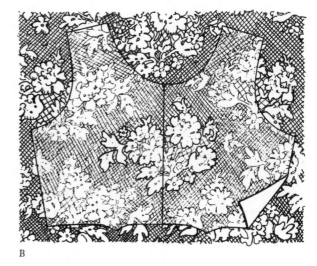

B

Duplicate Pattern Pieces

A number of special fabrics should be cut in a single layer instead of on the fold. In order to do this, you will need duplicate or whole pattern pieces, since the printed tissue pattern includes only half a garment. If you've made a muslin dress, then you already have duplicate pattern pieces where they are needed. When using a tissue paper pattern, you can make duplicates (so that you have two sleeves, an entire front, and so on) by tracing your pattern onto ordinary tracing paper, using a tracing wheel without dressmaker's carbon paper. Large-size tracing paper is available on rolls in art supply stores. To make an entire front, trace the pattern and tape each half along the center front line (*Figure 36A*). Be sure you mark each of your pieces RIGHT BACK, LEFT BACK, and so on, so that you don't cut two of the same side. Fabrics that need duplicate pattern pieces include slippery sheers, heavy velvets and brocades, and beaded fabrics, as well as some metallic fabrics and laces.

Transparent Patterns

If you are working with lace or a printed fabric that has a large or obvious design motif, the motif should be positioned carefully for a professional look. Usually the best placement is to center the motif at the center front line of the pattern so the entire motif is attractively placed on the bodice, not chopped through the middle (see *Figure 36B*). Position motifs on the skirt, back, and sleeves the same way.

You can make this job easier by using sheer nylon pattern tracing fabric, such as Trace-a-Pattern, to make a transparent pattern. Because you can see through it easily, you will be able to place your pattern so that the design of your lace or print is shown to its best advantage. You will need an entire pattern, not just the usual half. Fold the pattern tracing fabric in half lengthwise. Pin your pattern to the tracing fabric and cut it out as you would a garment. Mark the darts and other information with tracing wheel and carbon (the carbon will go through the tracing fabric, so protect your work surface). Crease and center front line sharply with your fingernail. Unpin the pattern pieces and mark the center front line with a ruler and ball-point pen. Usually you will need only transparent bodice, skirt, and sleeve patterns.

MARKING METHODS

Many sewing books advocate marking your garment with tailor's chalk or carbon and tracing wheel all over the place, but I believe that this should be avoided. In the sample room in the garment industry, markings are kept to an absolute minimum because excessive marking makes a garment look unprofessional. Many of the fabrics used for wedding gowns and special occasion dresses are very sensitive to marking and will quickly begin to look overhandled. This is why tracing wheel and carbon are seldom used except for marking a lining or underlining. (If you are using an underlining with a sheer fabric, even marks on the underlining can show through.) Notches should be cut out, rather than in, and other necessary marks should be made with tailor's tacks.

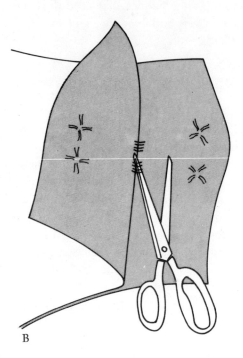

A

B

FIGURE 37

Tailor's Tacks

Tailor's tacks should be made using silk thread and a fine needle, size 9 or 10. For best results, make your tailor's tacks very close to the time when you will be sewing so that they will not mark the fabric or slip out. To make a tailor's tack, see *Figure 37*. You can use a double or single layer of fabric. Using a long double strand of thread without a knot, make a small stitch through your pattern and fabric at the point where you need a mark (such as the point of a dart). Then sew another stitch crossing over the first. Pull on the thread until a large loop is formed, as in *Figure 37A*. As you go to the next mark, leave a loose thread and make another tailor's tack the same way. When you have finished making the necessary loops, clip all the loops and also the long threads connecting the tacks. Remove the pattern carefully. If you are using two layers of fabric, slowly separate the two layers, clipping the connecting threads (*Figure 37B*). This will leave a little tuft of thread as a mark. Once you have sewn your dart, remove the thread tufts. This type of marking is necessary only at the inner part of the garment, not at the edge. Marks needed at the edge of the garment can be made with outward notches.

Thread Tracing

Thread tracing is a basting stitch used to mark grain lines and indicate trimming position on the right side of the garment. For example, by thread-tracing a line indicating the center front of your bodice and skirt, when you try on the dress you can see if the skirt is hanging correctly. By marking the center line of a sleeve with thread tracing, you can see if the sleeve is twisting or pulling. When you are using lace appliqués, the center front line of the dress should be thread-traced so you can be sure of positioning your appliqués symmetrically. A line of thread tracing can also be used to indicate where bands of lace or other trimming should be placed. If you are applying narrow lace in an intricate design, such as a swirl or scallop shape, you will definitely need to follow a thread tracing. Thread tracing is made by using silk thread with no knot on the end. Begin by taking a small backstitch. An uneven basting stitch is used (see *Figure* 38). A long stitch is taken on the top and a short stitch through the fabric. Thread tracing should not be left in the garment any longer than necessary because it may eventually cause marks. Once you no longer need the thread tracing, remove it by clipping the thread carefully every few inches and pulling out the threads. Don't yank out the thread in one long piece. (Test thread tracing on a scrap first to be sure the needle doesn't leave a mark.)

FIGURE 38

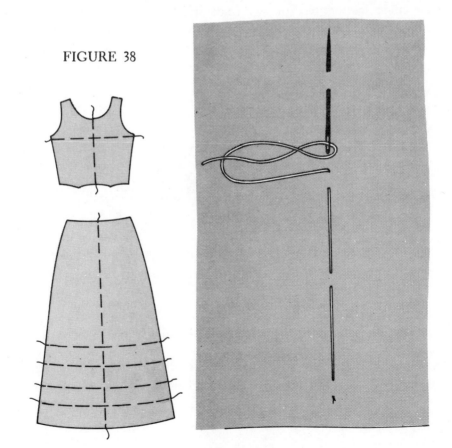

MAKING A TEST SEAM

Before you begin to sew your dress you should make a test seam to check the stitch length, tension, and pressure. Making a mistake on a scrap is not serious—you can just throw the scrap away. If you make a mistake on your dress, you have to rip it out carefully and run the risk of permanently marring the fabric. To make a test seam, cut two strips of fabric 3 inches wide and 8 inches long. The long side should be on the lengthwise grain with woven fabrics, and on the crosswise grain with knits. Place the strips together with the edges even. Pin and stitch the seam. Then check the following:

STITCH LENGTH If the seam is puckered, it could be because the stitch length is too short. (It could also be incorrect machine tension: see below.) If the seam is not held together securely, then the stitch is too long.

PRESSURE The pressure refers to how firmly the presser foot holds the fabric as you stitch. If the presser foot holds the fabric too tightly, the upper layer of fabric will drag, so that at the end of your seam the upper layer will be longer than the bottom layer (*Figure* 39A). If this occurs, loosen the pressure on the pressure foot. If the fabric does not feed through smoothly as you sew and the stitches are of uneven length, the pressure foot pressure is too light and is not holding the fabric securely enough to produce even stitches. Tighten the pressure slightly.

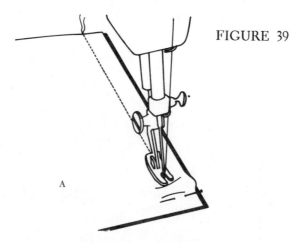

FIGURE 39

A

TENSION Tension refers to how tightly the thread is held as it moves through the tension guide. The tension is regulated by a dial on the machine for the upper tension and a screw on the bobbin case for the lower tension. When the thread tension is correct, or balanced, the stitching looks the same on both sides of the fabric (*Figure 39B*). If the thread tension is too tight, tiny loops will appear on the upper side (*Figure 39C*). If the bobbin tension is too tight, loops will appear on the underside (*Figure 39D*). If the tension is just a little too tight, it will cause a puckered seam.

Once you make an adjustment, trim off the first line of stitching and stitch again to check the adjustment. If your dress uses two different kinds of fabric, make a test seam for each of the fabrics as well as a test seam joining pieces of each fabric. You may find that you will have to make adjustments when you switch from one fabric to the other.

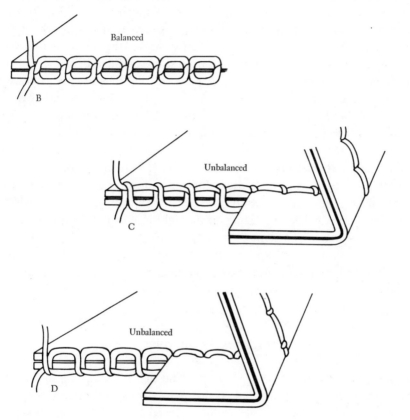

PRESSING

Pressing is extremely important to the final appearance of your dress. No matter how beautifully you sew, if you do not take the time to press carefully, your dress will not look professional. If you are a sewer of average skill, you can upgrade the quality of your garment considerably by careful pressing. You must press as you sew, and it is important to have good pressing equipment in order to do a proper job. (Refer to Chapter 1 for more information on pressing equipment.)

Remember that pressing is not the same thing as ironing. When ironing, you glide the iron over the fabric to smooth it and remove wrinkles. In pressing, the iron is lifted and placed without sliding it back and forth. One of the major aims in pressing is to mold and shape the garment. The body is curved and rounded, while fabric is flat. Sewing darts and seams is the beginning of shaping the fabric to the body; the rest is done by pressing. As you press, think of rounding and molding, not flattening. Use only the tip of the iron as much as possible. Press gently and lightly. The weight of the iron is not what is used to do the work—it is heat and moisture. Pressing the weight of the iron down on the fabric will only result in flattening the fabric and forming ridges from seams and darts.

During the fitting stage of construction, press very lightly and only as much as is needed to judge the fit of your garment. Well-pressed seams and darts may leave marks that will be difficult to remove if further adjustment is needed. Never press with pins in the fabric, since this will result in an impression of the pins being left. Where possible, also remove basting before pressing. If you do press with basting threads in, use silk threads because they are less likely to leave a mark.

Always pretest on a scrap of fabric before pressing your garment (temperature indications on the iron are not always accurate). Fabric should be pressed on the wrong side whenever possible; pressing on the right side can cause shininess and an overpressed appearance. To dampen your press cloth, use a water spray misting bottle or wipe it with a damp sponge. Depending on your fabric, very slight dampness or substantial dampness may be best. Certain fabrics, such as satins and some synthetics, should be pressed with no moisture at all.

Pressing Techniques

FLAT SEAMS A straight flat seam is so mundane that it's tempting to want to zip the iron over it and let it go at that. If not pressed well, however, a long straight seam will be quite conspicuous and really can spoil the look of your dress. Seams should appear as fine, smooth lines with no ripples or waviness. Press the seam flat before pressing it open, pressing with the grain. Turn the garment over and press again on the other side. All seams should be pressed flat before being pressed open to smooth out any puckers that may have occurred during the stitching and to make the seam smooth. Next, press the seam open with no moisture. Use the tip of the iron along the seam line. For hard-to-reach places, a small travel iron is handy. The best way to press open a flat seam is with a seam roll (see *Figure* 40A). When using a seam roll, only the seam itself is pressed. The surrounding fabric rolls over the seam roll and you do not risk making an impression of the seam allowance on the right side of your garment. Another way to avoid making a seam allowance impression is to cut strips of brown paper and insert them between

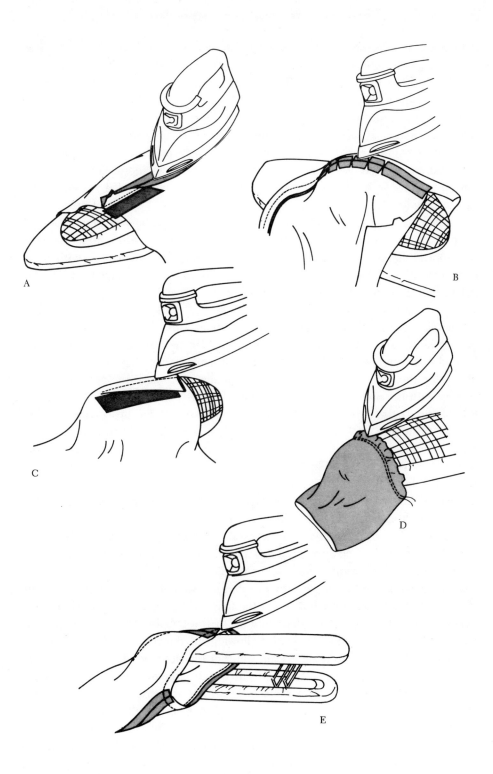

FIGURE 40

the seam allowance and garment fabric before you press, as in *Figure 40A*. Once you have pressed the seam open, press once again using moisture, if your fabric permits. For the final step, turn the garment right side up and press once again, using a pressing cloth and a light touch. Do not use a seam roll for this last step.

CURVED SEAMS Curved seams such as princess seams or the waist and hip area of side seams must be pressed over a curved surface to preserve the shape of the garment. Pressing a curved area on a flat surface will spoil the fit and also give a puckered appearance. For a curved surface you can use a tailor's ham or pressing mitt. Begin by pressing the seam closed flat, as explained for flat seams. When you are ready to press the seam open, lay the seam over a curved area of the ham that conforms to the shape of the garment. *Figure 40B* shows the bust area of a princess seam placed over a tailor's ham. Using only the tip of the iron, press the seam open, clipping or notching if needed. First press dry, then press with moisture, if possible. Turn the garment right side up and fit the shaped area to the tailor's ham and press again, using a pressing cloth.

DARTS A dart should have a softly rounded shape, not a sharp arrow point. The tip should curve gently and blend into the garment. First press the dart flat in the same position as it was stitched. Do not press a crease into the dart fold or press beyond the point of the dart. Turn the garment over and press again on the other side the same way. Next, using the tailor's ham, place the garment wrong side up with the point of the dart at the end of the ham (*Figure 40C*). Turn the fold of the dart away from the direction it will lie in the finished garment. With the tip of the iron, press along the stitching line from the wide end to the point. Next, turn the dart fold toward the direction it will lie in the finished garment and repeat, pressing from the wide end to the point. With the dart folded in the direction it will be in the finished garment, press a crease along the dart fold. Turn the garment right side up and, using the tailor's ham, mold and press the dart with a pressing cloth and moisture, if appropriate. If the fabric is hard to press and does not mold well, hold the iron 1 or 2 inches above the fabric and steam well. Using your hand or a tailor's clapper, press down on the dart seam until it is smooth and the point is molded. Do not press down with the iron.

SET-IN SLEEVES A set-in sleeve with an eased cap should mold smoothly over the shoulder. Stitch between the notches at the top of the sleeve before joining the underarm seam. Have the fabric right side up so the bobbin thread will be on the wrong side. Join the underarm seam. Following the direction for flat seams, press the underarm seam open, using a seam roll. Pin the sleeve in at the armhole with the right side of the sleeve and the right side of the garment together. Gently draw up the bobbin thread to ease in the cap. Distribute the ease evenly, then tie the ends of the easing thread. Remove the pins and take out the sleeve. Place the sleeve cap right side out over the end of tailor's ham or pressing mitt (see *Figure 40D*). Using steam and the tip of the iron, shrink and smooth along the stitching and the seam allowance. Do not let the point of the iron touch the fabric beyond the stitching line. Steam the fabric beyond the stitching line by holding the iron 1 or 2 inches above the fabric. Do not touch the fabric with the iron. There can be creases and puckers in the seam allowance, but not beyond the line of stitching. Shrink the cap of the sleeve between the notches.

Once the sleeve cap is smooth and molded, pin and baste the sleeve into the garment. After the sleeve is stitched into the armhole, trim the seam allowance of only the sleeve to ⅜ inch. Do not trim the seam allowance of the bodice armhole. The armhole at the underarm of the sleeve is not pressed. Turn the garment wrong side out. Place the armhole on your sleeve board, as you see in *Figure 40E*. Press along the line of stitching and along the seam allowance with the tip of the iron. Do not press beyond the line of stitching. Turn the garment right side out. Do not press the cap on the right side of the garment. The seam allowance of the bodice and the sleeve cap should turn toward the cap of the sleeve.

KEEPING YOUR SEWING MACHINE HAPPY

For your sewing machine to do its best job, you have to help it by oiling it, keeping it clean, and using the correct needle and thread for the job. Sewing machine needles come in a number of sizes—fine, medium, or heavy-duty. American and European needles are sized differently. A fine needle is size 10 or 11 in American size, 70 or 75 in European. Medium is size 14 American, size 80 or 90 European; and heavy-duty is size 16 American and size 100 European.

The needle of your sewing machine must go through the fabric, puncturing a hole and picking up the bobbin thread, in order to form a stitch. If you use a fine needle with heavy fabric, it will not make a large enough hole to pull the bobbin thread back up, so the result will be skipped or poorly made stitches. If you use a heavy-duty needle on a lightweight fabric, it will make too big a hole in the fabric, which will result in an unattractive seam. The needle should be replaced regularly. A tiny nick or blunted point will cause skipped stitches. A needle with a rough burred surface or a tiny hook on the end will cause snags and puckers to develop along the stitching line. Sewing on synthetic fabrics dulls the needle more quickly than sewing on natural-fiber fabrics.

In machine sewing, the thread is pulled back and forth through the needle eye many times before it is formed into a stitch. "Bargain" thread will not withstand this abrasion and will break easily, either during the stitching or shortly afterward. Polyester or cotton-wrapped polyester thread is used for sewing medium- to heavy-weight and knit fabrics made of synthetics or blends. Cotton sewing thread is used for sewing light, medium, and heavy cotton fabrics. Silk thread is used for sewing fine fabrics, such as sheers, laces, and other special fabrics. Silk thread comes in two sizes. Size A is fine thread used for regular sewing. Size D is called buttonhole twist and is used for decorative top stitching, handmade buttonholes, and thread loops.

When you select your thread to match your fabric, do not simply pick up a spool of thread and hold it against your fabric. When the thread is wound many times around the spool, the color cannot be perceived accurately. Unwrap the spool of thread and place a strand of thread across a swatch of your fabric to see whether the colors match. If you can't find an exact match, pick out two or three colors that appear the closest, compare them on the swatch together, and then pick the one that blends the most inconspicuously.

During sewing, lint from your fabric will build up underneath the throat plate and around the bobbin, especially when you are using pile fabrics and synthetics. This dust build-up is not good for the machine and will cause poor stitching. Clean the dust frequently, using the little brush that comes with your machine or an old toothbrush.

Following the directions in your sewing machine manual, oil your machine regularly. A machine in need of oil will rattle as it stitches. Do not let it get to this point. Also, do not overoil—this does not help the machine and you run the risk of having oil drops on your fabric. After you oil the machine, stitch for a few minutes on a scrap to pick up excess oil.

SPECIAL CARE FOR YOUR WEDDING GOWN

When making a wedding gown, some special care is needed to keep it clean and fresh-looking.

FABRIC STORAGE The best way to store most special fabrics is rolled on a tube to avoid forming wrinkles and creases. When you buy your fabric, see if you can get a long cardboard tube from the fabric store. Carefully roll your fabric and store it on a shelf—do not stand it up on end. If you can't get a roll, then spread layers of tissue paper on your fabric and fold the fabric with the tissue paper to prevent creases.

CUTTING Do all your cutting in one session, if possible. Cutting on the floor should be considered a last resort. It is very tiring, makes it hard to cut accurately, and invites getting your fabric dirty. Try to use a large table (even if you have to use a friend's Ping-Pong table). Be sure that your cutting table is smooth. You can cover rough edges with masking tape, or use one of those folding cardboard cutting boards. If you are working with a slippery or shifting fabric, such as chiffon, organza, or taffeta, place a clean sheet or felt over your table to protect the fabric and keep it from sliding around.

KEEPING THINGS CLEAN Be sure that your hands are clean and smooth. Some fabrics are so delicate they will actually catch on a hangnail or a rough fingernail. Clean the bottom and inside of your iron. Scissor blades should also be clean and sharp. Make it a rule to keep soda bottles, coffee cups, children, cats, and dogs as far away from where you are working as possible. You should have one or two old sheets that you can use to cover the floor around the cutting table, under the iron-ing board, and at the sewing machine. To keep your cut pieces organized and fresh, wrap cut parts carefully in tissue paper. Small pieces, such as facings, can be placed in plastic bags. Be sure to label each bag or wrapped part so you will know what it is. Store the pieces flat on a shelf, in a box, or in a drawer.

GOWN STORAGE When you store your gown during its construction, use tissue paper for folding the cut pieces, to prevent creases. Once the bodice and skirt are assembled, you can keep them on hangers. The skirt can be clipped to a skirt hanger. The bodice can be carefully pinned on a padded hanger and filled in with crumpled tissue paper, or kept on a dress form. Stretchy knits should not be hung but should be placed in a drawer.

SHEERS

Sheer fabrics are among the most popular for spring and summer weddings. They include chiffon, georgette, organza, satapeau, voile, and organdy. Georgette and chiffon are soft sheers. Both are transparent and clingy. Chiffon has a smooth surface and georgette has a slightly crepy texture. Organza and satapeau have more body than the soft sheers. Satapeau has a satiny appearance and is heavier and less transparent than organza. Refer to satins as well as sheers when using satapeau. Voile and organdy are crisp sheers. Silk or silk blends make the nicest chiffon, georgette, and organza. Real organdy is made of cotton. Nylon, rayon, and poly-ester are the most commonly used fibers for sheers.

Special Considerations

PATTERN SELECTION The beauty of sheer fabrics is their airy, gossamer quality. Make the most of this by selecting a pattern with softly gathered or flared fullness. You can use billowy bishop or circular cape sleeves, ruffles, or full skirts. Draped effects such as cowl necklines work beautifully with chiffon or georgette. Because all seam allowances and darts will show, avoid princess seams and intricately seamed patterns. Also avoid narrow shapes and closely fitted styles. Many sheer dresses use several layers of fabric for a luxurious effect. Each layer can be the same color, or the layers can vary in color for a rainbow effect. The bottom layer can be of an opaque fabric such as silk or taffeta. When using the soft sheers, chiffon or georgette, as many as ten layers can be used in a skirt. Remember that if you use more layers than the pattern calls for, you will have to figure how much extra fab-ric will be needed (see index, *Estimating yardage*). Sheers are often combined with other fabrics such as lace, velvet, or satin. Lace or velvet could be used for the bodice and sleeves and several layers of organza or chiffon for the skirt.

INTERFACINGS AND LININGS Refer to the chart near the beginning of this chapter. Interfacings are not used with sheers unless the dress is completely underlined in an opaque fabric. Facings should be eliminated and replaced by a narrow binding or hand-rolled hem. Chiffon or georgette are often underlined by using several layers of self fabric. For a sophisticated look, select a lining fabric in flesh tone, rather than matching the fabric color. You can underline some of the sheer fabric and leave other parts of the dress unlined. Or make a separate underdress of opaque taffeta, satin, or lining fabric and leave the dress itself sheer. Better wedding gowns with full skirts of organza, organdy, satapeau, or voile have an underskirt of one or two layers of net or tulle as well as the bottom underskirt of taffeta. For an opaque train, cut the lining the same length as the train. For a sheer train, make the lining floor length.

LAYOUT AND CUTTING Chiffon, georgette, satapeau, and organza should not be cut on the fold because they shift and slip. Before cutting, cover your work surface with felt or a sheet and pin the edges of the fabric to the felt or sheet. Pin your pattern to the fabric (but not the sheet), using fine silk pins inserted in the seam allowance only. Cut carefully, with very sharp shears or lingerie scissors. The crisper sheers can usually be cut without using any special techniques.

Chiffon and georgette are often made into garments that use several layers of fabric. When cutting layers, see *Figure 41A*. Cover your work surface with a sheet or felt, then place one layer of fabric on your cutting surface, right side up. Be sure that it is smooth and not stretched. Place the second layer on top of it, right side up, and continue placing the layers, being sure that each one is smooth and not shifted or pulling. Pin the layers together and then, with silk thread and a fine needle (size 10), use long basting stitches to "quilt" the layers together. Then lay out your pattern and cut, as explained above.

MARKING Mark underlining only, if possible. Use silk thread and tailor's tacks to mark all sheers.

Construction

Keep in mind that with sheer fabrics all your construction details will show, so they should be done neatly and carefully.

GENERAL SEWING Size A silk thread is best, or fine No. 60 thread, if available; coarse thread will cause puckered seams. Use a size 9 or 11 sewing machine needle and size 10 hand sewing needle. Set the machine for about 15 stitches per inch. If you have trouble with the fabric slipping or puckering as you stitch, place a strip of tissue paper underneath the fabric and stitch through it. Tear away the paper when you finish the seam. Because sheer fabrics can be very slippery, you may need to baste more than usual. In sewing a multilayered dress, the bodice layers are basted together and treated as one. The skirt layers are stitched and hemmed separately. Sleeves may be separate layers or treated as one, depending on the style and the effect you want.

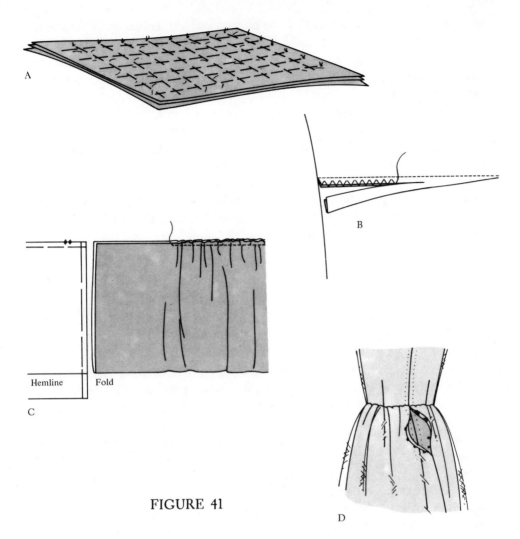

FIGURE 41

CONSTRUCTION DETAILS Seams should be narrow and carefully finished. Use one of the seams for lighter-weight fabrics. Darts should be finished with a straight or zigzag stitch and trimmed to ¼ inch, as in *Figure 41B*. A horsehair braid hem is used for crisp sheers with flared or gathered skirts. Chiffon and georgette require a very narrow hem. Use a hand-rolled hem or one of the narrow hems. All of these finishing techniques are covered in Chapter 8. A dress of chiffon or georgette should hang at least forty-eight hours, preferably a week, before marking the hem. On crisp sheers with a straight hem, a wide hem, as much as 12 inches, can be used for a luxurious look. A hemless double skirt can be used with a gathered skirt made of crisp sheer fabric that has a straight hem. Fold the fabric crosswise and place the pattern so that the fold forms the bottom edge of the skirt (see *Figure 41C*). Be sure that the length of the pattern is correct and the hem allowance has been removed before cutting. This will take more yardage than the usual skirt. For unlined sheers, a zipper would look too obvious and also be too heavy for the fabric. A closing of tiny snaps, hooks and eyes, or thread loops with tiny buttons would be better. For an underlined sheer, use a lightweight zipper, preferably inserted by hand. A couture finish for a dress with an underlined bodice and an underskirt of several layers is to insert the zipper in the skirt in the bottom layer only and have the overskirt opening closed by hooks and eyes (see *Figure 41D*). To insert the zipper this way, stitch the zipper to the bodice down to the waistline seam. Remove the dress from the machine and cut the threads. Pick up the overskirt and then continue stitching the zipper to the underskirt only.

PRESSING Test the iron heat and use of steam on scraps. On some fabrics, the steam may cause puckering. If your sheer is embroidered or beaded, place it face down on a pressing pad or folded towel to avoid flattening the embroidery or causing puckering around the beading.

VELVETS

Velvets include velvet, crushed velvet, sculptured velvet, panne, and velveteen. Velvets range in weight from heavy and stiff to light and soft. These fabrics are used for fall and winter weddings, for both brides and bridesmaids. Most velvet is made of nylon or rayon. Good-quality velvet has a dense pile and a luxurious feel. Lyons is a heavy velvet and one of the better types. Crushed velvet has the pile pressed in various directions, giving a texture somewhat like tree bark. Sculptured velvet has a subtle pattern created by varying the length of the pile. For example, a floral design can be made with flowers and leaves of long pile and the background of a short pile. Panne velvet has the pile pressed flat, which gives it a shimmery appearance. If you are using a knit panne, also read about knit fabrics in this chapter. Velveteen is usually made of cotton. It has a shorter pile and is considered less formal than velvet. The best velveteen is twill-back.

Special Considerations

PATTERN SELECTION A rich heavy velvet is very elegant and formal. It has the body for A-line and other structured styles and for a long train. Dense-pile velvet in a dark color may not show intricate seaming to its best advantage. Crisp Venise lace and sleek satin are good as trim or accents. For heavier velvets, choose a pattern with ease or a small amount of gathers rather than a great deal of fullness. Sculptured or crushed velvet has so much texture that you should select a simple pattern and use a minimum amount of trimming. Soft panne velvet is especially suited to drapey, wrapped, or sleek styles.

INTERFACINGS AND LININGS Refer to the chart near the beginning of this chapter. Do not use fusible interfacing with velvet. If the fabric has a great deal of body, it may not require interfacing. Underlinings are usually needed for A-line and other structured styles. For extra body in a structured style, use a light- to medium-weight woven interfacing as underlining. If your velvet is especially thick and bulky, you can cut facings from the lining fabric.

LAYOUT AND CUTTING All velvets have a nap. Because of the way velvet reflects light, the color will appear a different shade depending on whether the pile runs up or down. To see which way the pile is running, brush your hand over the velvet parallel to the selvage. Brushing one way will feel rough and the other way will feel smooth. The smooth way is the direction of the nap. Mark the nap direction on the selvage in pencil or chalk. When velvet is cut with the pile running up toward the face, it will appear a rich, deep color. When it is cut with the pile running down toward the floor, it will appear smooth and shiny. Velvet is usually cut with the pile running up, but with light colors you might prefer the effect of the pile running down. Cut panne velvet with the pile running down. Be sure you follow the with-nap layout when you cut any velvet fabric. Fold the fabric with the right sides out. If you put the right sides together, the velvet pile will stick to itself, causing ripples and shifting and making it difficult to cut accurately.

When cutting thick fabrics such as velvet, it is very important that you position the center line of the pattern piece carefully. Because of the thickness of the fabric, the fold itself can be as much as ½ inch wide. If you don't position the center front line of your pattern on the fabric to allow for this, you could add as much as an extra ½ or ¾ inch to the center front of your garment. This will make the neckline too big and spoil the fit. Place your pattern so that the center line of the pattern extends slightly beyond the fold of the fabric to allow for the thickness of the fold, as you see in *Figure 42A*. If the pile is especially dense or the fabric very heavy, it would be better to cut using a single layer rather than fold the fabric. Do not use a crosswise fold with a nap fabric, as this will result in the nap running up on one piece and down on the other. (An exception to this is a full circular skirt. The pattern piece is placed on a crosswise fold, but this will work here because the nap will be running across the skirt rather than up and down.)

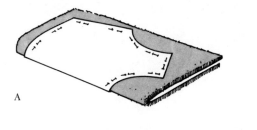

A

FIGURE 42

B

MARKING Make all your marks on the underlining if your dress has one. Otherwise use tailor's tacks or a tailor's chalk pencil. Test the tailor's chalk pencil first to be sure the mark does not show through or mar the pile on the right side. Do not use a tracing wheel and carbon on velvet.

Construction

GENERAL SEWING Use polyester thread with synthetic velvet, size A silk thread with silk or very fine velvet, and cotton thread with cotton velveteen. Use a size 14 sewing machine needle for most velvets. For hand sewing, select a size 6 needle for heavy velvet and 8 for medium-weight. Use a fairly long machine stitch, about 10 to the inch. If you find that your fabric is shifting as you stitch, hand-baste first. Whenever possible, stitch in the direction of the pile. Lessen the pressure on the presser foot so that it does not crush the pile.

CONSTRUCTION DETAILS Use one of the seam finishes in Chapter 8 to prevent the raw edges from shedding pile and raveling. Slash darts, trim to ⅝ inch, and press them open to reduce bulk (see *Figure 42B*). For structured styles, use a horsehair braid or interfaced hem. Use a padded or inside-stitched hem for softer styles (see instructions in Chapter 8). Stitch loosely and pick up the tiniest stitch on the back of the velvet, so the pile will not dimple. A zipper should be inserted by hand. Satin can be used for bound buttonholes or button loops. Thread loops with satin-covered buttons are an elegant closing for a velvet wedding gown.

PRESSING Velvet must be pressed quite carefully to avoid flattening the pile— once it is flattened, it cannot be revived. The best pressing aid for velvet is a needle board (see equipment in Chapter 1). If you don't have a needle board you can substitute a thick, folded terry-cloth towel. Always press velvet with the pile face down on the needle board or towel. Use steam rather than the weight of your iron to do the pressing. Hold the iron just above the fabric and let the steam penetrate, then use your finger to press the seam open. You can use a needle board or towel over a seam roll. Never use a dry iron and damp pressing cloth on velvet, as this will flatten out the pile. A velvet dress that looks rumpled can be refreshed by hanging it in the bathroom while you shower. The steam from the shower will fluff up the pile.

SATINS

Satin-weave fabrics include satin, peau de soie, satin-back crepe, satapeau, sateen, and satin stripes. Satins are probably the favorite of all bridal fabrics: smooth, lustrous, and rich-looking, they form a perfect background for almost any lace or trimming. The best satins are silk or silk-faced; others are made of Qiana, polyester, acetate, or rayon. Satins vary from very soft and lightweight to quite heavy and stiff. Some have a high sheen, others are low-luster.

Satin can mar and snag very easily. Be sure that all your work areas, including your sewing machine table and cutting table, as well as the sole of the iron, have no rough edges. The sewing machine needle must be very sharp or it will cause snags and puckers. Try to handle the fabric as little as possible to avoid having it look worked-over. It is important to make a fitting muslin for a satin dress unless you know the pattern fits perfectly. Ripped-out stitches can leave permanent marks. Needle holes in the fabric can sometimes be minimized or eliminated by scratching the fabric very lightly with a fine needle.

Special Considerations

PATTERN SELECTION For soft satins, choose a pattern for a soft, drapey style. Look for design features such as gathered, circular, or softly flared skirts, un-stitched pleats or released tucks, bodice shirring, ruffles, or pretty, full sleeves. Heavy, crisp satins are very regal and are among the most formal of fabrics. Choose an A-line, princess, or other sculptured shape. This fabric is a good choice for a simple, elegant pattern with unusual seaming. Look for one with ease or only slight gathers; a lot of gathers will not work well. A dress with a separate panel train or long cathedral train looks beautiful in heavy satin. The cap of a set-in sleeve may be difficult to ease smoothly in a heavy satin. You may want to elimi-nate some of the ease from the cap by lowering it, as you see in *Figure 43A*, or to select a pattern that does not have a set-in sleeve. Satins of all weights are often combined with sheers or lace. You might make the sleeves, bodice, or yoke of lace.

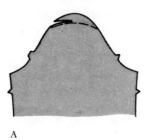

A

FIGURE 43

B

INTERFACINGS AND LININGS Refer to the chart near the beginning of this chapter. If the fabric is quite stiff, you may not need interfacing at all. Underlining is not generally used in soft, gathered, drapey styles. For structured styles, underlining is strongly recommended to give the dress body. For extra shaping, light- to medium-weight woven interfacing is used as underlining in better wedding gowns.

LAYOUT AND CUTTING Because of the sheen of satin fabrics you must use a with-nap layout, which means that the tops of all pattern pieces run in the same direction. If your pattern does not include this kind of layout, you can make your own (see index, *Estimating yardage*). Be sure that all of your pattern pieces are marked with arrows showing the direction to place them. Pin your pattern using fine silk pins placed in the seam allowance only.

MARKING Satin should be marked as little as possible. Use tailor's tacks and silk thread. Do not leave the tailor's tacks in the fabric for very long, as they may leave needle holes. Do not use tracing wheel and carbon.

Construction

GENERAL SEWING Use size A silk thread or polyester thread, with a size 11 sewing machine needle for lighter-weights and a size 14 sewing machine needle for heavier-weight satins. For hand sewing, use as fine a needle as possible. For seams, use about 14 stitches per inch. Hold the fabric securely as you stitch so it doesn't slip. Presser foot pressure should be just enough to hold the fabric securely, and tension somewhat loose.

CONSTRUCTION DETAILS If seam edges ravel, use a hand-overcast, straight stitch, or zigzag seam finish (see seam finishes in Chapter 8). Lightest-weight satins can be hemmed with a blind hem or hemming stitch. Use seam binding or lace for an edge finish. For medium-weight satins, use an inside-stitched hem. Heavy satins should have a horsehair braid or interfaced hem. (See Chapter 8 for hems.)

Use an invisible or hand-applied zipper; a machine-sewn zipper would be quite conspicuous on a satin dress. Thread loops and tiny satin-covered buttons are the finest closings for a wedding gown. Jewel trims or buttons may snag your fabric. Heavy or rough buttons can be sewn to the top layer and snaps hidden underneath. (Fabric-covered snaps are best.) This avoids having to make buttonholes and keeps a smooth look (see *Figure 43B*).

PRESSING Be sure to test first on a scrap. Use a warm, dry iron and light touch. Too high a heat will cause the fabric to become overly shiny. Some satins can be marked by steam, and a heavy pressure will cause unattractive ridges and sharp edges. When pressing on the right side, be sure to use a pressing cloth.

TAFFETA

Crisp, smooth, rustly taffeta comes in a variety of weights, from heavy to the lightest tissue taffeta. It is usually made of rayon or acetate. For bridesmaids, taffeta is available in prints and in woven plaids.

Special Considerations

PATTERN SELECTION Taffeta is especially appropriate for nostalgic designs, such as those with leg-of-mutton sleeves and Victorian neckbands. Depending on the weight, taffeta can be used for many styles: flared shapes or gathered, tailored or feminine are all suitable for this fabric. Gathered skirts will stand away from the body rather than drape. To make a taffeta skirt stand away even more, use an inside peplum ruffle (see *Figure 160*) or a net underskirt. Taffeta is often used with lace or sheer fabric. You could use taffeta for a simple dress and a sheer or lace for an overdress, jacket, or cape. A taffeta skirt goes well with a bodice of Alençon or Cluny lace. You might make a lace dress with a shawl, stole, or cape of taffeta. Medium- to heavyweight taffetas are used as an underlayer with sheers. Also see pattern suggestions for satin.

INTERFACINGS AND LININGS Interfacing is usually necessary with taffeta to maintain the crispness at buttoned openings, collars, necklines, and cuffs. Underlining will give body to structured styles. Refer to the chart near the beginning of this chapter.

LAYOUT, CUTTING, AND MARKING Taffeta is handled in much the same way as satin. Follow the directions given above for satin. Use the fabric direction test (page 75) to decide whether a one-way layout is needed. When using a slippery tissue taffeta, see cutting directions for sheers in this chapter.

Construction

GENERAL SEWING Use size A silk thread or polyester thread and about 12 to 15 stitches per inch. Use a size 11 machine needle and a size 9 or 10 hand sewing needle. Be sure that the presser foot is tight enough to hold the fabric, but not so tight that one layer slips over the other.

CONSTRUCTION DETAILS Refer to the directions above for sewing satin.

PRESSING Some taffetas may water-spot, so be careful when pressing. Follow the methods given for pressing satin.

BROCADE AND OTHER JACQUARD FABRICS

Jacquard fabrics include brocade, damask, brocatelle, and matelassé.

Jacquards are richly textured because the design is created by a complicated weaving process, rather than by printing. They are among the most formal and elegant fabrics. Brocade is heavy and satiny, usually with an intricate floral or scroll design. Damask is a lighter-weight version of brocade. Brocatelle is a type of brocade that has a raised bubbly texture as part of the design motif. Matelassé has an allover bubbly texture. Jacquards are usually made of silk or acetate and many include metallic threads. These fabrics are reversible but vary from one side to the other. For example, in a two-colored brocade one side could have a flower design with white petals and blue background, while on the other side the flower would appear with blue petals on a white background. In a one-color brocade the texture will vary on each side. You can use whichever side you prefer or use both sides of the fabric for different parts of your garment as a design feature. You might make your dress using one side and a matching jacket using the other.

PATTERN SELECTION Most jacquards are quite elaborate, so choose a pattern with simple lines. Avoid small details or involved seaming. Satin is often combined with brocade. The smoothness of satin provides a good contrast to the texture of the jacquard. You could make a dress with the bodice and sleeves of satin and the skirt of brocade, or a dress of brocade with accents such as collar, cuffs, or hem banding of satin. Also see pattern suggestions for satins of comparable weight.

CUTTING AND SEWING Jacquard fabrics are handled the same way as satins. Follow the instructions given for satin in this chapter. If your brocade has a large or prominent design that needs to be positioned carefully, see page 79. When using a jacquard with metallic threads in it, also read about metallic fabrics in this chapter.

A REMINDER Because jacquards are reversible, it is easy to place the wrong side out when sewing. Since each side is somewhat different, the result will be obvious on the finished dress although you may not notice it at the time of sewing.

PRESSING Follow the directions above for pressing satin. When pressing a fabric with a three-dimensional design, place it face down on a pressing pad to avoid flattening it.

FAILLE, OTTOMAN, AND MOIRÉ

Faille and ottoman both have crossways ribs. Faille is a light- to medium-weight fabric with a fine rib; ottoman is heavier and has a wide, prominent rib. Authentic moiré is a special finish applied to taffeta or faille that gives the fabric a shimmery watermarked appearance. Imitation moiré effects are created by printing or weaving.

PATTERN SELECTION Faille is suitable for soft or tailored styles. See suggestions for taffeta. Because of its distinctive texture, a simple style would be best for ottoman. By placing some of your pattern pieces on the cross grain or bias, you can use the ribs of the ottoman as a design feature. Smaller parts such as yokes, cuffs, plackets, belts, or midriff insets can be cut so the ribs run vertically or diagonally, instead of crosswise. Also see the suggestions given for satins.

When using moiré, select a style with a minimum number of seams to show off the fabric texture. A design with intricate seaming will appear too chopped-up. Faille and moiré combine well with organza, chiffon, and heavy- or lightweight laces. Also see pattern suggestions for taffeta.

CUTTING AND SEWING Faille, ottoman, and moiré may be directional and require a one-way pattern layout. See the fabric direction test on page 75. Follow the layout, cutting, and sewing directions given for satin.

CREPES

Crepe has a slightly pebbly surface texture. It is soft and drapes beautifully. Heavier-weight crepe is used for fall and winter weddings. Lightweight crepe, called crepe de chine, is used more in spring and summer. Satin-back crepe is crepe with a satiny, lustrous surface and should be handled as satin. Knitted crepe should be treated as other knits.

Special Considerations

PATTERN SELECTION See the suggestions given for soft satin if you are using a light- to medium-weight crepe. Crepe de chine is suitable for lingerie-inspired styles, such as lace-edge slip-dresses, and for sophisticated draped or wrapped styles. Lightweight crepe does not have the body for more than a short train unless it has an underskirt. Heavier crepes also drape nicely, but have more body than the lighter-weights. They can be used for somewhat more tailored or fitted styles. Heavier crepe has the weight for a train. Most patterns that say "Suitable for Knits" (not "For Stretch Knits Only") will work well with medium-weight crepes.

INTERFACINGS AND LININGS For crepe de chine and other lightweight crepes, use only the softest featherweight interfacing. Do not use fusible interfacing with crepe. Underlining is seldom used for gathered or draped styles. Refer to the chart near the beginning of this chapter.

LAYOUT AND CUTTING Some crepes have directional shading, which would require a one-way pattern layout. To check your fabric, see the fabric direction test on page 75. Crepe tends to shift, so be sure that the underlayer is smooth and stays on grain as you lay out and cut your pattern. Shears must be sharp to cut synthetics.

If crepe de chine is a problem to cut because of the way it slips, follow the suggestions in this chapter for cutting sheers.

MARKING Make all your markings on the underlining if there is one. With lightweight crepes, mark sparingly, using tailor's tacks of silk thread. On heavier crepes you might be able to use a tailor's chalk pencil, but test first on a scrap to be sure that it doesn't show or press through. Avoid using tracing wheel and carbon.

Construction

GENERAL SEWING For lightweight crepe de chine, use silk thread with a size 11 sewing machine needle and a size 10 hand sewing needle. For medium- to heavier-weight crepes, use polyester thread for sewing synthetics and cotton thread for wool crepe. Use a size 14 sewing machine needle and a size 8 hand sewing needle. Stitch length should be about 12 to 15 stitches per inch. Be sure that you do not stretch the seam as you stitch.

CONSTRUCTION DETAILS For lightweight crepes, use one of the seams for lighter-weight fabrics shown in Chapter 8. With heavier crepes, finish the seam edges with one of the seam finishes in Chapter 8 for a neater appearance and to prevent raveling. In addition to a regular hem, crepe de chine can be finished with a hand-rolled hem for a fine look or a shell edging. Heavier crepes should have an inside-stitched hem. For extra body, a horsehair braid hem or a padded hem could be used. See Chapter 8 for hems. The hem should be softly rounded, not pressed to a sharp edge. Let the finished dress hang at least overnight before marking the hem. A hand-applied zipper or buttons with thread loops would be the best closing. Machine buttonholes may ripple—be sure to use interfacing and test on a scrap first. You may need seam binding stays at the shoulder seams and waistline if your crepe is very stretchy (see *Figure 44*). When you sew the seam, pin the strip of seam binding along the stitching line and attach the seam binding as you sew your seam. Do not pin the seam binding between your two layers. For a finer finish at the waistline, use a ribbon stay (page 241). Stitch the ribbon to the seam allowance at the waistline instead of catching it only at the darts and side seams.

PRESSING Test the iron temperature and use of steam on a scrap first. Steam will cause some crepes to shrink and pucker. Do not overpress. Also see the pressing suggestions given for satin.

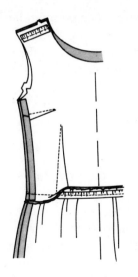

FIGURE 44

METALLIC FABRICS

Although not worn by brides, sparkly metallics are popular for special occasions. Metallic refers to any type of fabric that contains metal threads. It can be all-metallic, such as lamé, or have just a few metal threads for glimmer. Many different fabrics such as knits, sheers, brocades, and laces can be metallic. Read about the basic fabric you are using (chiffon, jersey, or whatever), as well as about metallic fabrics here.

Special Considerations

PATTERN SELECTION For style suggestions, refer to those given for the basic fabric. If the fabric has an elaborate design, choose a dress with simple lines. Metallic fabrics can be combined with plain fabric or another metallic. For example, you might make a bodice and skirt of gold-threaded chiffon and the sleeves, underskirt, and sash of matching plain chiffon.

INTERFACINGS AND LININGS Metallic fabrics often need a lining to cover scratchy seams and prevent the hem from snagging stockings. Also use lining fabric to cut facings. If the fabric is especially scratchy, you can finish neckline and sleeve edges with a satin piping. Lining fabric should be woven firmly enough so you won't feel the rough seam edges through it. Refer to the chart near the beginning of this chapter for linings and interfacings recommended for the weight of your fabric.

LAYOUT AND CUTTING Metallic fabrics must be cut using a one-way pattern layout. This is explained on page 75.

When cutting, use old but sharp shears, as the metal threads have a dulling effect. Insert your pins in the seam allowance only. For heavy or hard-to-cut fabrics, cut a single layer, making duplicate pattern pieces as explained on pages 78–79.

MARKING Use tailor's tacks. A tracing wheel can cut metallic threads.

Construction

GENERAL SEWING The metal threads may cause your sewing machine needle to get dull quickly, so change it often. Remove the throat plate from your sewing machine and clean bits of metallic thread out of the feed dog fairly often. If your fabric has loose metallic threads that catch in the presser foot or feed dog as you sew, stitch using tissue paper. Refer to information on the basic fabric for stitch length, needle size, and so on. Be sure first to make a test seam using a scrap.

CONSTRUCTION DETAILS If your dress is unlined and the fabric lightweight, use one of the seams for lighter-weight fabrics in Chapter 8. When using medium-weight fabric, neaten seam edges with one of the seam finishes shown in Chapter 8. A bound edge or Hong Kong finish would be best for heavy fabrics. Use a hem appropriate to the weight of your fabric. A faced hem can be used if the fabric is scratchy. (See Chapter 8 for information on hems.) A hand-applied zipper or button and loop closing is usually the best choice. Bound buttonholes can be made using plain fabric. Test bound or machine-made buttonholes on a scrap first. For another button closing, see *Figure 43B*.

PRESSING Test to see whether steam will tarnish or damage the fabric. Use a pressing cloth, as metal threads may catch on the iron or scratch the sole plate. In some cases it is better to finger-press seams, using a thimble to protect your finger.

BEADED FABRICS

Beaded fabrics may be decorated with rhinestones, sequins, pearls, or other beads applied solidly or used only as accents. For bridal gowns, white fabrics are beaded with pearls, crystal beads, or crystal sequins. The base fabric (the fabric that the beads are applied to) may be almost any type from sheer to heavy, and knit, woven, or lace. Unless your fabric is solidly beaded, also read about sewing the type of fabric used as the base.

Special Considerations

PATTERN SELECTION Since beaded fabrics are usually quite expensive, you can use the beaded fabric for only part of the garment and use matching unbeaded fabric or a contrasting fabric for the rest. If you are making the entire dress of beaded fabric, choose a simple style with a minimum of details and seams. Avoid set-in sleeves, gathers, and buttonholes with heavily beaded fabrics. Some beaded fabrics may lend themselves to being cut into bands or pieces for trimmings. Also see pattern suggestions given for the base fabric.

INTERFACINGS AND LININGS Most beaded fabrics need a closely woven lining or underlining to cover the threads or prongs used to attach the beads. Cut facings from lining fabric also. To prevent irritation, the garment edges can be finished with satin piping. Refer to the chart near the beginning of this chapter for lining and interfacing suitable for your fabric.

LAYOUT AND CUTTING Beaded fabrics must be cut using a one-way layout (see page 75). Cutting beaded fabrics is hard on shears, so don't use your best pair. If cutting is difficult, remove beads from the cutting line, using shears or embroidery scissors, before cutting out the pattern (*Figure 45*A). Unless you know your pat-

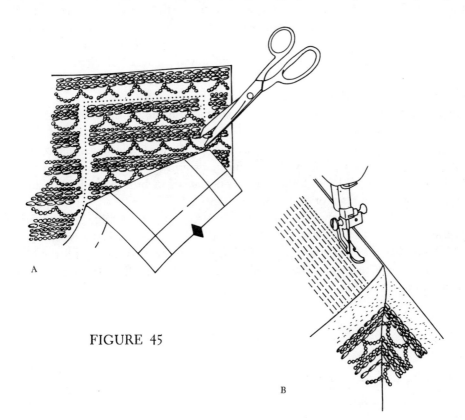

FIGURE 45

tern fits perfectly, it is important to make a fitting muslin first. Once a seam is sewn on a beaded fabric, it cannot be ripped out without leaving permanent marks. Also check your fabric to see that the beads don't fall off when it is cut. If this happens, leave extra seam allowance (at least an inch) and immediately stay-stitch around each piece. Most beaded fabrics must be cut in a single layer. To do this, you will need duplicate pattern pieces (see pages 78–79).

MARKING Tailor's tacks are best. Tailor's chalk may work in some cases. Avoid using a tracing wheel.

Construction

GENERAL SEWING Sewing beaded fabrics can dull or damage the needle, so change it frequently. Basting is strongly recommended. You may find that you must stitch with tissue paper because the fabric catches. If the beads are too thick to sew over, carefully remove beads from the seam allowance and dart area and stitch with a zipper foot, positioning your fabric so that the zipper foot is in the seam allowance (*Figure 45B*). Refer to information about your base fabric for thread, needle size, and so on. Be sure to make a test seam first.

CONSTRUCTION DETAILS If your dress isn't lined, use one of the seam finishes shown in Chapter 8. Beads can be removed from the seam allowance after the seam is sewn. A faced or horsehair braid hem would be a good choice if appropriate for your fabric. An interfaced or padded hem can be used with heavier fabrics. Remove beads from hem allowance to prevent snagged stockings and to reduce bulk. (See Chapter 8 for specific information on hems.) Buttonholes should not be used except with sparsely beaded fabrics where the beads can be removed from the buttonhole area. Buttons can be stitched on the upper layer of fabric and snaps sewn underneath (see *Figure 43B*), or button loops can be used. If you choose a zipper closing, remove the beads from the seam allowance before applying the zipper by hand. Once you have finished your garment, fill in any bald spots by hand-sewing beads taken from scraps. Any cracked or broken beads at a finished edge or caught in a seam or dart should be replaced.

PRESSING Place the fabric face down on a pressing pad or folded towel. Use a pressing cloth and a low heat. Do not press on the right side. Test first on a scrap to be sure that the beads or sequins will not discolor or melt. Press as little as possible, using only the tip of the iron along the seam or dart, or try finger-pressing seams, using a thimble.

SILK

Silk is the most luxurious of all fibers and, although it is more expensive than synthetics, its beauty and sensuous feel make it worth the extra cost. Almost any of the special fabrics can be made of silk from the most gossamer chiffon to heavy brocade. The French word for silk is *soie*, so a fabric with that word in the name (such as peau de soie) should be made of silk. However, these names are misused, so check the hang tag or fabric bolt to be sure that the fabric really is silk, not an imitation.

There are two types of silk, cultivated and wild. Cultivated silkworms eat mulberry leaves and produce an even, delicate thread with a great deal of sheen. It is used to make fine, luxurious fabrics such as satin, brocade, surah, and organza. Cultivated silk takes dye well, which is why these fabrics come in such beautiful colors. Wild silkworms eat oak leaves or whatever else they can find, so the thread they produce is rough and uneven, with a distinctive texture. Wild silk is often called raw silk, although this term is incorrect. ("Raw silk" refers to either type of silk cocoon before it has been processed.) Since they are difficult to dye, wild silk fabrics are usually sold in natural beige and brown colors. Real tussah, shantung, and pongee are made of wild silk.

Special Considerations

Refer to information on your specific fabric for pattern selection, layout, and cutting directions.

The lighter-weight silks take beautifully to fine detailing, such as tucks, pleats, shirring, and gathering. Alençon or Chantilly lace is the traditional luxurious trimming used with fine silks.

Use sharp shears and cut with smooth, even strokes.

Marking should be done with silk thread and tailor's tacks.

Construction

Follow instructions for your specific fabric. Use size A silk thread and a fine needle for hand and machine sewing. Most silks fray quite a bit. For lightweight silks, use a French, self-bound, or clean-finished seam. For heavier silks, use a seam finish to prevent raveling. Lightweight silks can be hemmed with a hand-rolled hem. See Chapter 8 for seams and hems.

Silk will water-spot, so it should be pressed with a dry iron on the wrong side.

KNITS

The most important consideration when using a knit fabric is the amount and the direction of the stretch. Don't confuse weight with stretch. A lightweight sheer knit may have only a little stretch, while a heavy, thick knit may stretch quite a bit. You should be familiar with the different types of knits because each has different stretch characteristics. A knit that stretches a great deal is referred to as unstable. A knit that stretches only slightly is referred to as stable. There are two basic types of knits, circular and warp.

Circular Knits

Circular knits are also called tubular or weft knits. They are constructed on the same principle as hand knitting, using knit and purl stitches (see *Figure 46A*). They are called circular knits because they are knit in a large tube. Circular knits have no selvage. They are sometimes sold in tubular form, but more often the tube is cut open. Most have a crease down the middle of the fabric that cannot be com-

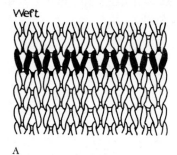

Weft

FIGURE 46

A

pletely pressed out or removed. They stretch in both the lengthwise and the crosswise directions, but more in the crosswise. Circular knits include:

SINGLE KNITS, usually soft and drapable, with a good deal of stretch. Jersey is the best-known single knit. Sweater knits are the loosest and stretchiest. Single knits can be recognized by a fine lengthwise rib on the right side and a purl-stitch crosswise rib on the wrong side, like those you would see in hand knitting.

INTERLOCK, a fine, soft knit similar to jersey.

RIB KNIT has vertical ridges like ribbing on a sweater. It stretches a great deal in the crosswise direction. It is used mostly for trim, or for parts, such as cuffs, bands, bodices, and sleeves. Ribbing is sometimes sold to match a single or double knit.

DOUBLE KNITS, called double because they are made using two sets of needles. This type is the most stable of all knits. Double knits can be plain or resemble woven fabrics such as crepe, piqué, or brocade.

PATTERN KNITS Because single knits are made from the basic knit and purl stitch, a great many patterns such as cable stitch and other hand-knit designs can be made by machine. They are usually of a much finer gauge than hand knits.

Warp Knits

Warp knits are knitted flat so that the side edges look like a selvage rather than the cut edge that you find in circular knits. Warp knits stretch crosswise but have little lengthwise stretch. Except for lacy patterns, warp knits have fine ribs running lengthwise on the right side and crosswise on the wrong side (see *Figure 46B*). Warp knits do not ravel or run.

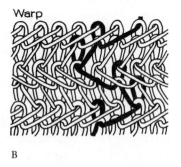

B

TRICOT is the best-known warp knit. Besides the familiar nylon tricot used for lingerie, tricot knits are also made as opaque fabrics that resemble jersey and are used for dresses and tops. It is easy to confuse warp knit that looks like jersey with a true jersey knit. Remember that warp knit stretches only crosswise and jersey stretches both ways.

RASCHEL KNITS are open, lacy fabrics that range from fine and delicate to heavy crochet types. (Raschel machines are also used to make lower-priced laces, but these have no stretch.) See *Figure 46C*.

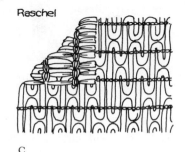

C

Pattern Selection

Selecting the right pattern to use with knit fabrics is important. Depending on your fabric and the fit you want, you can choose from three pattern categories:

FOR STRETCH KNITS ONLY These patterns have significantly less wearing ease than other patterns, to take advantage of the stretchiness of knit. They fit closely to the body and usually have no darts. All double knits, as well as some warp knits, do not have enough give to use with this type of pattern. Patterns marked "For Stretch Knits Only" have a gauge on the pattern envelope that indicates how much stretch is required for that particular pattern. When using the stretch gauge, measure on the crosswise grain and be sure not to overstretch the knit. You want to measure only how far the knit will stretch easily. If the fabric curls, it has been stretched too much. If your fabric stretches more than is indicated, that is all right, but it must stretch at least up to the mark indicated on the gauge. If you use a pattern marked "For Stretch Knits Only" with a fabric that does not stretch enough, it will not fit properly and will be very uncomfortable.

SUITABLE FOR KNITS These are regular patterns that will work in knits as well as in wovens. Patterns marked "Suitable for Knits" or "Recommended for Knits" have the normal amount of wearing ease. Depending on whether the style is soft or tailored, you can use stable or unstable knits. These styles will not fit as closely to the body and may require some extra fitting if you use a very stretchy knit.

REGULAR PATTERNS Many patterns that are not marked "Suitable for Knits" can be used with knit fabrics. Some list specific knits along with wovens under fabric suggestions. Patterns that do not suggest knits but call for soft wovens such as crepe or challis can sometimes be used with soft knits, such as jersey, interlock, or tricot. Patterns that call for medium-weight wovens such as wool, flannel, piqué, or heavy crepe can usually be made in double knit. Most patterns that suggest fabrics such as soft satin, peau de soie, and crepe are suitable for maracaine.

When choosing a pattern for knits, it is best to avoid a full, circular skirt because it is apt to hang unevenly. Stay away from intricate seaming unless you are using a double knit. Knits are often combined with wovens or lace for wedding gowns and formal dresses. Do not use a pattern designed "For Stretch Knits Only" if you are cutting part of it from a woven fabric.

Interfacings and Linings

Dresses made from patterns designed "For Stretch Knits Only" should not be lined or underlined because that would eliminate the stretch. Many patterns marked "Suitable for Knits" do not need lining or underlining. If you are using a regular pattern with a knit fabric, you have to consider the effect you want when deciding whether or not to line or underline. Unlined knits (except double knits) will mold to the body and cling and drape softly. Lined knits will not stretch and will have more body. A good compromise between clinginess and rigidity is to use a lightweight knit such as tricot or jersey as a lining. This reduces cling but retains the soft knit look. Openwork raschel knits need a lining or underdress if they are too see-through.

If you are using a woven underfabric with a knit, a lining is usually preferable to an underlining. Because the knit will stretch somewhat and the woven won't, the knit might ripple over the underlining. If a separate lining is used, the knit is free to give and should not form pulls or ripples. Lining can be cut on the bias to mold better with knits. Stable knits can be lined in light- to medium-weight polyester or rayon lining, China silk, or lining crepe.

Dresses made of maracaine or jersey are sometimes lined with a petticoat of taffeta or crepe attached only at the waist seam. If the dress has a gathered skirt, you can use an A-line skirt pattern for the petticoat to eliminate fullness (see *Figure 47*). You might also make the petticoat of a lightweight lining fabric, gathering it separately and attaching it to the waistline seam. A separate underdress or slip can be made of taffeta, satin, or crepe.

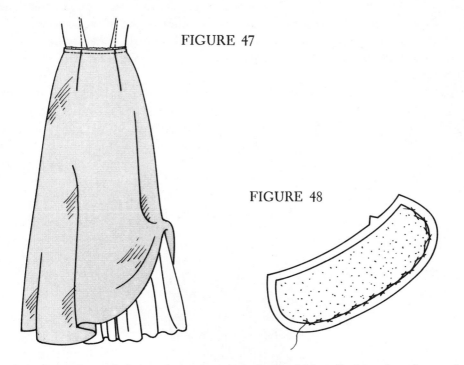

FIGURE 47

FIGURE 48

Interfacing is needed any place where stretch should be eliminated, such as collars, cuffs, buttoned openings, necklines, yokes, and pockets. Use featherweight non-woven bias interfacing for stretchy knits. Use light- to medium-weight woven or non-woven for stable knits. (Refer to the chart near the beginning of this chapter.) On collars, trim seam allowances from interfacing and catch-stitch interfacing to the collar, as in *Figure 48*.

Layout and Cutting

Before laying out and cutting you must first determine the right and wrong side of your fabric. Smooth knits have very fine ribs, which you can see by looking closely under good light or by using a magnifying glass. The lengthwise ribs are the right side of the fabric and the crosswise ribs are the wrong side. On warp knits, crosswise ribs have a zigzag appearance. Plain double knits have a slightly different texture on the right and wrong side. The fine lengthwise ribs are considered the right side, but you can use whichever side you prefer. (Just be sure to use the same side throughout your garment.)

Most knits have directional shading to some extent. To check your fabric, see the fabric direction test on page 75. Smooth knits, especially those with a sheen, such as maracaine, and synthetic jerseys, should be cut using a one-way layout (page 75).

If your knit fabric has special properties such as nap or metallic threads, you will also have to apply the same considerations to the knit as to a woven of the same type. For example, knit panne velvet and velour must be cut in the same way as a velvet or other woven pile fabrics. If your knit falls into this category, read about knits here and also read the information that applies to wovens with the same characteristics.

The lengthwise and crosswise ribs of knit fabrics are used in laying out your pattern in the same way as the lengthwise and crosswise grains in woven fabrics. As with wovens, the grain of knit fabrics must be straightened. To straighten the ends of knit fabric, working on the wrong side, carefully mark a crosswise rib, using a light-colored pencil and ruler, or with thread tracing (see *Figure 49*). Cut across on the line. Straighten both ends of the fabric, then follow the directions on pages 70–72 for checking the grain of woven fabrics. A few synthetic knits have a heat-set process applied to them and the grain cannot be straightened.

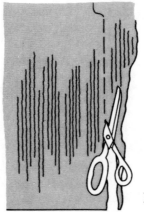

FIGURE 49

When laying out your fabric, use a large flat work surface. Don't let one end of the fabric hang over the edge of the table or it will stretch out of shape. Fine synthetic knits can snag easily, so be sure the edges of the table are smooth. Never use the center crease of a knit as the center fold line when placing your pattern. This crease is often permanent and discolored, so it should be avoided altogether or placed in an inconspicuous part of the garment. Be careful not to stretch your knit as you pin the pattern. Use ball-point pins in the seam allowance only. If the fabric curls, pin it to tissue paper. When working with slippery knits, see cutting instructions for sheers (see index). For synthetic knits, you must use very sharp shears, preferably knife-edge, or they will chew and shred the fabric. As you cut, anchor the fabric with your left hand and be careful not to pull or stretch it.

MARKING Tailor's tacks are best in most cases. On fine knits, use silk thread so as not to mar the fabric. Tracing wheel and carbon can permanently mark and damage a knit.

Construction

GENERAL SEWING Use polyester thread with most synthetic knits because it can stretch. Silk thread can be used with very fine jerseys. For best results, use a ball-point sewing machine needle. A sharply pointed regular needle can cause skipped stitches and snags. Use a size 11 needle for lightweight fabrics and a size 14 for medium-weight. For hand sewing, use a size 9 or 10 needle for fine knits and a size 7 or 8 for medium-weights. Tension and pressure adjustments are very important with knits. The tension should not cause puckering. If the pressure on the presser foot is too tight, the two layers of fabric will not feed through the machine at the same rate and you will end up with the top layer extending beyond the bottom layer when you finish the seam. A roller presser foot or an even-feed presser foot can alleviate this problem.

If your fabric isn't feeding through easily and gets caught or tangled under the presser foot, try stitching with a strip of tissue paper underneath the fabric. Tear the tissue away once you have sewn your seam. To help prevent the fabric from being pulled down into the needle hole and the thread from tangling when stitching lightweight, slippery knits, hold both the bobbin and needle thread taut at the beginning of each seam. Turn the wheel by hand so the needle is lowered into the fabric (see *Figure 50*). Begin to stitch slowly, still holding the thread.

Some machines have a stretch stitch for sewing knits. When you are sewing special dresses, this stitch may not always be appropriate. The stretch stitch will not allow you to press seams open as smoothly as will an ordinary stitch. For seams where there is no stress, such as the side seam of a gathered skirt, a regular straight stitch would look better. In areas of stress, such as the side seams on a closely fitted bodice, a stretch stitch could be advantageous. You have probably read that you should stretch your knit fabric as you sew. This is not the greatest piece of ad-

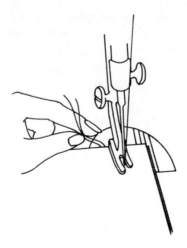

FIGURE 50

vice because more often stretching will result in puckered seams. What you should do is hold the fabric just taut enough so that there is no slack. Experiment on scraps to discover which type of stitch and stitch length produce the most attractive seam. For straight stitching, use about 12 to 15 stitches per inch.

CONSTRUCTION DETAILS Stay-stitch necklines, armholes, and other curves. For lightweight knits, use a double-stitched (*Figure 110*) or merrow seam (*Figure 111*). For light- or medium-weight knits, use a basic seam with a straight stitch, zigzag, or hand-overcast finish (see Chapter 8). There are a number of narrow hems and edgings such as shell, scalloped, and lettuce edging that are done on a zigzag machine and make an attractive treatment for knit fabrics (see Chapter 8). Hems appropriate for knits include inside-stitched and catch-stitch hems. For heavy knits, use a double-stitched or an interfaced hem. As a hem edge finish you can use stretch lace or machine zigzag. (See Chapter 8 for complete information on hems.) Let the dress hang for at least twenty-four hours before marking the hem to allow for any stretching that might occur.

The shoulder and waistline seams of a stretchy knit dress should be stabilized with ribbon seam binding (see page 100).

Buttonholes are seldom used on very stretchy knits because they are likely to gap. On other knits, position the buttonhole in the least stretchy direction of the fabric. The buttonhole area and underlap must be interfaced. You can use machine-stitched or bound buttonholes. The little strips that form the bound buttonhole can be stabilized with fusible interfacing. Button and loop closings (see index) work with most knits, except for the very stretchy, sweatery types. With a light knit, such as jersey, be sure to use one of the lightweight zippers that have a delicate zipper tape and a fine coil, not metal teeth. An invisible zipper will work on most knits, except for the very stretchy. Because the knit is apt to stretch while the zipper is being stitched to it, a hand-applied zipper (see index under *Zippers*)

will look much better and is highly recommended. The zipper opening can be stabilized by stitching woven seam binding to the seam allowance before applying the
zipper (see *Figure 51*).

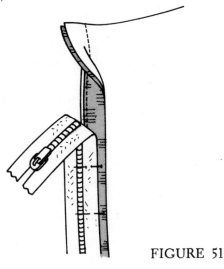

FIGURE 51

PRESSING Test pressing on scraps first. If your iron is too hot, the knit can become stiff and glazed-looking, and some fabrics will curl or pucker from steam.
Press on the wrong side with a light touch. When working with smooth, shiny
knits, such as maracaine and synthetic jersey, use a warm dry iron and a pressing
cloth. It is important to press carefully so that you do not cause ridges to appear
on the right side of the garment. Be sure the sole plate of your iron is smooth and
clean so that it does not snag or mark the fabric.

SEWING KNITS AND WOVENS TOGETHER When you are making a dress that uses
knit and woven or lace fabric both, the area needing special consideration will be
the seams that join the knit and the other fabric. If you are using sheer lace with
knit, back the lace with tulle or organza to give it a little more body. Stitch the
lace and backing together and use as one. (Read about lace in Chapter 6.) When
joining knit and woven together, be sure that the knit is not stretching as you
stitch. You may find it necessary to stay-stitch the knit first before joining it to the
woven, or to hand-baste the seams. Make a test seam on scraps using the knit and
woven fabrics together.

NET FABRICS

Net fabrics include net, tulle, illusion, and maline. English net is a high-quality
net used with lace in making wedding gowns. Net and tulle are used as underskirts
with crisp, sheer fabrics or lace. Tulle is also used as a backing and to make narrow

facings for fine laces. Illusion and maline are used for bridal veils and headwear (see Chapter 9).

LAYOUT AND CUTTING Net fabrics have no grain and the edges will not fray when cut. They do not need to be straightened.

If you are cutting several layers, pin the layers together before placing your pattern. Be careful not to snag or break the threads. Cut very carefully, using smooth strokes so you will not have a raggedy edge. If net slips, see instructions for cutting sheers (see index).

GENERAL SEWING Use silk thread and size 11 machine needle. You'll have to experiment on scraps to determine the stitch length. It should be small enough to hold the fabric securely but not so close that it causes puckering, probably around 15 to 18 stitches per inch. For gathering, use about 10 stitches per inch. When gathering several layers, gather each layer individually, then stitch the layers together. For seams that show, use a French seam; otherwise use a zigzag finish seam (see Chapter 8 for seams). The edge of an underskirt can also be finished with narrow lace. If you have trouble stitching because the net gets caught in the sewing machine, try stitching between strips of tissue paper. Press with a warm dry iron.

6

Lace

When you think of a wedding gown you probably think of lace. Lace is widely available now and reasonably priced, but it wasn't always so. During the seventeenth and eighteenth centuries, lace was so costly and so much in demand that it ranked with gold and jewels as a luxury item. It was handmade by a process so slow and painstaking that it could take weeks to make an inch of wide lace. The lacemakers worked by the light of a single candle and could have no fire for heat because the soot would soil the lace. The linen threads used in making the lace were so fine they had to be spun in a damp basement or they would dry out and break. Laws were passed by monarchs regulating who was allowed to wear lace and when. When the first lace machine was invented, the penalty for smuggling any part of the machine out of England was death. Different cities and areas in Europe invented and produced their own particular style of lace. Today, although lace is made by machine, most laces still retain the name of the place where a similar type was first made by hand.

If you are uneasy with the idea of sewing lace, let me reassure you: sewing lace is not terribly difficult and has a great many advantages. You may think that because it looks so fragile it would be hard to handle. Actually, lace is much easier to handle than most other sheer fabrics because it is not slippery and does not shift like organza or chiffon. Since lace is neither woven nor knitted, it does not fray and can be cut in any direction. Because of the intricate design and texture, small mistakes that would be obvious on a smooth-surfaced fabric often will not show on

PLATE 4
Alençon Lace

lace. If you should cut your lace incorrectly, it can be appliquéd back together. Or if you should even inadvertently cut a hole in your dress, a lace motif can be cut from a scrap and used to cover it. No hemming is required when a lace border is used at a garment edge, such as the hem or sleeves.

Many people think that good lace is very expensive. Actually, it is not so expensive when you realize you need only a small amount. One to two yards is enough for most dresses, and there is no waste because all the scraps can be used to make trimming for the gown and headpiece. Depending on the width, lace is used as both fabric and trimming.

PLATE 5
Chantilly Lace

TYPES OF LACE

Lightweight Laces: Alençon and Chantilly

Chantilly and Alençon (pronounced Ah-*len*-sun) laces are the most popular and traditional for bridal gowns. Both these laces consist of a design motif, usually floral, on a fine net background. Chantilly lace (*Plate 5*) has a fine threadlike cord outlining the design. Alençon lace (*Plate 4*) is also called re-embroidered lace be-

cause each design motif is outlined in a heavy satin cord. Because the satin cord outline must be applied by a hand-guided embroidery machine after the lace is made, Alençon lace costs more than Chantilly lace of equal quality. Chantilly and Alençon laces are available in all forms and widths.

The best of these laces are imported from Europe. Good-quality lace has a variety of textures. The ground net may be made up of two or three different net configurations and the design of the motifs should be intricate and varied. Lower-quality lace has a repetitious look. In fine lace, the motifs are well spaced; in less expensive lace, the design is crowded together. You can see the difference between fine and low-cost lace in *Plate 6*.

If you are buying re-embroidered lace, look to see that the satin cord is stitched securely to the lace and the ends of the cord are hidden. You may see the word "hand-clipped" referring to Alençon and Chantilly laces. This is an indication of good quality. When the lace is made on the machine, threads are carried loosely from one motif to the next. After the lace is finished, these threads must be carefully clipped by hand. On lesser-quality laces, these threads are clipped by machine, which restricts the type of designs that can be made.

Another way to distinguish the quality of the lace is by the fiber content. Blends that include silk or linen are used in good-quality lace. Nylon is used in both fine and lower-priced laces. Acetate and nylon-acetate blends are most often used in lower-cost laces. You may sometimes see lace referred to as "Leavers" or "Raschel." These terms refer to the type of machine that the lace was made on. The Leavers machine is used to make the best laces and the Raschel machine is used to make lower-priced imitations of Leavers laces.

Another lightweight lace, which is available only in narrow trimmings, is called Val or Valenciennes. It consists of a small design, usually simple flowers or dots, on a net ground.

Heavy Laces: Venise and Cluny

Venise lace (pronounced Ven-*neese*) has a rich, three-dimensional appearance. It is also sometimes referred to as guipure lace. Unlike the lightweight laces, it has no net ground and is almost always made of cotton (see *Plate 7*). Because of its weight, it is seldom used for an entire dress but can be used for parts such as yoke, sleeves, or bodice, as well as for trimmings. Along with Chantilly and Alençon, Venise is considered an elegant and formal lace.

Venise is made by an embroidery process, so you can judge the quality by looking at the stitches and the threads. In good Venise, fine threads are used and many small stitches are placed very close together, which gives it a richly sculptured look. The texture can vary from one part of the design to another or it can be the same weight all over. It should have neat, well-finished edges. In poor-quality Venise,

PLATE 6
Top: Fine Alençon Lace. Bottom: Low-cost Lace

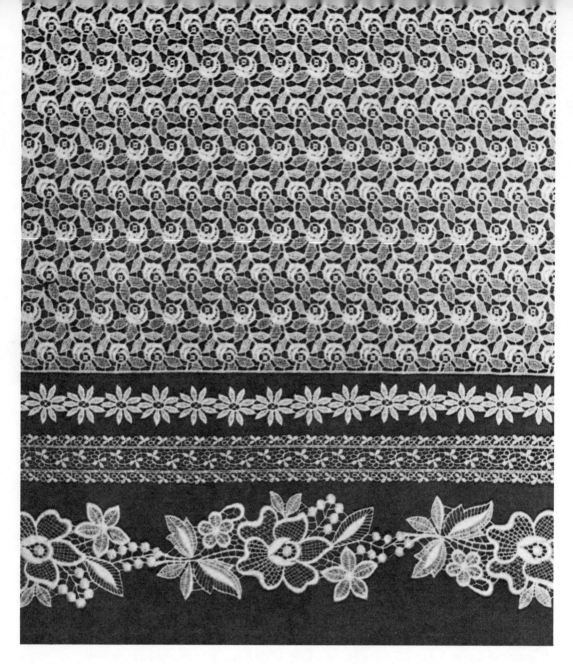

PLATE 7
Venise Lace

the stitches are spaced too far apart and a coarse thread is used, which gives it a flat or rough appearance.

Cluny has become a kind of a catch-all word for a number of heavier, less formal laces. Unlike the other types of laces, Clunies are generally made of a fairly heavy thread. Many have a hand-crocheted appearance (see *Plate* 8). Cluny is available in narrow trimmings and in fabric widths. Because it has a kind of nostalgic appearance and is not considered as formal as the other laces, it is often used with simpler fabrics such as dimity, voile, or muslin.

PLATE 8
Cluny Lace

LACE FORMATIONS

Lace is made in a number of different widths and forms for the most variety in designing. One lace pattern made up in several ways is called a set. The terms listed here refer only to the formations of the lace and should not be confused with lace types. A lace edge is still an edge whether it is Chantilly, Venise, or any other type. So you need not be confused by what seems to be a tremendous number of lace terms when you look through the bridal magazines or at bridal trim-

Appliqués

Beading

Insertion

Edge

Galloon

PLATE 9
Lace Formations

mings. Just remember that there are four major lace types : Alençon, Chantilly, Venise, and Cluny, and six major lace formations, listed below (see *Plate 9*).

WIDE LACE Wide lace usually measures 36 inches or more in width and is used like fabric. "Allover" refers to wide lace that has a straight edge on both sides. Wide lace that has a scallop on one side is called a flounce or edge. When it has a scallop on both sides it is called a galloon (rhymes with "balloon").

These terms refer to trimming laces :

EDGE A lace edge has a scallop on one side and a straight edge on the other. It can be used gathered or flat. Edges are used to trim necklines, sleeves, hemlines, and so on. Wider edges, 10, 12, or 18 inches, can also be used to cut out small parts of the gown such as sleeves or yokes. A picot edge is a very narrow trim made of little loops or points that is used around necklines, collars, and sleeve edges.

INSERTION An insertion has a straight edge on both sides and is used flat. For a sheer look, the fabric behind the insertion can be clipped away.

GALLOON As with a wide lace galloon, a trimming galloon has scallops on both sides. It is generally used flat. However, there are some galloons with a plain strip in the center so that the galloon can be gathered into a double ruffle. Lace bands of flowers are also called galloons. Galloons can be used as trim almost anywhere on the gown: around the skirt or the sleeves, across a yoke, and so on.

BEADING Beading refers to any lace that has a row of holes through which a ribbon can be woven. (This is quite different from jewel beading.) Beading is available as an edge, insertion, or galloon, which means you can purchase beading with a scallop on one side, scallops on both sides, or straight edges on both sides.

APPLIQUÉS Lace appliqués are also called medallions or motifs. They are individual lace designs that can be sewn to any part of the gown. You can buy appliqués, but the best way is to cut your own from wide lace (directions follow).

CLIPPING LACE

Here is the secret of making a truly professional-looking wedding gown. There are designers' methods of using lace that are quite simple, yet almost unknown to the home sewer. Because lace has no grain and will not fray, it can be cut and used in a completely different manner than are wovens or knits. You can, of course, cut a bodice, skirt, or sleeves of lace as you would regular fabric, but, in addition, lace can be clipped apart into sections consisting of panels, borders, and individual motifs, to be used to decorate the gown. This is the most important method of trimming a wedding dress. Once you become aware of this technique, you will see that it is done on almost all expensive gowns.

In order to do this, you must use good-quality Chantilly or Alençon lace with distinct motifs, not the lower-priced imitations, which have very small, simple designs. Clipping can also be done with Venise lace. Before you begin to clip your lace, refer to the photographs here. Although your lace will not be identical, the procedure is the same. After you look at the photographs, study your own lace. Pick out the individual motifs and the border. Some borders are a simple, narrow scallop; others include part of the main motif. Most laces can be clipped a number of ways. If you haven't yet bought your lace, study the pictures so you will be able to pick out a lace that is suited to your purpose.

Use small, sharp embroidery scissors for clipping the lace. First roughly cut the motif or border from the lace. Then cut carefully around the motif or along the shape of the band. You do not have to follow the exact shape of every detail. If you are using re-embroidered lace, follow the cord outline, being careful not to cut into the threads holding the cord. When the design of the lace has too many intricate leaves and curlicues to follow, you can leave net filling in complicated areas and cut around the basic shape.

Separating a Galloon

See *Plate* 10. Many galloons of medium width, 6 to 15 inches, consist of identical borders top and bottom. The borders may form the entire design, or there may be a motif between the borders. With this technique, the border on both sides is separated from the galloon. By doing this, you will have an interestingly shaped border that follows the contours of the motifs. Because the border has a zigzag shape it can be eased around the curved hemline of the gown. It is easier to apply this type of border than a straight galloon, which must be clipped and overlapped to fit a curve. This border requires only half the amount of lace you would need if you used the entire galloon. If the galloon has motifs between the borders, they can be used as appliqués on the gown or headpiece.

Clipping Motifs

Motifs can be clipped from pieces of lace after the larger parts of the gown have been cut, or you can buy a small amount of lace just for the motifs (see *Plate* 11). Notice that the lace design illustrated here is fairly large and intricate, so it can be cut in a number of different ways. With many laces, you can cut a large motif using the entire spray of flowers or smaller motifs comprised of parts of the spray or individual flowers. The larger motifs could be used on the skirt or bodice, and the smaller ones at the neckline or sleeves.

PLATE 10
Clipped Galloon

PLATE 11
Clipped Appliqués

PLATE 12
Clipped Border

Borders

In addition to separating a medium-width galloon, borders can be made by clipping wide lace, either a galloon or a flounce (see *Plate 12*). Galloon is usually the better choice, since it gives you two borders. With this system of clipping, the borders can be used at the hem of the dress, the bodice and sleeve cut from the main part of the lace, and appliques cut from the scraps. Borders can consist of a fairly narrow scallop or a scallop that also includes a larger motif.

Clipped Band

Bands

The design of some lace is made up of bands or strips instead of separate motifs. The bands are usually in a scallop or zigzag form (see *Plate 13*). With this type of design, the bands can be separated to use as trim. Individual motifs can be clipped from the bands to use as appliqués.

PLATE 14
Venise Galloons and Clipped Appliqués

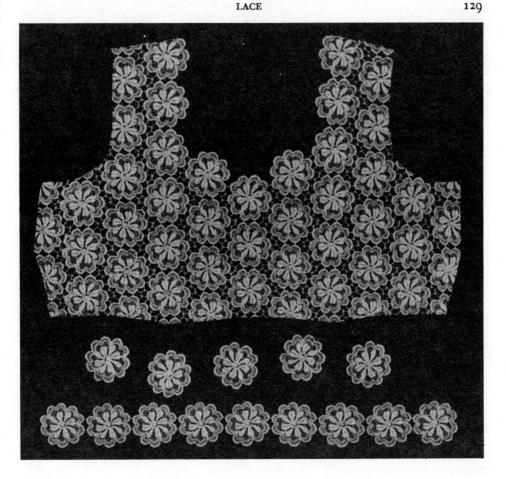

PLATE 15
Venise Bodice with Clipped Band and Appliqués

Venise Lace

Many Venise laces also lend themselves to clipping. Since Venise does not have a net background, the technique is simply to disconnect the motifs where they are joined by threads (see *Plate 14*). At first glance these laces look like band trims. They can be used that way, but in addition they can be separated into individual motifs, as you see in the photograph. When the motifs are elaborate, they can be further separated into smaller motifs. Another popular Venise trim is the daisy band. This lace can be both used as a band and separated into individual flowers. Bands and separated motifs are often used together on the gown.

Some wide Venise lace also lends itself to clipping. *Plate 15* shows a bodice cut in Venise. Notice how the scoop neckline follows the shape of the flower motifs. The individual flowers cut from scraps can be used as appliqués. Because of the way the flowers are arranged in rows, this lace can be cut into bands as well. A combination of all three could be used on one dress.

APPLYING LACE TRIMMINGS

Lace trimming can be applied by hand or machine. Hand application is generally best because it has a finer look and also gives you more control as you work. The trim should be basted first. To stitch by hand, use a whip stitch (see *Figure 153*). For machine application, in some cases a straight stitch is used, in other cases a fine narrow zigzag. If the trim is enclosed in a seam, it is applied during construction of the garment; otherwise it is usually stitched to the dress after construction. When stitching around the shape of lace motifs by machine, use a small embroidery foot, if your machine has one, rather than the regular presser foot. For re-embroidered lace, a cording foot sometimes works best. Try stitching with the feed dog lowered for easier maneuvering. Test stitch size and machine adjustments on a scrap first.

Lace appliqués and other small lace trimmings can be applied to some fabrics with a fusible web such as Stitch Witchery. Although this method is faster than sewing, it is not as nice a finish because it tends to flatten the lace somewhat and can look rather stiff. The appliqués cannot be removed once they are fused. Cut fusible web in the shape of the appliqué but ¼ inch smaller. Test on a scrap first. Follow the directions on the package, using a lightweight pressing cloth. Excess Stitch Witchery in the open areas of the lace should melt onto the pressing cloth. Do not leave any scraps of web on the ironing board because they will melt onto the dress if exposed to heat.

You should be aware that if you plan to use lace trim around a curve, special consideration must be given. Ruffles are flexible and can follow a curve with no trouble. Narrow loop edges also curve easily. Wider trims must be eased or otherwise shaped into a curve, as explained below for each type of lace.

If you apply lace trim to a bodice, especially large appliqués or any trim near the bust area, the trim should be pinned and basted with the gown on a dress form or your body. This is very important because the trim must conform to the shape of the body and may need to be eased or adjusted. If not, the shape and fit of the bodice can become distorted significantly and the dress will not fit properly or look right. It is impossible to get the correct body shaping while working flat.

Finishing the Ends of Lace

If the lace end is free, as at the end of a neckline opening, the end can be finished with a hand-rolled hem (*Figure 52A*). At a garment edge, the ends of

FIGURE 52

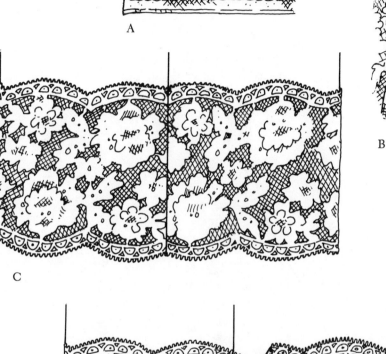

A

B

C

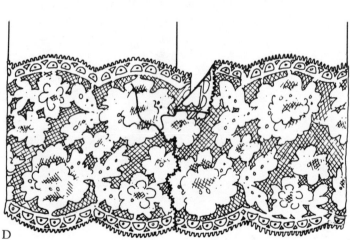

D

lace can be joined using a French seam (*Figure 52B*). If the lace is stitched to the garment, the ends can be enclosed in the seam (*Figure 52C*). When you are using wider lace, especially finer lace such as Alençon, Chantilly, and Venise, the appliqué method is the best and most attractive way of finishing the ends (see *Figure 52D*). After the lace is applied, trim the ends, following the shape of the motif. Overlap the motif and whip-stitch the end to the underlayer of the lace.

FIGURE 53

Lace Appliqués

Lace appliqués can be used anywhere on the gown. Generally, larger appliqués are used on larger areas, such as a skirt, and smaller appliqués are used on smaller areas, such as sleeves. To decide where to place your appliqués, put the gown on a dress form or on yourself and have someone pin and position the appliqués until you have a pleasing arrangement. If you are using scattered appliqués on the bodice or skirt, thread-trace (*Figure* 38) along the center front so that you can position the appliqués symmetrically. When appliqués are placed on the skirt, they are generally concentrated more closely toward the hem with fewer or smaller appliqués farther up the skirt to keep a balanced look (*Figure* 53). You can also use appliqués heavily on the bodice and let them trail down onto the skirt. Remember that the dress *must* be on your body or dress form when pinning appliqués to the bodice.

Large, elaborate appliqués that look like flower bouquets can be made by cutting the main motif from the lace, then cutting additional flowers and adding them at the top or sides of the motif, overlapping them so that they appear to form one very large motif. You can use motifs from more than one lace to do this (see *Figure* 54). For another pretty effect, appliqués can be used at the waistline to hold a sash.

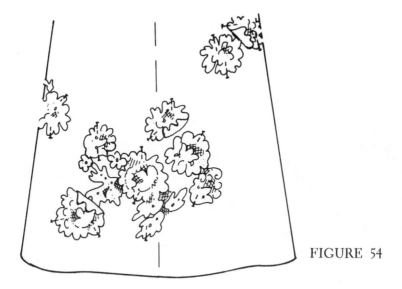

FIGURE 54

Once you have pinned the appliqués in their final position, baste in place and then stitch by hand or machine, as explained above.

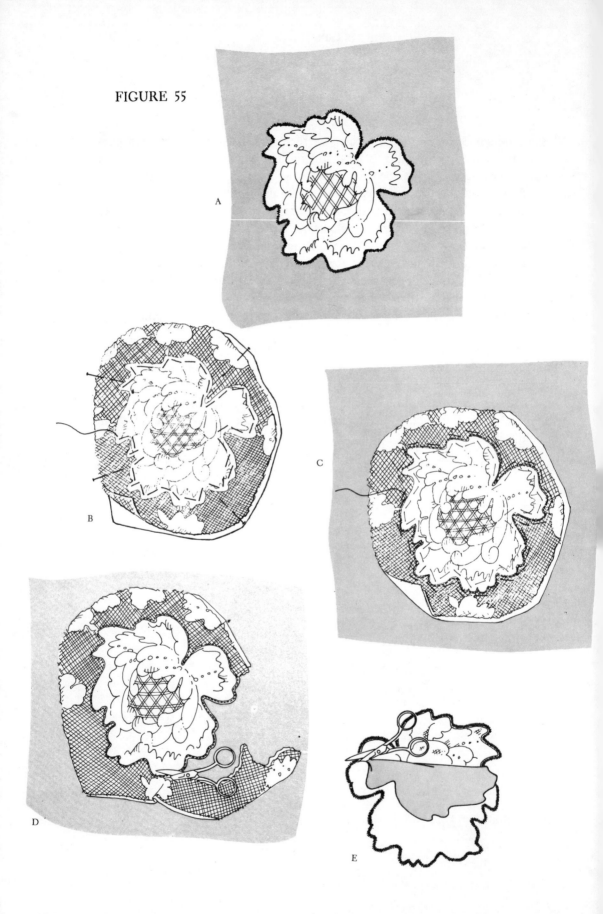

FIGURE 55

Cutaway Lace Appliqués

With this type of appliqué, the lace is stitched to the dress and then the backing fabric is trimmed away for a sheer effect (see *Figure 55A*). This is suitable for Alençon or Chantilly lace.

1. Roughly cut a lace motif, leaving about 1 inch of extra fabric all around the motif. Cut a piece of tulle or organza the same size to use as backing.
2. Pin the lace to the backing with the lace right side up.
3. Hand-baste the lace and backing together, about ¼ inch inside the shape of the motif, as you see in *Figure 55B*.
4. Pin the appliqué in the correct position on the right side of the garment.
5. Hand-baste the appliqué to the garment about ¼ inch outside the design outline of the motif (see *Figure 55C*).
6. Using a small straight stitch, sew around the motif, following the design outline. With re-embroidered lace, use a cording foot and stitch just to the outside of the cord.
7. With embroidery scissors, carefully trim away excess fabric from around the appliqué close to the stitching, as you see in *Figure 55D*.
8. Set your machine for a narrow satin stitch (very close zigzag). Follow the outline of the design, stitching over the edge of the lace.
9. Turn the garment wrong side out. Very carefully trim away the backing garment fabric, close to the zigzag stitch (see *Figure 55E*). Be sure that you do not cut into the tulle or organza backing the lace.

To cut away only the garment fabric, pinch up the garment fabric in the center and then slowly clip over toward the edge of the motif.

Lace Borders

Borders can be cut from wide lace or made by separating a galloon. Borders are used most often around the hem, on sleeves, and at the waistline (see *Figure 56*). Because the upper edge of the border usually has a zigzag or deeper scalloped shape, the border can be eased around curves.

When applying a border at the hemline, the dress should be hemmed first. The width of the hem should be less than the width of the narrowest part of the lace border. Spread the dress out on a large table. Pin the bottom edge of the border to the edge of the hem, aligning the upper part of the scallop with the edge of the

FIGURE 56

dress so the lower part of the scallop extends below the hem. After the border is pinned around the hem, begin pinning the upper part of the border to the dress, easing it in so that it lies flat. If it will not lie flat, clip into the lace around a motif and overlap the motif, as shown in *Figure 57*. Baste the border to the dress. If it

FIGURE 57

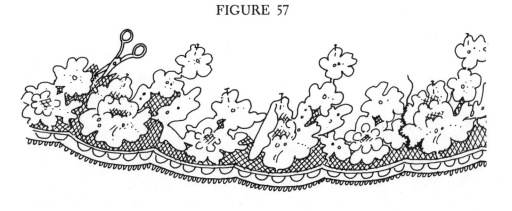

was necessary to clip and overlap lace motifs, hand-stitch along the motifs, using a whip stitch (*Figure 153*). Stitch the lace border to the skirt around the upper edge only. The bottom scalloped edge is left free.

For a sheer effect, the fabric backing the lace border can be trimmed away. When this is done, it is not necessary to hem the skirt first. The hem should be cut at the finished length of the dress. Follow the directions above for pinning the border to the dress, then stitch the upper edge of the lace border to the skirt, using a narrow, close zigzag stitch. Turn the dress wrong side out and carefully trim away the backing fabric close to the zigzag stitch. This type of cutaway border effect can be used along with the cutaway lace appliqués described previously.

To apply a border to the end of a sleeve, follow the directions above for applying a border at the hemline. The border should be centered on the sleeve. Fold the sleeve in half and mark the center with a pin. Place the center of a lace scallop at the center mark on the sleeve and pin from the center toward the sides of the sleeve.

Borders are also applied to the bodice at the waistline seam. You may have seen dresses that look as if the edge of the bodice pattern was placed on the scalloped edge of the lace, but that is not how it is actually done. The bodice must be sewn first, then the border is appliquéd to cover the waistline seam. For proper fit, the border must be pinned to the dress while the dress is on a form or on your body (see *Figure 72*). Stitch the upper edge of the border only, leaving the bottom scallops free.

Borders of any width can be applied in a double row, forming a panel effect, on the front skirt, as you see in *Figure 56*. In this case, both sides of the lace are stitched.

Narrow scalloped borders can be used to outline the edges of sleeves, neckbands or necklines, or waistlines. They can also be used for curved outlines on the skirt. A simple narrow scallop border will go with most types of lace.

Galloons

Galloons range from narrow Venise daisy chains to opulent bands 10 or more inches wide (see *Figure 58*). They are one of the most versatile lace forms. The daisy chain galloons are flexible. They can be made to curve around the neckline, or to form shaped designs on the skirt, which are often highlighted with an appliqué. Flower band galloons are used with individual appliqués cut from the band. Narrow and medium-width galloons are used to trim almost any part of the gown. Wide galloons are placed around the hem and at the ends of long sleeves. Some galloons look very pretty with a ribbon underneath so a hint of color peeks through. You can cut away the fabric from behind a Chantilly or Alençon galloon for a sheer look. Apply the galloon with a narrow, close zigzag stitch. Then turn the garment wrong side out and trim away the backing fabric close to the stitching.

The flowers of some daisy chains are joined with a single thread, while others are joined with two threads. When using the type joined with two threads on a curve, it may be necessary to clip one of the threads so that the chain will lie flat. To attach a daisy chain by machine, stitch once along the middle. This trim looks much more attractive when applied by hand, tacking the centers of the flowers. Depending on the size of the flower and whether the area is curved or straight, you may need to attach every flower or only every second or third flower.

Wider, more elaborate Venise flower galloons can be formed into a gradual curve but not a deep curve. For deep curves, cut the flowers apart and apply as individual appliqués. To use a flower band around a slight curve, clip into some of the threads attaching leaves or petals, but do not sever parts of the flowers from the bands. If the motifs are joined in one place only, then the band should curve without any clipping. This type of lace should be applied by hand.

Fairly narrow, simple galloons can be stitched in a straight line along the top and bottom edge. Wide galloons are stitched along the top and bottom following the shape of the scallop.

A wide galloon of Alençon or Chantilly lace looks beautiful around a hem of a gown. In most cases, the galloon must be shaped to follow the curve of the hem. The dress should be hemmed first. Place the dress on a large table. Pin the bottom edge of the galloon to the hem of the dress so the upper part of the bottom scallop is even with the edge of the hem and the lower part of the scallop extends below the hem. The upper edge of the galloon will be rippled. At the upper edge, cut into the galloon, following the shape of a motif and cutting as deeply as necessary

FIGURE 58

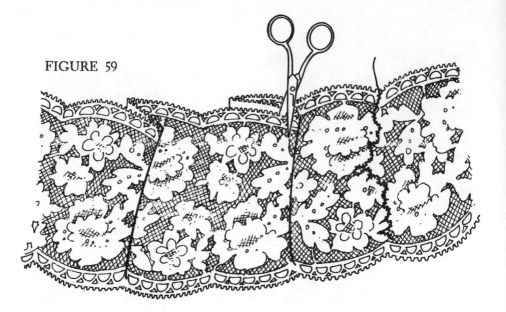

FIGURE 59

to enable the lace to overlap and lie flat, as shown in *Figure 59*. The sharper the curve, the deeper you will have to cut into the lace and the more overlap there will be. On a slight curve, you may need to cut only into every second or third motif. Once all the cuts have been made, overlap and pin the lace motifs, arranging the overlap so that the top edges of the scallop meet as neatly as possible. The scallops will probably not match perfectly. Once you have pinned the galloon in place, carefully baste the overlapped motifs to the lace only, not to the dress. Thread-trace (*Figure 38*) the side and center back seams of the dress onto the lace so you will be able to align the lace later when you repin it. Do not bring the thread tracing through to the dress fabric. Unpin and remove the lace from the dress. Stitch the overlapped basted motifs by hand with a whip stitch (*Figure 153*) or by machine with a narrow zigzag. If you are whip-stitching the motifs, you can leave the galloon pinned to the dress if you prefer. Repin the lace to the dress, aligning the thread tracings with the correct seams. Baste the lace at the top and the bottom. Stitch along the top of the galloon, following the shape of the scallop, and along the bottom.

Lace Edges

Lace edges range from the tiniest loops to wide, sumptuous bands. Edges are applied flat and are also gathered to make ruffles (see below). These trims can be used on any part of the gown. They can be applied to garment edges, such as neckline, sleeve edges, and hemline, as well as to the body of the dress (see *Figure 60*). Narrow to medium-width edges can be applied in single or multiple rows, flat or gathered, or in a combination of both flat and gathered. Wide, expensive bands are more often used flat. You can use an edge 5 inches or more in width for cuffs, small sleeves, or upper sleeves.

FIGURE 60

Edges can be eased into a gradual curve. To do this, run a stitch at the top of the lace as you would for gathering. Pull the thread slightly, just enough to make the lace curve but not to form gathers. If there are some puckers you can usually steam them out, but try this on a scrap first. Some laces have a heavy thread along the top edge that can be pulled with a pin to ease the lace instead of using a gathering thread. The wider the lace, the less it can be curved before it will begin to ripple.

Flat lace edges can be attached to the garment by machine-stitching along the top of the band only. Edges are not stitched along the bottom. At a garment edge, the lace is stitched ⅝ inch from the cut edge before the facing is applied. Then the facing is stitched directly on top of the line of stitching that holds the lace. The lace can be applied to a finished garment edge by hand, using a whip stitch (*Figure 153*), or by machine, using a fine zigzag. On sheer fabrics, make a hand-rolled hem (*Figure 130*) and then whip-stitch the lace to the rolled hem. For a pretty effect, stitch a narrow trim, such as ribbon or small daisy chain, covering the straight band at the top of the lace edge.

Mitering

When flat lace is applied to a corner, such as at a yoke seam or a square collar, the corners must be mitered (see *Figure 61*). To miter a corner, pin the lace around the corner, folding it as shown. Notice that a triangle is formed where the lace is folded. Be sure that the miter line runs directly from the inside to the

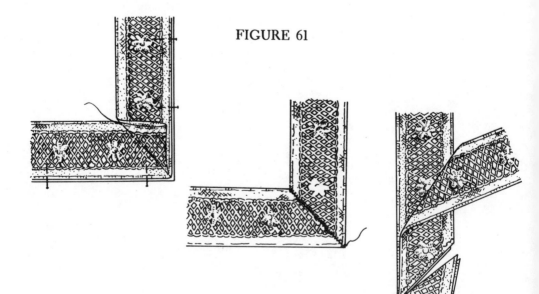

FIGURE 61

FIGURE 62

outside corner. Zigzag- or whip-stitch along the fold and trim away the excess lace from the wrong side. A corner can sometimes be turned by appliquéing the lace (see appliquéd lace finish in *Figure 52D*).

Lace Ruffles

Ruffles are made by gathering a lace edge. Pregathered lace ruffles can also be purchased, although many of these are made from a poor-quality lace and are gathered rather skimpily. Because of its weight and thickness, heavy Venise is not suitable for gathering. Ruffles can be used to trim any part of the gown, at garment edges or on the body of the dress (see *Figure 62*). A wide edge gathered slightly around a scoop neck or attached to a short sleeve looks very pretty. A ruffle can be used in a princess seam to give a pinafore effect. The seam or garment edge where the ruffle is attached is sometimes covered with another lace or trim.

Lace edges have a narrow strip along the top, which is where you should stitch the gathering thread. On most laces the strip is only wide enough to run a single row of gathering stitches. If the strip is wide enough to run a double row of gathering stitches, that would be preferable. Don't make the gathering stitch too long, especially on fine lace, or the gathers will be unattractive. If the lace gets caught in the machine as you stitch, use strips of tissue paper while stitching. If lace must be joined, use a French seam or appliqué method.

To figure the amount of lace needed for a ruffle and for directions on applying a ruffle, see Chapter 7, under "Ruffles."

Lace Insertions

Insertions can be used as vertical or horizontal bands on skirt, bodice, or sleeves. Bands of insertion lace can be alternated with bands of other trim such as braid or ribbon, or with rows of tucks (see *Figure 63*). Some can be eased into a slight curve, but they should not be applied to a sharp curve. Insertions can be topstitched directly onto the fabric or stitched with a band of ribbon or colored fabric underneath.

For an openwork look, the fabric behind the insertion can be trimmed away. Hand-baste the insertion in place. There are two possible methods of application.

METHOD 1 (*Figure 64A*). Topstitch the insertion along the top and bottom edges. Carefully trim away the backing fabric to within ¼ inch of the stitching. Hand-overcast or zigzag-stitch the raw edge and press it away from the insertion. You can also trim to ½ inch and hand-roll hem the raw edge up to the insertion.

METHOD 2 (*Figure 64B*). Apply the insertion with a narrow, close zigzag stitch at the top and bottom edge. Trim away the backing fabric from the wrong side close to the zigzag stitch.

FIGURE 63

FIGURE 64

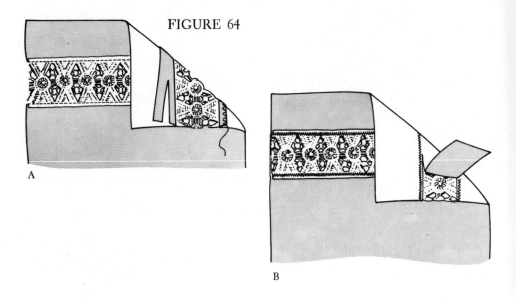

A

B

Lace Beading

Lace beading can be used to trim bodice, sleeves, yokes, cuffs, skirt, and so on (see *Figure 65*). Beading is available plain or with ribbon already woven through the holes. If you add your own ribbon, you can choose embroidered or colored ribbon, as well as white. You can also use a ribbon wider than the holes so it will have a softly crushed look, or you might weave a strip of your dress fabric or organza through the beading. The ribbon can be interlaced in and out of each bar, or in and out of every second or third bar, or farther apart. In some cases, the beading looks better stitched on top of the ribbon instead of the ribbon being woven through. Try a number of ways to see which looks best.

If you want the ribbon to tie in a bow, it is better to lace the ribbon through the beading and make a separate bow, which is hand-tacked on top of the beading.

Beading is stitched to the garment just above and below the ribbon. The scalloped edge is left free. Beading should be used on straight areas, or very slight curves.

SELECTING AND USING LACE TRIMS

When you select your lace it is not necessary to use matched lace sets. While lace sets are often used on wedding gowns, you will see just as many gowns using two or more different laces of the same type, or even several different types. Alençon or Chantilly lace is often trimmed with Venise. A bodice of allover Cluny lace

FIGURE 65

might have a Venise or Cluny edge trimming the neckline, sleeves, and skirt. A dress of Chantilly lace could be trimmed with a narrow Val edge gathered at the collar and sleeves.

Lace appliqués are nearly always used in combination with another form of lace, such as a border or allover. Appliqués cut from matching lace are most often used, but they may also be a different lace pattern or cut from two different patterns, one for large motifs, the other for small. Venise appliqués are used with all types of lace. You could use large Venise appliqués with a narrow Venise edge or a dainty daisy galloon.

Wide laces can be used for part of the gown, such as bodice, sleeves, bib, or princess panel, and a matching or co-ordinating edge, galloon, or border used to trim the rest of the gown. Another possibility is to use both sheer and opaque lace effects by cutting away the backing fabric behind some of the lace. You might trim away the backing fabric behind the lace border of a skirt so that it would appear sheer and then use matching solid appliqués on the skirt, or you could use cutaway appliqués on the sleeve and regular appliqués on the bodice.

EMBELLISHING LACE

On the most expensive gowns, the lace is usually embellished with additional touches of pearls, beads, rhinestones, sequins, or individual fabric, lace, or embroidered flowers (see *Plate 16*).

For information on applying beads to your lace, see the section on "Jewel Trims" in Chapter 7. Small lace flower motifs can be added to Alençon, Chantilly, or Venise laces. The lace appliqué does not have to be the same type as the lace fabric. For example, Chantilly and Alençon laces are often embellished with tiny Venise flowers. The flowers are hand-stitched at the centers only so that the free petals are three-dimensional. The centers of the three-dimensional flowers can also be embellished with pearls or beads. On some embroidered fabrics or sheer lace, organdy flowers or satin buds can be used for added decoration. Purchased silk or other delicate flowers are also used as embellishments. Refer to the section on "Flowers" in Chapter 7.

PLATE 16
A. Alençon Lace Appliqué with Pearls on English Net
B. Venise Lace Appliqués with Sequins and Pearls
C. Three-dimensional Flower Appliqués
D. Alençon Lace with Pearls

DYEING LACE

Small amounts of lace for trimming can be dyed quite easily. Cotton lace takes dye the best, but nylon and other fibers can usually be dyed successfully. Always test a scrap first and be sure the scrap is dry to judge the color.

Dyeing lace ivory is done by using tea. Make a strong brew of tea and filter it so there are no tea leaves. The tea should be warm but not boiling hot. Wet the lace first in cool water. Place the wet lace in the tea and let it steep for a few minutes. Take it out, roll it in an old towel, and check the color. The wet color will be darker than the dry color. When you think the color looks somewhat darker than you want, take the lace out and dry it to see the true color. Once the color has been tested on scraps, you can dye the rest of the lace.

For bridesmaids' and other dresses, you can dye lace in a color to match the dress. Wet the lace first and use liquid dye, not powder. You can mix dyes to get the color you want. Use warm but not boiling water. Follow the steps above for using tea, testing a scrap and drying it to check the color.

CUTTING AND SEWING LACE FABRICS

Before you begin cutting your lace, read the general information about sewing special fabrics at the beginning of Chapter 5. Except for fabric preparation, this information applies to sewing lace as well. If you are using lace that is beaded or contains metallic thread, also read about working with beaded or metallic fabrics.

Pattern Selection

The design of the lace is the most important consideration in selecting your pattern. Many laces have scalloped border edges that can be used as ruffles, hem or sleeve edges, and so on. You can buy a pattern that shows a border view or you can adapt a pattern to incorporate the scallop of the lace into part of the design of the dress. Information on revising a pattern to use a lace border is found in this section.

The weight of the lace should also be considered in selecting your pattern. Chantilly and Alençon laces are lightweight and sheer, so are suitable for patterns that suggest lightweight fabrics. Venise and Cluny are heavier and more suited to patterns that suggest crisp fabrics. The lightweight laces can be used with patterns for crisp fabrics if a taffeta lining is used. Lighter-weight laces can be used to make an entire dress or only parts of the dress. In choosing a pattern for an all-lace dress, select a style with simple lines and a minimum of details and seams. The design of the lace should be the main feature of the gown.

Combinations of lace and fabric are almost unlimited. If you look at the brides' magazines, you will see that the majority of gowns are designed this way. Lace combines well with any fabric that is formal enough and doesn't have a design or surface texture that would compete with the design of the lace. Let the lace be the focal point and the other fabric form the background. You can use a lightweight fabric such as organza or chiffon for a delicate look, or a substantial one such as satin or velvet for a stately appearance. Combinations of lace with soft knits such as jersey or maracaine are popular.

Most Venise lace is too heavy to use for an entire dress. It is generally used for smaller parts and accents, such as bodice, yoke, bib, sleeves, and cuffs. Venise combines well with most dressy fabrics, including velvet, satin, crepe, taffeta, organza, and jersey. Only the lightweight, flatter Venise will gather well, so do not choose a pattern with gathers for a heavy Venise.

Cluny is less formal and less expensive than Venise. The heavier weights are more often used for parts, while the lighter weights can be used for parts or for the entire dress. Use the heavier crochet type of Cluny with the less dressy fabrics, such as dimity, dotted swiss, or leno. The more delicate Clunies can also be used with formal fabrics, such as velvet, taffeta, satin, and moiré.

Using Expensive Lace on a Budget

Don't be tempted to buy a low-priced lace to save money. A yard or less of quality lace will give you enough to create an elegant, expensive-looking dress. If your budget is limited, you are much better off buying a small amount of a fine lace and using it carefully than buying yards of a low-priced lace. With good lace, there is no waste because appliqués are cut from the leftover pieces. Also, because fine imported lace is usually available in a number of widths, it is often possible to buy the width that is just the size of the piece you want to cut, such as 18 inches wide for a bodice or 30 inches wide for long sleeves. Smaller parts—a yoke, neckband, or cuffs—can be cut from even narrower lace.

Many expensive dresses use lace for a small area like the bodice alone or bodice and sleeves. The rest of the dress might be made from satin, organza, or English net trimmed with co-ordinating lace. For added richness, the lace can be beaded with pearls or crystal beads (see the section on "Jewel Trims" in Chapter 7).

FIGURE 66

Figure 66 shows some ways to use a small amount of lace. Approximately ¾ yard of 45-inch lace will enable you to cut a yoke, neckband, and long sleeves of lace. Only ⅝ yard of 45-inch lace is needed for an Empire bodice and neckband. From ⅞ yard of 45-inch lace you can cut short sleeves and an Empire bodice. You can make long fitted sleeves from ⅞ yard of 36-inch lace. With larger motifs, somewhat more would be needed for centering the design or matching seams.

English Net

English net is a fine-quality, closely spaced cotton net that is used as a background fabric with lace trimmings. It looks exactly like the net background found on many of the best Chantilly and Alençon laces. By cutting a border and motifs from lace and applying them to English net, you can lighten the effect where a solid-lace dress would be too heavy-looking. You can also save money because you can achieve almost the same effect as solid lace at a considerably lower cost. This is not just a budget trick. Many expensive dresses are made this way, often with the lace or net embellished with pearls or beads (see *Plate 16*).

The English net should be backed with tulle or organza. If you sew lace trim to English net by machine, you will have to place a strip of tissue paper under the net and stitch through the net and paper together. Tear away the paper when you finish.

Interfacing and Lining

INTERFACING Sheer laces are not interfaced. With heavier laces, interfacing is used only if the lace is underlined in opaque fabric, as otherwise the interfacing would show. Where interfacing is necessary, use a fairly crisp, light- to medium-weight woven or non-woven. You can sometimes use the underlining fabric as interfacing.

UNDERLINING Gathered sheer laces may or may not be underlined. Fitted parts such as bodices or fitted sleeves are underlined for strength. To preserve the delicate look, lace is most often underlined with a sheer, such as organza or tulle. Where coverage is needed, the lace is underlined in an opaque fabric. For a sheer effect with coverage, use a flesh tone opaque lining. Refer to the chart on page 69 for specific fabrics.

LINING With expensive sheer lace dresses, the lining is sometimes made as a separate underdress. The sheer lace overdress is underlined in tulle or organza to give it a little extra body. China silk or lightweight silk-like crepe lining fabrics are suitable for either lining or underdress for soft styles. For crisper shaping, taffeta or satin are used.

A gathered skirt made of sheer lace will fall beautifully and look very professional if you include an underskirt made of one or several layers of net or organza over a bottom layer of silk or taffeta. Gather and seam each of the layers separately and then join all of the underskirts together at the waist. Attach the underskirt only at the waistline of the gown. When hemming, be sure that your underdress or lining is shorter than the dress itself by ½ to 1 inch.

If you are using an underlining with a scalloped-edge lace, the edge of the underlining can be finished with a straight line even with the top of scallop, or in a curved line following the shape of the scallop. For the straight-line method, see *Figure 67*A. Pin or baste the underlining to the scalloped edge just above the scallop. Cut the backing ¼ inch longer than the inner point of the scallop, then turn the raw edge under and hand-stitch to the lace. For the scalloped-edge method, see *Figure 67*B. Baste the lining to the scallops, following the shape of the scallop, about ¼ inch from the edge. Clip the edge of the underlining ¼ inch longer than the scallop. Fold the edge under and stitch, following the shape of the scallop. After you have basted the underlining to the lace but before you cut the underlining, try on the dress to be sure that the underlining is not pulling or straining. If there is any strain on the underlining you will see ripples on the lace and the dress will not hang nicely. Release the basting and have the underlining pinned to the hem while you wear the dress.

FIGURE 67

A

B

Layout and Cutting

Before cutting, you should first determine which is the right side of your lace. With Alençon this is easy because the motifs of the lace are outlined on the right side in a very obvious cord. Chantilly lace motifs are usually outlined in a fine cord on the right side. If there is no cord, look closely at the design on both sides. The right side has more texture and is finished better—the wrong side is flatter. The right side of Venise lace is smooth and sculptured in appearance. The wrong side is coarser and duller-looking. Some Cluny laces have a cord outlining the design on the face. Others have popcorn bumps on the right side. The texture on the right side should be more apparent and varied. The back is flatter and more monotonous.

For cutting fine lace, you will need sharp scissors such as lingerie or polyester shears. Sharp, heavy-duty shears are best for Venise. Since lace has no grain, it does not need to be straightened. Lace can have a directional design that would require a one-way pattern layout. See fabric direction test on page 75. If the lace has a scalloped edge that you plan to use as part of the garment, see "Cutting Border Laces," below. Lace can be cut either lengthwise or crosswise, whichever shows the design to the best advantage. You should cut all the pieces on the same grain so that the motifs all run the same way. When cutting on the crosswise, the grain line arrows on your pattern pieces (whether muslin or paper) should be changed to make the pattern positioning easier (see pages 76–77).

Lace with small, closely spaced designs does not need special consideration in laying out the pattern unless it has a one-way design. Lace with large or prominent motifs, however, requires extra care in layout and cutting. With a large, distinct motif, the position of the motif is very important to the over-all professional look of your dress. Major motifs should be centered or positioned to their best advantage on bodice, sleeves, skirt, and so on (see *Figure 36B*). The lace should be cut in a single layer. In order to do this, you will need duplicate pattern pieces. If you have not made a muslin pattern with duplicate pieces, refer to page 78. You can place your muslin pattern underneath the lace and cut with the lace face up to position the design. Because of its thickness, Venise lace should be cut in one layer, whether positioning is needed or not.

Also consider whether the design of your lace is such that the motifs should be matched. You can match the design and also make the seams invisible by using appliquéd seams (see below). Remember that extra yardage will be needed for matching, for special motif placement, and for making appliquéd seams. When pinning lace, use fine silk pins in the seam allowance only. Pins with large-size colored heads are easy to see. Lace should be marked with tailor's tacks (*Figure* 37) or thread tracing (*Figure* 38) only. Do not use chalk, tracing wheel, or dressmaker's carbon.

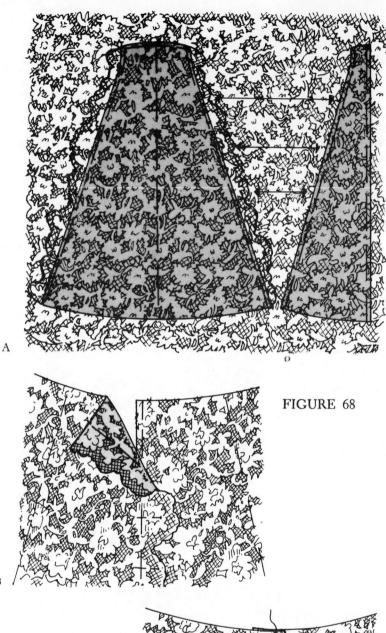

A

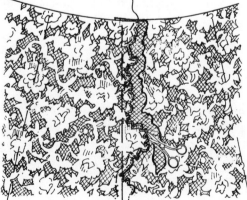

B

C

FIGURE 68

Appliquéd Seams

In a fine lace dress, a conventionally stitched seam would detract greatly from the beauty of the lace by abruptly cutting through a motif and interrupting the flow of the design. Conspicuous seams, such as side and center back, should be joined by the appliqué method, which makes an invisible seam. This technique applies to Alençon, Chantilly, and Venise laces. With this method, the seams are overlapped and the top layer of the seam follows the design motifs. The under-layer has conventional seam allowance.

Place the pattern pieces so that the center line of the pattern runs through the center of the main motif. The front and back of the skirt or bodice should be aligned so that the motifs at the seam to be joined will match, as you see in *Figure 68A*. Leave at least one motif between each pattern piece. Pin the pattern pieces. Cut around waistline and hem for a skirt, and neck, armholes, and shoulders for a bodice, where conventional seam allowance will be used. Cut the side seams of the front pattern, following the design motif, as shown. Cut the back pattern with conventional seam allowance. Thread-trace (*Figure* 38) the stitching lines of the side seams of the front and back, as you see in *Figure 68B*. If the pattern has straight seam lines, the design will match. However, if the seam is curved or at an angle, such as on an A-line skirt, the design motifs will blend together but not match exactly. Baste the two layers together along the seam line. Baste again, this time following the shape of the motifs and using a small stitch, as you see in *Figure 68C*.

Appliqué the edges of the lace motif to the underlayer, either by hand-stitching with a whip stitch (*Figure* 153) or by machine with small, narrow zigzag or straight stitch. With embroidery scissors, trim excess lace close to stitching, as shown in *Figure 68C*. Turn the garment wrong side up and trim excess lace from the wrong side close to the stitching line.

If your pattern has a center back seam, position the right and left back as explained above for front and back skirt. The center back seam of the right side would have the conventional seam allowance, while the left side would be cut following the lace motifs.

Cutting Border Laces

Using the lace scallop at a garment edge will be easier if your pattern has a straight edge to coincide with the edge of the lace. A sleeve pattern with a slight curve at the bottom can be straightened (*Figure* 69). Curved patterns such as flared skirts can be used with lace borders by making some adjustments (see next page).

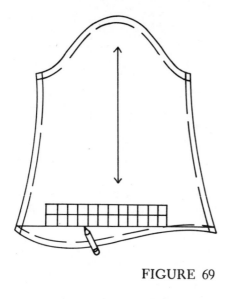

FIGURE 69

Because the scalloped border of the lace is used as the finished edge of the garment, any alterations in the length of the pattern must be made before cutting. The hem or seam allowance should be removed from the pattern at the edge that will be placed on the scallop. Position the pattern edge midway between the upper and lower part of the scallop.

When using the scallop of the lace at a garment edge, the scallop should match at the seams so that you won't end up with half a scallop on one side of the seam, as in *Figure 70*. The seam may be at the high or low part of the scallop or in between, as long as both sides are the same. Position the pattern so the center of the pattern piece is at the center of the scallop, as in *Figure 71*. See that the stitching

FIGURE 70

FIGURE 71

line (*not* the cutting line) at the side seam falls at the same position on the scallop on each side of the pattern.

In the case of a gathered skirt, you can add or subtract a small amount at the side seams in order to make the pattern piece fit the scallop, as in *Figure 71*. Remember there must be seam allowance beyond the scallop. The *stitching* line should end at the top or center of the scallop, not the cutting line.

If you want to use border lace with a curved pattern, such as a flared skirt or a cape sleeve, the border is first cut from the lace (*Plate 12*) and the skirt is cut with no hem allowance. You will need to use a galloon (double-border lace) to have enough lace. After the garment is sewn and the hem length marked, the lace border is appliquéd to the skirt, following the directions on pages 136–37. Trim away excess lace fabric under the lace borders. Because the border must curve, measure the hem of the skirt pattern to be sure that you have enough border on your lace. A sleeve or any other curved pattern with a border would be cut the same way.

To use a border at a waistline or Empire waist, clip the border from the lace and cut and sew the bodice. After the bodice is joined to the skirt, pin the border so the scallops cover the waistline seam. Be sure to center the border at the center front of the dress (see *Figure 72*). The border must be pinned with the dress on a dress form or your body for proper shape and fit.

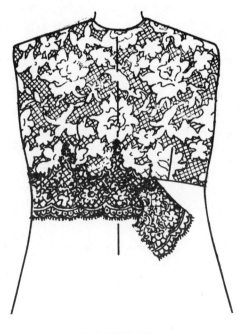

FIGURE 72

There is another cutting method that can be used for a flared skirt with no train (*Figure 73*).

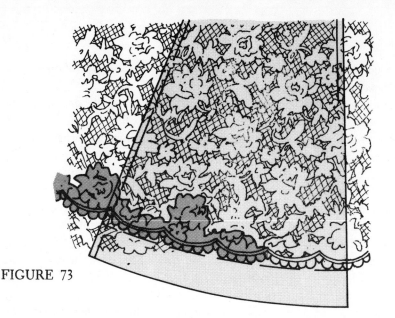

FIGURE 73

Place the lace face up on top of the pattern. Pin the pattern to the lace so the center front of the pattern is centered on a motif and the finished hemline at the center front is positioned at the bottom of a scallop, as shown. Roughly cut out the skirt front, leaving one motif excess at each side of the pattern. Unpin the skirt pattern near the hem only. Beginning at the side seams, carefully clip the lace along the top of the border design. Clip only as far as where the skirt hem begins to curve up, as you see in the drawing. Raise the lace border until it follows the same curve as the hemline on the skirt pattern. The border will overlap the lace. If the border will not lie flat, make small clips around the motifs on the upper part of the border. Overlap and ease in the upper part of the border. Baste into place. Cut along the waistline of the skirt, but do not cut the side seams. Thread-trace (*Figure 38*) the side seams and remove the pattern. Hand- or machine-stitch the lace border to the lace. Trim excess lace from the wrong side.

To cut the back skirt, follow the above steps using the back skirt pattern, except cut the side seams using conventional ⅝ inch seam allowance. Join the side seams by the appliqué method explained above.

Construction

GENERAL SEWING Use size A silk thread when sewing fine lace. Heavier thread will result in unattractive-looking seams. Be sure your needles are new and sharp: rough needles can snag the lace. Use a size 9 or 11 sewing machine needle and a size 10 hand sewing needle. Sew with small stitches, 15 to 20 per inch. Test your stitch size and tension on a scrap first. If the lace catches or the machine does not stitch neatly, place a strip of tissue paper under the lace and sew through the tissue paper. If it is needed, you can place a paper strip on top of the lace as well. When you have finished sewing, tear away the tissue paper.

For heavy lace (Venise or Cluny), use cotton or polyester thread with a size 11 or 14 sewing machine needle and a size 8 hand sewing needle. Set your machine for about 12 to 15 stitches per inch. If you must rip out a seam, be very careful to avoid breaking the threads of the lace.

CONSTRUCTION DETAILS Lace that is underlined with opaque fabric will not show construction details. With sheer lace, all construction details are visible, so darts, seams, and hems should be stitched neatly and carefully. Use a French, double-stitched, or merrow seam. Refer to seams for lighter-weight fabrics in Chapter 8. Darts should be double-stitched and trimmed (see *Figure 42B*). If you are not applying a lace border to the hem, use a horsehair braid hem (see *Figure 127*) or a sheer shaped or bias facing of tulle or organza.

To make a hem facing, cut a bias strip of organza for a curved hem. For a straight hem, use a straight strip of tulle, net, or organza. The strip should be 2½ inches wide and of a length equal to the circumference of the skirt hem. Trim away hem allowance, leaving only ¼ inch for attaching the facing. Fold the strip in half lengthwise and press. For a curved hem, shape the facing into a curve as you press. Pin the strip to the right side of the garment, matching the raw edge on the facing with the raw edge of the garment. Stitch ¼ inch from the edge. Stitch a second row ⅛ inch from the edge. Press the facing to the wrong side and blind-stitch by hand (see *Figure 74*).

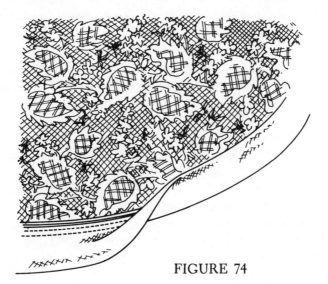

FIGURE 74

Conventional facings at necklines, armholes, sleeves, or other garment edges should be eliminated and replaced by satin or organza piping or a narrow bias organza facing.

For closings, use thread loops and buttons (page 230). Use an organza facing at the button opening. With lace underlined in opaque fabric, you can use a hand-applied zipper (see *Figure 144*).

PRESSING Three-dimensional lace, such as re-embroidered and Venise, should be pressed face down on a pressing pad or towel to avoid flattening or puckering. Use a transparent pressing cloth. Test the heat of the iron and the use of steam on a scrap. Press seams with tip of the iron only. Read complete pressing directions in Chapter 5.

HANDMADE LACE

For a truly heirloom gown, consider handmade lace for part of the gown or for trimming. Maybe you have a grandmother or aunt who knows how to do fine needlework such as tatting or Irish crochet. The materials and instructions for the following should be available at needlework shops or can be ordered by mail (see the Shopping Guide).

CROCHET Directions for lace tablecloths can be adapted to make the skirt for a gown. Most tablecloths have a border that can be used for the hem of the skirt. The tablecloth will show a border on all four sides. To adapt it for a skirt, crochet the border on one long side only. As a guide, use a pattern for a gathered skirt that is not too full. The pattern should be rectangular, not curved. Crochet the skirt to fit the pattern piece.

Crochet can also be used to make lace edges and motifs. For motifs, follow the directions given for making motifs that are used for delicate afghans or the center part of a doily. Instead of joining the motif for an afghan or completing the doily, the individual motifs can be used as lace appliqués.

IRISH CROCHET This is an especially rich-looking, beautiful type of crochet, consisting of three-dimensional flower designs with raised petals. You could use Irish crochet for a skirt or bodice, or crochet just the three-dimensional flowers to use as motifs.

FILET CROCHET This lacy crochet is used for edges and trimming. The design is formed from a series of solid and open squares.

HAIRPIN LACE Motifs and trimmings are made using a crochet hook and a hairpin lace loom—which is not really a loom but a simple U-shaped wire.

TATTING Delicate lace edgings and motifs can be made by this method, which uses a tatting shuttle and tatting cotton thread.

EMBROIDERED FABRICS AND TRIMMINGS

Like lace, embroideries are available as fabrics and trimmings (see *Plate* 17). The quality of embroidery varies tremendously. Select one that is of good quality; poor-

PLATE 17
Embroidered Fabrics and Trimmings

quality embroidery looks terrible and is not worth the money at all. Most important are the stitches, which should be made with a fine thread and placed very close together to give a rich, finished appearance. If you are buying eyelet, look at the holes in the eyelet designs to see that the stitching finishes the holes neatly and that there are no loose threads hanging. In the lower-priced embroideries, the stitches are spread too far apart so the design looks flat and ragged. The finest machine embroideries are made in Switzerland.

Embroidered Fabrics

Embroidery can be applied to almost any fabric from velvet to knit. The most popular embroidered fabrics for bridal wear are the lightweights—organza or organdy, as well as eyelet. For bridesmaids, there are embroideries and eyelets made on gingham and dainty floral-printed fabrics, in addition to solids. Eyelet fabrics look very pretty underlined in a contrasting color so the underlining color peeks through the holes of the eyelet. Embroidered fabrics are sometimes sold with matching plain goods. You can use the embroidery for some of the dress and the plain for other parts, such as an embroidered skirt with a plain bodice, or a plain dress with just embroidered sleeves (see *Figure 75*).

If your fabric has a scallop or border, you will have to cut it on the cross grain. Be sure to cut the remaining parts of your dress on the cross, even if they do not utilize the border. Otherwise there can be a difference in appearance or shading if some parts are cut on the cross grain and others are cut on the lengthwise grain. See page 75 for instructions on border designs. If your embroidery has a finished scalloped edge, see "Cutting Border Laces" in this chapter. You will not be able to use a curved pattern with an embroidered border as you can with a lace border. For sewing directions, follow the instructions in Chapter 5 for the base fabric.

Embroidered Trimmings

Embroidered trimmings come in most of the same forms as lace trimmings and are generally handled like lace trimming of the same type.

EYELET The most popular eyelet trimmings are edges, galloons, and beading. Eyelet edges can be used gathered or flat. Galloons are usually applied flat, but some have a plain strip along the center so the galloon can be gathered into a double ruffle. Eyelet beading is used in the same way as lace beading. To apply these trims, refer to information in this chapter on lace of the same formation.

EMBROIDERED FLOWER CHAINS Galloons made of embroidered flowers joined together are very delicate and pretty. Many of these are from Switzerland. Some are embroidered on organdy and have batting stuffed in the flower to give a three-dimensional appearance. These trims are handled the same way as a Venise flower

FIGURE 75

chain. They can be clipped apart between the motifs and used as individual appliqués (see *Plate 14*).

EMBROIDERED APPLIQUÉS Embroidered appliqués are available ranging in size from tiny flower buds to large elaborate shaded roses. A few are also available embroidered in white. These are used more on bridesmaids' and other formal dresses than on wedding gowns. They are applied by pinning in place, basting, and then stitching by hand.

EMBROIDERED BANDS Some embroidered bands have a finished edge and some have a raw edge. The type with a finished edge can be applied the same way as a lace insertion. If you have the type with a raw edge, turn the edge under and top-stitch the band to your fabric, or join the band to the garment with a seam.

7

Trimmings

Trimmings are what make a wedding gown. Selecting or making your trimmings is a chance to let yourself go and create something really beautiful and unique. Many of the decorations and trimming techniques used on wedding gowns are not seen on any other type of garment. This is your most special dress, unlike anything you will ever wear again. Some trimmings, such as hand embroidery, are not used on ready-made gowns because the cost would be prohibitive. Others, such as hand beading, are found only on the most expensive gowns costing many hundreds and even thousands of dollars. Although some are time-consuming, most of the trimmings listed here are not difficult to apply and do not require a great deal of skill or fancy sewing ability. If you are interested in creating an heirloom gown, the time spent on such things as hand beading or making organdy flowers will be well worth the effort. Lace trimmings are covered in Chapter 6.

While I certainly don't advocate cluttered and overdone dresses, the fact is most amateur designers use too little trimming rather than too much. It is the extra added details that make the difference between a professional and a homemade looking dress. The reason that many homemade dresses don't quite come off is because the ideas weren't developed far enough. For example, maybe the same lace was used everywhere on the dress when two different widths of lace or even two different styles of lace would have been more interesting. Or maybe only one trim was used when adding a second or third would have given the gown real excitement. Study the pictures in brides' magazines and you'll see that most gowns use a number of different trimmings to create a rich effect. Lace appliqués are often embellished with pearls or sequins. Silk flowers are used with embroidery, tucks are combined with lace inserts, and so on. While trimmings are used in abundance on many gowns, a few guidelines should be considered to keep the gown from becoming overdone. Generally, the simpler the dress pattern, the more trimming is used; the more elaborate the dress pattern, the less trimming is used. A plain satin A-line style covered with lace appliqués and pearls would look rich and elegant, while a fluffy organza dress with gathered tiers and puffed sleeves would look like a lampshade if covered with trim. A lightweight or sheer fabric may not support the weight of a lot of heavy trimming without drooping.

Be aware that some trims are flexible and some are not. Flexible trim must be used at curves such as the neckline or the hem of a flared skirt. Ruffles, some beaded bands, flower strips, some feather bands, and rickrack, as well as sequins and beads on a string, are flexible. Non-flexible trims include woven band trims, ribbons, and most straight, wide trimming. Some straight trims can be eased into a gradual curve, but the wider the trim, the less it can be curved.

Be aware also that different types of trim must be made or added before, during, or after construction of the dress. Trimming that changes the dimension or surface of the fabric generally must be done before the dress is cut. This would include embroidery, smocking, shirring, some appliqués, quilting, patchwork, tucking, and dyeing. Trimmings added during the construction include most machine-applied trims, such as ruffles, some band trims, piping, cording, and some appliqués. Trims added after construction include most hand-applied trims, such as beads and pearls, some appliqués, flowers, feathers and fur.

In a number of instances you can apply your trim either by hand or by machine. I would highly recommend applying it by hand for several reasons. Handwork is always considered finer than machine work and will give your gown a quality appearance. Because handwork proceeds slowly, you have much more control and are less apt to make mistakes. With hand application, you can do a much neater job because hand stitches are usually far less conspicuous than machine ones.

RUFFLES

Ruffles of fabric or lace are among the favorite wedding gown trimmings. For lace ruffles, see Chapter 6. Ruffles can be used to trim almost any place on your gown, such as necklines, sleeves, sleeveless armholes, front openings, hems, collars, and around yokes (see *Figure 76*). There are several different types of ruffles to choose from, depending on the kind of fabric you are using and the effect you want. The three basic kinds of ruffles are bias fold, straight grain, and flared. Bias fold and straight grain ruffles are gathered, while flared are not.

FIGURE 76

To figure the amount of fabric you need for a gathered ruffle, first measure the place on your gown where you want the ruffle to be—around neckline, hem, or wherever. For a light- to medium-weight fabric and a full-looking ruffle, multiply the measurement by 3. When using heavy fabric or for a less full ruffle, multiply the measurement by 2. Wide ruffles need more fullness than narrow ruffles to keep them from looking skimpy. For example, suppose you want to make a ruffle of velvet to go around the hem of a skirt and the circumference of the skirt at the hemline is 54 inches: 54×2 equals 108 inches or 3 yards needed for the ruffle strip. To make a ruffle of organza, you would multiply 54 inches×3, which equals 162 inches or 4½ yards needed for the ruffle. If you are using a ruffle at the garment edge, such as sleeve or hem, and the pattern does not include a ruffle, you will have to shorten the pattern piece by the same amount as the width of the ruffle (see page 46).

The edge of the ruffle can be trimmed with lace, braid, or ribbon, and the seam where the ruffle joins the garment can also be trimmed. If the gathered raw edge of the ruffle is not enclosed in the seam (for example, on a skirt with rows of ruffles around the hem), using a band of trim such as ribbon or braid will conceal the raw edge of the ruffle and look pretty as well.

Gathered Ruffles

If your ruffle will have a hem or edge applied, this should be done before gathering. Use a strong thread in the bobbin for gathering ruffles. Clear nylon thread is good for sheer fabrics because it is fairly lightweight but strong. Buttonhole twist or heavy-duty thread can be used with heavier fabrics. You should not always use the longest stitch—stitch length depends on the fabric. For heavier fabric, the longest length is all right; but for light, sheer fabric, too long a stitch will not produce attractive gathers. Use a somewhat shorter stitch, around 10 to the inch. Stitch the ruffles right side up so the bobbin thread will be on the wrong side of the ruffle. Make two rows of stitching, ¼ inch apart. Place the first row of stitching on the seam line and the second in the seam allowance. The two rows will distribute the fullness better and there will be less chance of the thread breaking. When you are gathering a long ruffle it should be divided into segments. Stop every yard and a half or so, pull the fabric out of the machine, and cut the thread. Go back a few stitches and begin stitching again so you have separate gathering threads to pull. Loosen the upper tension slightly so fabric slides over the bobbin threads, and distribute the gathers evenly and smoothly. Always stitch the ruffle to the garment with the ruffle face up so you can stitch exactly on the gathering line. If you are using a facing, pin the facing in place and turn the garment over so the stitching line attaching the ruffle is face up. Sew the facing on the ruffle stitching line. If you stitch the ruffle below the gathering line, it will cause little tucks and pleats to form, which will look awful. If you stitch above the gathering line, the threads used to gather the ruffle will show. Once the ruffle is attached, be sure to pull out any gathering stitches that show on the right side.

Ruffles can also be gathered using the gathering foot if your machine has one. In order to make the gathers amount to something more than a slight ripple, the fabric has to be fed into the machine a certain way. Keep the tension tight and the stitch fairly long. Hold the first finger of your left hand directly behind the foot as you stitch. Meanwhile, hold a small pointed tool such as an awl or crochet hook in your right hand and use it to help feed the fabric under the presser foot as you run the machine. You really have to push the fabric into the presser foot and stitch fast to make this work. If the gathers are too loose, run the ruffle through the gathering foot a second or third time. The thinner the fabric, the more it will gather. The foot may not work on heavier fabrics.

If you have an attachment for your machine that makes tiny pleats, you can use this to make ruffles too.

FINISHING ENDS OF RUFFLES If the ruffle ends at an opening, such as the center back, you can finish the ends with a narrow hand-rolled hem (*Figure* 130). A folded ruffle can be finished by turning the raw edges inside and slip-stitching (*Figure* 152). If the ruffle has no opening, such as one used around the hem of a skirt, the ends can be joined with a French seam (*Figure* 108). For a nicer finish, you can join all the ruffle strips first so the ruffle is in a ring when you gather it.

Bias Fold Ruffle

One of the loveliest ruffles is made of a folded strip of bias (*Figure* 77A). This works especially well for sheers and lighter-weight fabrics because it does not need a hem. Since the ruffle is cut on the bias, the gathers are softer and prettier than one cut on the straight grain. To figure the width to cut the bias strip for the ruffle, decide how wide you want the finished ruffle to be, double that amount, and add 1½ inches. For example, for a ruffle 2 inches wide: double 2 is 4, plus 1½ equals 5½ inches, which is the width to cut the bias.

When you make a bias ruffle it is very important that the bias strips be cut on the perfect true bias, otherwise the ruffle will not look right. Before the true bias can be located, the fabric must be straightened (see pages 70–72). Locating the true

FIGURE 77

A

bias and marking bias strips will be much easier and more accurate if you use a drafting triangle. By placing the triangle on the selvage of your fabric, the long side of the triangle will automatically fall on the true bias (see *Figure 77B*). Mark the bias line with pencil. If the line is too short, extend it by using a ruler or yardstick. If you do not have a triangle, locate the true bias by folding the fabric so the cross grain end meets the selvage, as you see in *Figure 77C*. The fold will be on the bias. Pin the selvage and cross grain edges together and cut along the fold.

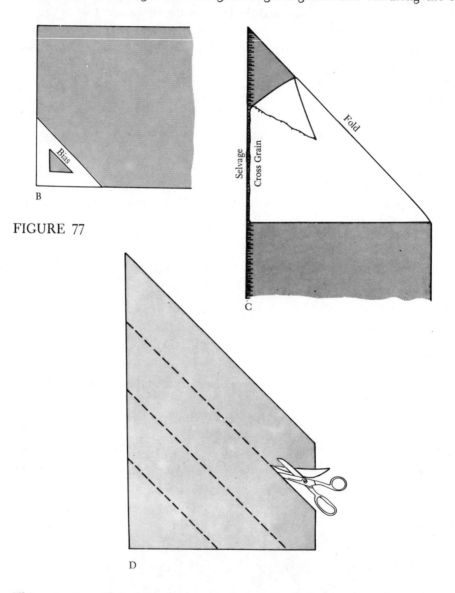

FIGURE 77

This cut edge will be bias. Once you have located the true bias, mark the ruffle strips parallel to the bias line or edge (*Figure 77D*). For longer strips, you will usually have to join or piece the bias. Joining must always be done on the straight grain. Be sure that the bias pieces are at a right angle when you sew your seam, as you see in *Figure 77E*, so that when the seam is pressed open the bias piece will be straight. Notice that a small triangle of seam allowance will extend on each side of the bias edge.

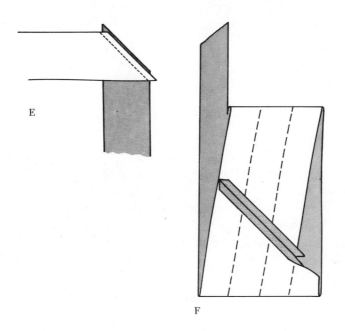

If you need a long piece of bias, the bias can be joined first and then cut into one long continuous strip. Prepare a rectangle of fabric, marking true-bias, parallel lines from selvage to selvage the correct width for the ruffle strip. Cut the fabric on the bias along the first and last line. With the right sides together, pin the selvages, forming a tube. Notice that the width of one strip extends beyond the seam at each end. Stitch a ¼-inch seam and press the seam open. Beginning at the first line, cut around the tube following your marked lines, as you see in *Figure 77F*.

Once you have joined the pieces into one long strip, or into a ring, fold the strip in half lengthwise, right side out. For a sharp edge on the ruffle, press the bias, being careful not to stretch it. For a softer edge, just steam it very lightly or finger-press. Gather the ruffle as explained above.

Lined Bias Ruffle

If you are using a fabric such as velvet or brocade, which is too heavy to fold but where a hem would be unattractive, you can make a lined bias ruffle (*Figure 78*). Use a lightweight lining fabric or organza for the backing. Following directions

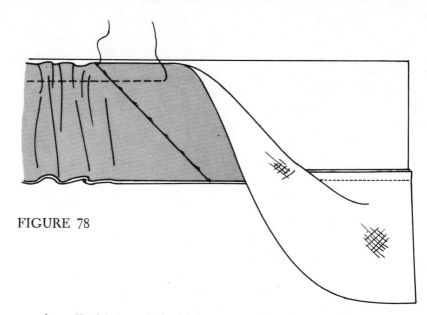

FIGURE 78

above, cut the ruffle fabric and the backing the width of the finished ruffle plus 1 inch. For a 2-inch ruffle, you would cut a bias strip of fabric and backing each 3 inches wide. Place the lining and ruffle fabric right sides together and join them with a seam ¼ inch from the edge. Press the seam open, turn right side out, and press again. Gather as explained above.

Tapered Ruffle

In some cases you may want a ruffle that does not end abruptly but tapers off at the end, such as an armhole ruffle or jabot ruffle, shown in *Figure* 79A. For this, you make a bias fold ruffle, as explained above, but run your gathering stitch grad-

FIGURE 79

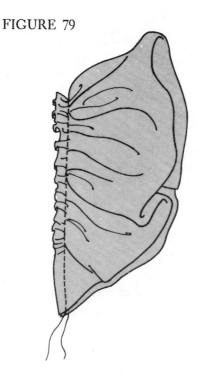

A

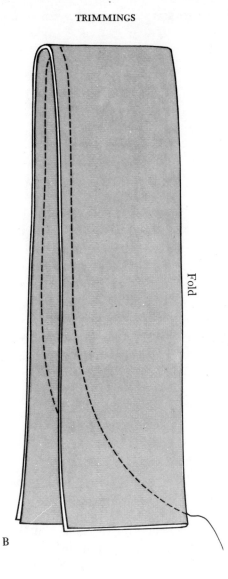

Fold

B

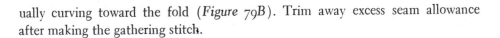

ually curving toward the fold (*Figure 79B*). Trim away excess seam allowance after making the gathering stitch.

Straight Ruffle

A straight ruffle should be cut on the cross grain from selvage to selvage. A ruffle cut on the lengthwise grain (along the selvage) will not gather nicely at all. The ruffle can be hemmed on one side or folded. If the ruffle is hemmed, for best results use a hemmer foot to make the narrowest hem possible. You could also apply a satin ribbon, narrow lace, or other band trim to the edge of the ruffle before it is gathered (see *Figure 80*).

FIGURE 80

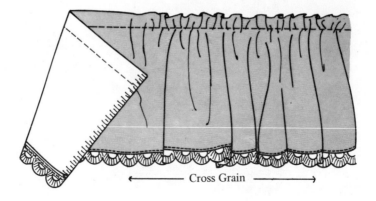

Cross Grain

To determine the width to cut your fabric strips for a hemmed ruffle, add 1 inch to the amount you want your finished ruffle to be. For example, if you want your finished ruffle to be 2 inches, cut the fabric strips 3 inches wide. After hemming or finishing one side, gather as described above. For a folded ruffle, figure the width as explained above for bias fold ruffles.

Header Ruffle

This type of ruffle is finished on both sides and gathered to form a double ruffle. The gathering thread can be placed near one edge for a narrow header, as you see in *Figure 81* or in the middle of the strip for a ruffle that is the same width on both sides. The ruffle strip is cut on the cross grain. To figure the width to cut your fabric, decide how wide you want the ruffle and the header to be and then add ¾ inch. For example, for a ruffle 2 inches wide with a header ¾ inch: 2+¾+¾ equals 3½ inches, which is the width to cut your ruffle. Hem both sides of the ruffle and then gather it, using only one row of stitching. After you have gathered the ruffle, pin it to the garment and topstitch directly on the gathering thread.

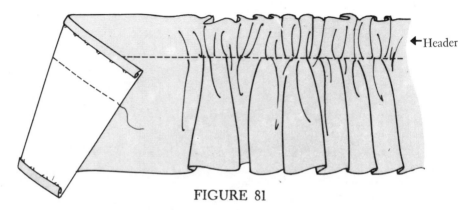

←Header

FIGURE 81

Flared Ruffle

This ruffle has no gathers. The fullness comes from the circular shape, the same way the fullness is formed in a circular skirt. This type of ruffle is often used on chiffon or other soft fabrics because of the pretty way that it drapes. The ruffle is made by joining a series of circles. You will need to make a circular pattern using a compass (see *Figure 82*). The dotted line close to the inside circle indicates the stitching line of the ruffle and the outside circle indicates the outside edge of the ruffle. The slash should be placed on the straight grain of each ruffle. The smaller the inside circle of the pattern, the more flare the ruffle will have and the more circles you will need. The edge of the ruffle can be finished with a narrow hand-rolled hem (*Figure 130*), or the ruffle can be lined. If you are using sheer fabric, join the ruffle circles with a French seam (*Figure 108*) or simulated French seam (*Figure 109*). After the circles are joined, run a stay stitch ⅝ inch from the inside edge. Clip into the seam allowance of the ruffle so it will straighten and lie flat when you attach it to the garment.

FIGURE 82

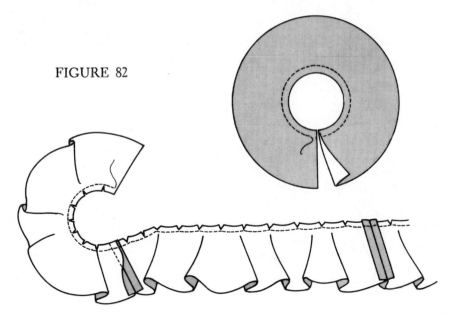

Purchased Ruffles

You can buy many different ruffles ready-made. They range from quite attractive to absolutely awful. Some of these ruffle concoctions can really make a dress look homemade, so be careful in your selection. Many are gathered much too skimpily; others are decked out with very cheap trims. If you are buying ready-made ruffles of organza or other fabric, be sure that the shade of white or ivory matches your dress fabric.

FIGURE 83

HAND EMBROIDERY

One of the most popular adornments for wedding gowns is embroidery. On ready-made gowns, embroidery must be done by machine, but you can add the personal touch of hand embroidery to your gown. Beaded embroidery is found under "Jewel Trims," on page 184, and embroidered fabrics and trims are covered in Chapter 6. White embroidery on white fabric is delicate and beautiful. Select fabric and embroidery thread with enough contrast so the embroidery will show. Organza is a good background fabric; the solid texture of the embroidery will stand out against the sheer fabric. Silk or rayon embroidery works well on velvet with a short pile, or on velveteen. Fabrics with a slight texture, such as dimity or piqué, also look pretty with embroidery. Pastel embroideries as well are appropriate for wedding gowns.

The embroidery designs are almost always floral. You might choose individual flowers or small bouquets scattered about, a single rose or bouquet on the bodice, a trellis along the sleeves, or a band around the skirt (see *Figure 83*). Embroidery can be placed almost anywhere on your gown. I have included some embroidery designs here that you can use (*Figure 84*). For more ideas, look in the 700's section in the library for art and design books on such subjects as Chinese antiques, oriental porcelains, styles of ornaments, or even folk art. You do not need to copy every detail. Pick the major design elements or the part you especially like and use that. Photos in garden books and seed catalogues will give you a feeling for color, shading, and detail in flowers. You can also trace designs from wallpaper books, gift wrap, or printed motifs on fabrics, as well as crewel kits or books. Iron-on transfers for embroidery designs are available in pattern catalogues in the accessories section, and in patterns for children's clothes. For enlarging designs, you can buy paper marked off in a 1-inch grid.

Embroidery Threads

There are many different kinds of threads that can be used for embroidery. The most popular is embroidery floss, which is usually made of cotton. Floss comes with six strands of thread loosely twisted together. For fine work, you should use only two or three strands, separating them from the larger strands. Embroidery floss is also available in variegated colors, which are very pretty for embroidering flowers. They are shaded from light to dark tones of the same color—yellow would be shaded gradually from the most delicate maize to a deeper yellow, green would shade from very pale to olive, and so on. You can combine variegated and solid-color threads for some attractive effects.

Silk embroidery floss creates extremely fine embroidery with a beautiful smooth luster. Rayon floss is similar to silk, being smooth and lustrous, but it has a higher sheen and is not as subtle and delicate. Pearl cotton is somewhat heavier than embroidery floss and does not separate into strands. Silk buttonhole twist can be used for embroidery accents, such as French knots. Needlepoint yarn called Persian wool comes as three strands loosely twisted together. A single strand of Persian can also be used for embroidery.

Marking

The garment part to be embroidered should not be cut out until after the embroidery is completed. Cut a piece of fabric larger than your pattern piece and mark the outline of the pattern piece on the fabric. Be sure to mark the darts if there are any. The embroidery design itself should not be marked directly on the garment fabric because the marks could show after the embroidery is finished and also cause the dress to look handled. If you are using a sheer fabric, draw the design on tracing paper and baste this to the back of the fabric so you can see the design through the fabric. Embroider through the fabric and the tracing paper. When you have finished embroidering, tear away the paper. The best way to mark an embroidery design for opaque fabric is to use Stitch Witchery, available at the notions counters and in interfacing departments. Do *not* follow the directions on the Stitch Witchery package. The Stitch Witchery is not fused or ironed to anything—it is used just as it is. Mark the embroidery design on the Stitch Witchery, using a ball-point pen. You can see through it like tracing paper. Pin the Stitch Witchery with the traced design to the right side of your fabric and baste into place. Embroider the design through the Stitch Witchery and the garment fabric. Once the embroidery is complete, tear away the Stitch Witchery from around the embroidery. Be sure not to let any little bits of the Stitch Witchery cling to the fabric or the outside of the embroidery because they will melt with the heat of an iron. If you choose to mark directly on your fabric, use only dressmaker's carbon paper—never use regular carbon paper. An old, used piece is preferable because it is not so apt to smudge.

When embroidering on a stretchy knit fabric, baste a piece of organza or batiste larger than the embroidery motif to the wrong side of the fabric. After you have embroidered your design, carefully clip away the excess backing fabric from around the design.

Embroidery Hoops

If you use an embroidery hoop or frame, it should be used only while you are actually embroidering. Do not leave your work in the hoop, as this will cause it to stretch and may leave permanent marks. A frame that leaves both hands free is

FIGURE 84

much more convenient than a hoop. Use tissue paper to protect the fabric from being marred by the hoop while you are working on it. Place the fabric over the first hoop, then place a sheet of tissue paper over the fabric. Slip on the second hoop and tear away the tissue paper from the work area, leaving paper between the hoop and the fabric.

Embroidery Stitches

There are a tremendous number of different embroidery stitches. I've included here a number that are not difficult and that are most suited to delicate floral designs. For the most interesting-looking embroidery, combine several different stitches and vary the type of embroidery thread. This is especially important with white-on-white embroidery, so that it does not look monotonous. You can use regular satin stitch for some parts of the flowers and padded satin stitch for others. Make some of the centers using clusters of French knots. If you use only one or two strands for smooth petals, use two or three strands or a different thread for the stems. French knots should be made with a heavy thread or they will look insignificant.

STEM STITCH (*Figure 85A*). This stitch is worked from left to right. Insert the needle to the right of the previous stitch and bring it out to the left through the hole made by the previous stitch, as shown. This stitch is used for stems and outlines.

SPLIT STITCH (*Figure 85B*). This is also used for stems and outlines. It is worked similarly to stem stitch, but when the needle is brought out, it is inserted through the center of the thread, splitting the thread, instead of being brought out through the hole made by the previous stitch.

FRENCH KNOT (*Figure 85C*). These little knots are generally used for flower centers. Use a heavier thread or more strands than you have been using for the rest of your embroidery. Bring the thread up through the fabric and wrap the thread over the needle, as shown. Insert the needle back into the fabric next to where you brought it up.

SATIN STITCH (*Figure 85D*). This is the basic stitch for filling in solid areas. When you have a large area, divide it into smaller sections and embroider each section. Do not use long stitches, as the stitches will snag and become messy-looking very quickly. When embroidering complicated flowers, such as roses, embroider individual petals with the satin stitch running in a different direction on each petal. The satin stitch should have a neat, clean outline. The easiest way to maintain a neat outline is to outline the design first, using split stitch, then satin-stitch over the split stitch. Satin stitch can be made straight across, straight up and down, or on a slant. Bring the needle up on one edge outside the split stitch and insert the needle on the opposite edge, covering the split stitch. The stitches should be very close together so the threads lie one against the other.

FIGURE 85

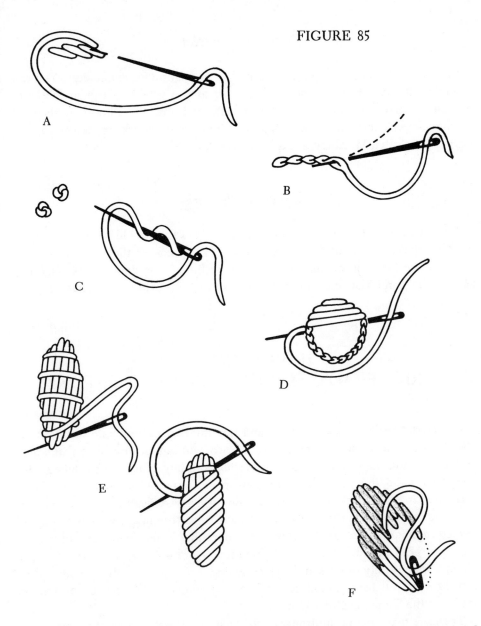

A

B

C

D

E

F

PADDED SATIN STITCH (*Figure 85E*). For extra-rich-looking, more dimensional embroidery, the satin stitch can be padded with an underlayer of satin stitch. Make the first layer of satin stitch in a different direction from the final layer.

LONG AND SHORT SHADING (*Figure 85F*). This is a variation of satin stitch used for shading flower petals. Outline the shape in split stitch; then work a row of long and short stitches, using the first shade, along the outside of the shape. Fill in between the long and short stitches with a second shade. You can use a third and even a fourth shade as you work toward the center of the flower.

Embroidery on Net

English net or tulle can be used as a background fabric for embroidery. You can embroider flowers or other designs on the net as you would on regular fabric, or use the holes of the mesh as a fine needlepoint canvas and use needlepoint stitches. Select fine or heavy threads and a blunt needle. Mark the design on tracing paper or Stitch Witchery, as explained above.

Other Needlework

There are many traditional needlework techniques that would be beautiful for a wedding gown. If you, or a relative or friend, know any of these, consider using one or more for your wedding gown. Such techniques as drawn work, fagoting, hemstitching, and Madeira cutwork would create lovely, heirloom touches.

JEWEL TRIMS:
PEARLS, BEADS, SEQUINS, AND RHINESTONES

Pearls, crystal beads, delicate sequins, and tiny rhinestones are found on the finest gowns. By adding a touch of these to your gown, you can create a dress that would cost many hundreds or even thousands of dollars to buy. Since most beading must be done by hand, it is very costly for a gown manufacturer to do in a factory. However, you can do beading yourself quite easily: it is not difficult and takes less time than you probably would think. Ready-made beaded trimmings, such as bands and beaded appliqués, are quite expensive, but the basic ingredients—loose or prestrung pearls, beads, sequins, and rhinestones—are not. These trims are available in a wide variety of sizes and shapes, and several types are often combined on one dress. If you have trouble finding beading supplies, they can be ordered by mail (see the Shopping Guide).

There are two types of prestrung jewels, each meant for a different purpose. One type is strung loosely on a thread meant only to contain the beads until they are applied. If the string is cut, the beads will fall off. The other type has the beads permanently strung and is designed to be applied as is. The beads will not fall off if you cut the string because they are glued or knotted in place. Most permanently strung beads cannot be removed singly for individual application.

PEARLS Pearls are available in oat, round, and teardrop shapes. Round pearls come in a variety of sizes, ranging from pinhead size (1½ mm) to very large (10 mm). (A millimeter—1 mm—is the tiniest space on a metric ruler; 25 millimeters, or mm, equal 1 inch). For wedding gowns, the most popular sizes are 2½, 3, 4, and 5 mm. The small round pearls often referred to as seed pearls are 2½ mm. Strung pearls can be used to outline necklines, sleeves, cuffs, hems, and so on.

BEADS Beads are available in three main shapes—bugle, faceted, and round—as well as novelty shapes. Bugle beads are tube-shaped, faceted beads are round with flat surfaces, and round beads are smooth. Crystal beads, which come in all shapes, are the most popular for bridal wear.

SEQUINS When you hear the word "sequins," you probably think of the sparkly, metallic kind, which of course would not look right. There are, however, two sequin colors that are used quite often on wedding gowns. One is crystal iris, which is almost transparent and has an iridescent look. The other is white iris, which is pearly and white. Sequins are available flat and faceted (also called cup). As with pearls, sequins come in various sizes, indicated in millimeters. They vary from a tiny 3 mm to a large 12 mm. The small to medium size, 6 to 8 mm, are most commonly used. Paillettes are large sequins with the hole at the side, instead of the center.

RHINESTONES There are two rhinestone colors: crystal, which is clear and icy-looking, and aurora borealis, which reflects more colors and is fiery-looking. Crystal is more subtle for bridal use. Rhinestones are also sized in millimeters; the tiny sizes are usually prettiest. They can be purchased with a flat back, to be glued on, and with slots, to be sewn on.

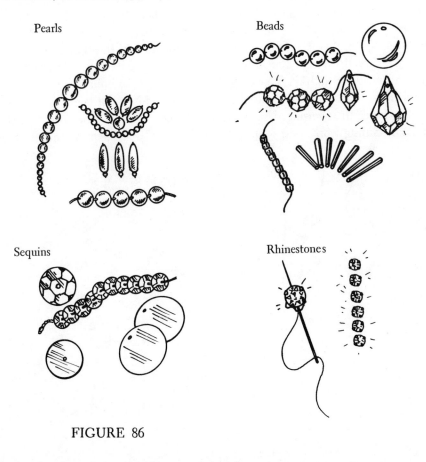

Pearls Beads

Sequins Rhinestones

FIGURE 86

Applying Beads

You will need a fine needle to slip easily through the beads. Special beading needles are available. Use a single strand of polyester thread for sewing lighter beads, a double strand for heavier beads. Sewing will be easier if you run the thread through beeswax first, to make it stronger and less apt to tangle. The thread should be fairly short. Loose beads can be kept organized in a plastic egg tray. Use tweezers to pick up tiny beads. When stitching the beads, do not pull your thread too tight, which will cause puckering. Where possible, adjust the bead so that the holes are at the side, not on top. Depending on the design effect you want, beads can be applied in a number of different configurations (see *Figure 87*).

SPOTTING Individual beads are sprinkled about to accent fabric, net, or lace motifs. Individual pearls, seed beads, and bugle beads are applied with a backstitch. If the next bead is fairly close, you can carry the thread to the next bead on the wrong side of the fabric. When there is a lot of space from one bead to the next, you should knot off your thread and sew each bead separately (see *Figure 87A*).

Flat faceted jewels, such as rhinestones, have a slot in the back, or sometimes two slots in a crisscross. Bring the thread up through the fabric and pass it through the slot. Sew several stitches each way to fasten the jewel firmly.

Individual sequins are generally applied with a bead; otherwise you would have to take a stitch over the edge of the sequin, which would not look attractive. Bring the thread up through the fabric and through the hole in the center of the sequin. Bring the thread through the bead and insert the needle into the center of the sequin again. Backstitch on the wrong side of the fabric to hold firmly.

Individual beads can also be applied with glue. This is not the greatest method, but it is faster than sewing. Use white glue, such as Elmer's or Sobo, which will dry clear. Gluing works best with beads with a flat back, such as sequins or rhine-

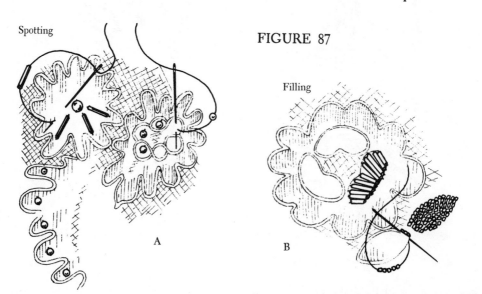

Spotting

FIGURE 87

Filling

A

B

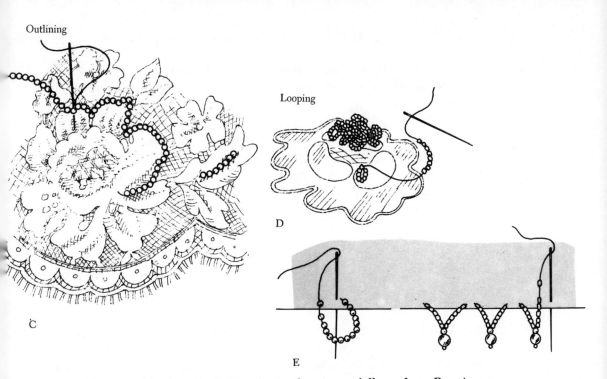

Outlining

Looping

D

C

E

stones. Because of the texture, it is easier to glue successfully on lace. Practice on a scrap first. Apply a tiny drop of glue to the dress and use tweezers to place the bead in the glue. Allow it to dry thoroughly. You can also apply an individual sequin with a pearl or bead in the center this way. First glue the sequins, then glue the pearls. Gluing is for wedding gowns only, since it is not washable or dry-cleanable.

FILLING (*Figure 87B*). Beads are applied solidly to fill in areas such as flower centers or leaves. Use the methods above for applying individual beads, stitching the beads very close together.

OUTLINING A single line of beads is applied in a straight row or following the outline of a motif. Outlining is easiest if you use prestrung beads, but it can also be done with individual beads, stringing them as you sew them on. To outline with prestrung beads, sew over the threads holding the beads (see *Figure 87C*). If you are applying the beads in a straight line, you do not have to make the stitches as close together as when applying the beads around a curve. When outlining a curved shape, some waviness and irregularity is perfectly acceptable. For intricate shapes, outlining should be done with individual beads. To do this, take a tiny stitch, then string one or several beads onto the thread and take another stitch. The number of beads you can string with each stitch will depend on the weight of the beads and whether the line is curved or straight.

LOOPING This is one of the most opulent and expensive-looking forms of hand beading. Prestrung or loose beads are formed into three-dimensional loops (see *Figure 87D*). Clusters of loops are used to accent lace flower motifs and to form flowers in beaded embroidery. Beaded fringe loops can also be applied in a straight row at sleeves, hem, or neckline (*Figure 87E*). If you use this technique, apply it only to select motifs or areas so that it will stand out. Use a double strand of thread. Pull the needle through from the wrong side. String a number of beads and insert the needle back in the fabric close to where the thread was brought out. Secure with a backstitch. Bring the needle out again and continue making loops in this manner. If you pull the thread tightly, the loops will stand up away from the fabric. If you leave the thread looser, the loops will lie against the fabric. For flower petals, vary the size of the loops slightly. For beaded loop fringes, count the beads for each loop to keep the loops uniform in size. You can embellish the loops by adding drop pearls or larger beads in the middle of the loop. When using loop fringe, you can also add outlining to make a more interesting design.

Beading Lace

All forms of Alençon, Chantilly, and Venise lend themselves to beading. The beads are used to accent and embellish the design of the lace, giving a very rich and formal look. For beading lace, a number of different types of beads or several sizes of beads are generally used, as otherwise the beading would tend to look monotonous. It is not necessary to bead all the motifs or all of the dress. If you are using lace appliqués, you might bead only those around the neck or the hem. On an all-lace dress, you could bead only the bodice. For one attractive method of beading, cut a bodice of lace, centering the major lace motif, and bead the center motif only. On lace borders, the scallops can be outlined along with some of the motifs. If you are beading a skirt, increase the amount of beading toward the hem for a balanced effect. Of course, you can bead all of the dress, if you prefer. Refer to *Plate 16*.

Spotting, filling, outlining, and looping are all appropriate for beading lace. To decide where to bead, study the motif of the lace. Outline the important motifs, such as the main flowers and leaves. Stems, leaf veins, and scrolly lines also lend themselves to outlining. The centers of larger flowers lend themselves to filling. A few flower motifs embellished with looping of pearls or crystals are an elegant touch. Small buds and smaller flower centers can be spotted with individual beads or sequins. In addition to the main motifs, smaller motifs and net areas can be spotted. For outlining and three-dimensional effects, strands of seed pearls, crystal seed beads, or crystal bugle beads work well. For spotting, use larger individual pearls, sequins with a tiny bead or pearl in the center, or small rhinestones. Pearls or crystal beads work well for filling. Oat and drop pearls are good for filling and spotting areas where the shapes coincide. For example, small flower petals or leaves might be the same shape as an oat pearl.

Most beading is applied last, after the gown has been sewn.

Beaded Embroidery

You can make your embroidery entirely with beads or combine beaded areas with regular embroidery. Organza and chiffon are popular background fabrics for

FIGURE 88

beading. The contrast of opaque beads with gossamer fabric can be very attractive. Beaded designs on the bodice can be in the form of a single motif or an allover embroidery. Scattered motifs might be used on the skirt, or a long-stem flower on the sleeves (see *Figure 88*). For information on embroidery designs and marking the fabric, see "Hand Embroidery" in this chapter. If you are using a fairly simple scrolly or outline design, you can mark the design on tracing paper, then thread-trace the design through the paper and fabric. Tear away the tracing paper and apply the beads following the thread tracing (see *Figure 89*).

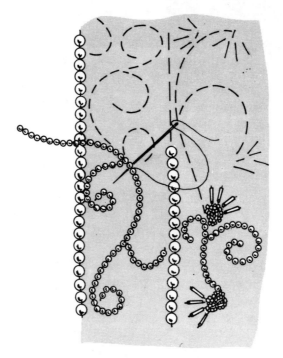

FIGURE 89

Beaded embroidery is done on the fabric before the dress is cut. If you are beading a large area, it is very important to check your pattern in muslin before the embroidery is done, because you cannot make alterations after the beading has been applied. Be sure that you do not use any beads within seam allowance or dart areas. You can bead right up to the seam allowance and then stitch using a zipper foot or cording foot to avoid running the presser foot over the beads. On a sheer fabric, use a double layer for extra strength or back the sheer with tulle. Use several different types of beads for textural interest. Crystal seed beads, crystal bugle beads, and crystal sequins work well together. Bugle beads, because of their tube shapes, lend themselves to stems, leaves, and other outlines. You can combine tiny pearls with larger pearls. Oat pearls, with their elongated shape, lend themselves to flower shapes. Any of the four beading methods—spotting, filling, outlining, and looping—are appropriate for embroidery. To avoid puckering, use an embroidery hoop and do not pull your threads tightly. When embroidering a large area that will not fit in an embroidery hoop, the entire piece of fabric can be stretched and stapled to a frame, called a canvas stretcher, available at art supply stores.

Another way to do solid beaded embroidery is to embroider the design on a piece of organza. Then, once the embroidery is complete, the organza is trimmed, leaving a small seam allowance. The seam allowance is turned under and the embroidery stitched to the garment like an appliqué.

When beaded embroidery is used on the gown, the neckline and sleeve edge can be trimmed with rows of matching beads.

Beaded Band Trimmings

Beaded band trimmings are used for an elegant and sophisticated look. Choose a dress pattern with simple lines and embellish it with bands at the hem, neckline, waistline, or sleeves. Most of the wider trims are fairly heavy, so select a fabric that can support the weight. If you are planning to use a beaded trim around the neckline or a curved hem, you must first be sure that the band is flexible. Some of the wider jewel trims are rigid and cannot be eased around a curve. The narrower trims are usually flexible and can be used on curves without a problem.

Beaded band trimmings must be sewn by hand. In most cases they are difficult to pin, so will have to be basted first. Many are stitched to an organza or net backing so you can attach the bead trim to the garment by stitching through the backing. Where there is no backing, there will usually be some kind of cord or heavy thread that you can catch with a hand stitch. The beads will fall off the ends of some bead trims when they are cut. If you have this problem, wrap the ends of the trim with Scotch tape while you are working. When you finish, apply a small amount of white glue or clear nail polish to hold the beads. To finish the ends, remove the beads or sequins from the backing, if glue was not used. Turn under the raw end and stitch securely (see *Figure* 90). Do not enclose the ends in a seam. If you are going to miter a corner, remove the beads from the backing at the area that will be enclosed in the miter.

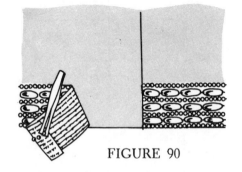

FIGURE 90

APPLIQUÉS

There are many different appliqué techniques. Some are very sophisticated and were originated with Paris designers, others have been derived from Indian and African folk crafts. The word "appliqué" comes from the French word meaning "to put on." Appliqué is simply applying a shape cut from one fabric onto another fabric. Given a variety of materials, of machine and hand stitches, and of embellishments such as beading or padding, the number of different design effects is almost limitless. Because an appliqué is a silhouette cut in fabric, the design should be a simple, clear shape. For designs, you can use the patterns in *Figure 91*, enlarging if necessary, or appliqué and embroidery transfer patterns, available in the pattern catalogues. See the design suggestions given for embroidery as well.

Fabrics for wedding gown appliqués can be white or a delicate color. A number of lovely white-on-white effects can be created by the contrast in the texture and weight of several different white fabrics. On sheer fabric, such as organza, you might try appliqués of satin or other opaque fabric. For a shadow effect, organza can be appliquéd with another layer of organza. Satin appliqués are also interesting on velvet or a simple allover lace. Velvet appliqués can be used on sheer fabrics, lace, or satin (see *Figure 92*). For best results, the background fabric should be woven or lace and not too stretchy. Where possible, cut the appliqué so the grain of the appliqué coincides with the grain of the background fabric.

The shape of the appliqué can be transferred to the fabric by using dressmaker's carbon and tracing the design with a dry ball-point pen. Since the edge of the fabric will be covered or turned under, you do not have to worry about the carbon marks showing. With white fabric, use yellow or light blue carbon. Use thread tracing or tailor's tacks to mark the appliqué placement on your garment. You should not put any permanent marks on the garment in case the design has to be rearranged. Be sure that you avoid darts and seam allowances and do not place appliqués close to an area that will be gathered or tucked or have other work applied to it.

Machine-stitched Appliqués

If you have a zigzag machine, you can use satin stitch (very close zigzag stitch) to apply the appliqués. For best results, use machine embroidery thread or silk thread. Ordinary polyester or cotton sewing thread is too coarse-looking. For an interesting effect, vary the width of the satin stitch by turning the stitch width dial slowly as you stitch. Another attractive effect can be achieved by stitching over a

FIGURE 91

FIGURE 92

very fine cord (see corded satin stitch hem, *Figure 138*). Follow the same procedure, using the pearl cotton to outline the shape of the motif as you satin-stitch. If
your appliqué fabric is flimsy or frays, you can stabilize it by applying iron-on interfacing to the back of the fabric before you cut out your appliqué shapes. For machine embroidery, you can use a hoop or not, depending on your preference and
on your machine. See your sewing machine manual for special instructions. Be
sure to try each technique on scraps first before you apply it to your garment.

Because they are stitched on the raw edge, machine-stitched appliqués do not
need any seam allowance. This type of appliqué is stitched twice. The first time is
to hold it in place—especially important if the appliqué consists of several pieces.
The second time is the finished satin stitch.

1. Trace your appliqué onto fabric and cut out the shapes.
2. Position the appliqué pieces. If there are overlapping parts to the appliqué,
   be sure that you have the right part under or over. Pin or hand-baste.
3. For the first stitching, use regular zigzag, not satin stitch, in a narrower width
   than the finished satin stitch. The stitch must cover the raw edge of the
   appliqué, as you see in *Figure 93A*.
4. For the second row of stitching, adjust your machine to satin stitch and
   stitch very carefully, covering the raw edges and the first line of stitching (see
   Figure 93B). Do not satin-stitch areas that will be covered by another part of
   the appliqué.

FIGURE 93

A

B

Hand-stitched Appliqués

There are two methods of making hand-stitched appliqués and also two methods of applying them. For the first method, the shape is cut with seam allowance and the raw edge is turned under as you stitch. For the second, the appliqué is lined and the shape is stitched and turned before it is applied to the garment. I think the second method is preferable because you can make curves and flower petals that would be difficult to turn under neatly by hand. Hand-stitched appliqués can be applied either invisibly with a slip stitch (*Figure* 152) or by using a variety of decorative embroidery stitches.

UNLINED METHOD Trace the appliqué onto the wrong side of your fabric. Add ⅜ inch seam allowance. Machine-stitch on the first line, indicating the finished shape of your appliqué. Cut out the appliqué on the unstitched line (see *Figure* 94A). Where the appliqué is curved, clip into the seam allowance almost up to the stitching line. The remaining steps can be done using an embroidery frame if you prefer. Pin the appliqué in place and hand-baste ½ inch in from the machine stitch (see *Figure* 94B). Turn the raw edge of the appliqué under up to the line of machine stitching and slip-stitch the appliqué to your fabric.

FIGURE 94

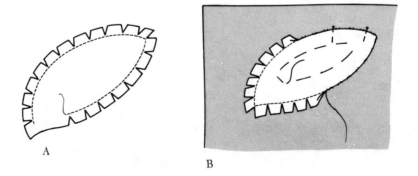

A

B

LINED METHOD For this you will need a lightweight lining fabric, such as batiste or organdy. Cut one piece each of lining fabric and appliqué fabric about 1 inch larger all around than the appliqué. Trace your appliqué onto the lining fabric. Pin the lining to the appliqué fabric so that the appliqué fabric is wrong side out and the traced outline on the lining is face up. Using very short machine stitches, 18 to 22 per inch, carefully stitch all around the shape, following the traced outline, as in *Figure* 95A. Trim the appliqué so there is ¼ inch seam allowance or less. In the center of the appliqué lining, make a slit in the lining only.

This is used to turn the appliqué right side out. Clip into the seam allowance all around curved areas (see *Figure 95B*). Turn the appliqué right side out through the slit in the lining. Use a blunt-pointed instrument such as a crochet hook or a retracted ball-point pen to push out the corners. Press the appliqué. Once all the shapes are stitched and turned, pin and baste them in position on your fabric. You can use an embroidery frame or not, as you wish. The appliqués can be attached invisibly by using a slip stitch (*Figure 95C*) or by using decorative embroidery stitches.

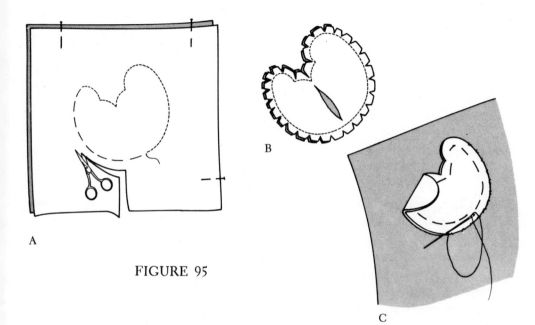

FIGURE 95

Padded Appliqués

Rich-looking raised effects can be created by padding certain areas of an appliqué with polyester batting. Do not use sheer appliqué fabric, since the batting would show through. For more interesting results, pad some areas more than others and leave other parts completely flat. For example, in a bouquet you might have the leaves unpadded, some flowers highly padded, and other flowers slightly padded. This can be done with hand or machine appliqués. For machine appliqués, after the motif is applied, very carefully make a slit in the garment fabric behind the appliqué. Using a knitting or tapestry needle, push the stuffing into the appliqué a small amount at a time. Hand-stitch the slit. With unlined hand-stitched appliqués, no slit is needed. Insert the stuffing from the right side under the appliqué when stitching is almost completed. For lined appliqués, insert the stuffing through the slit made in the lining to turn the appliqué. Smooth the stuffing, then stitch the opening.

FIGURE 96

Sheer Inset Appliqués

This type of appliqué is made from sheer fabric with the garment fabric in back of the appliqué trimmed away. The sheer appliqués contrast with the opaque dress fabric. Use organza or organdy for the appliqué; cotton organdy is easiest to work with. For the dress fabric, use a medium to heavy weight, such as satin, velvet, or piqué. You will be making two rows of stitching. The first row is to hold the appliqué in place; the second row is satin stitch to cover the raw edge and finish the appliqué (see *Figure 96*).

1. Cut two pieces of appliqué fabric, 1 inch larger all around than the appliqué.
2. Lightly trace the appliqué outline onto one layer of the sheer.
3. Pin the two layers of sheer fabric together with the appliqué outline face up.
4. Hand-baste the two layers together, stitching about ¼ inch inside the design outline.
5. Position the appliqué and pin to the right side of the garment fabric.
6. Hand-baste the appliqué piece to the garment fabric about ¼ inch outside the design outline, as you see in *Figure 96A*.
7. For the first row of stitching, use a narrow zigzag, not satin, stitch. Carefully stitch around the appliqué motif, following the traced outline. Remove basting.
8. Using embroidery scissors, trim away excess appliqué fabric very close to the zigzag stitch, as you see in *Figure 96B*. Be careful not to cut into the garment fabric.

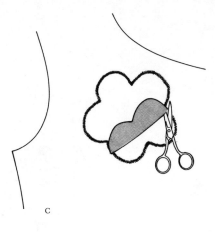

c

9. Reset your machine for satin stitch. Stitch around the appliqué, covering the raw edge and the first zigzag stitch.

10. Turn the garment wrong side out. Using your embroidery scissors, cut away the backing fabric as close to the zigzag as possible, as in *Figure 96C.* You must be careful not to cut into the sheer appliqué fabric when you do this.

Print Motif Appliqués

Another way to make an appliqué suitable for bridesmaids' or other formal dresses is to cut a motif or part of a motif from a print and appliqué it to solid fabric. For example, you might make a bridesmaid's dress with the bodice in a floral print and the skirt of a matching solid, then cut a number of the motifs from the floral print and scatter them on the skirt. The appliqués could be applied by hand or machine, as explained above. They could also be padded or embellished with beads or embroidery.

Using Appliqués with Other Needlework

A number of other needlework techniques can be combined with appliqués for some beautiful effects. Appliqués can be embellished with hand or machine embroidery. Use hand stitches such as buttonhole, couching, feather, or chain to attach and outline the appliqué shapes. For accents, use satin stitch or French knots for flower centers, and stem stitch for details such as lines on leaves or petals. Use embroidery for part of the design and appliqué for other parts, such as embroidered flowers with appliqué leaves, or a bouquet with appliquéd large flowers and embroidered small ones. Three-dimensional effects are especially pretty and expensive-looking. You might attach real satin ribbon bows to the stems of appliquéd flowers, or use three-dimensional flowers combined with appliqué motifs. Fabric appliqués can be accented with beads and pearls in the same way as lace appliqués.

FIGURE 97

FLOWERS

Three-dimensional fabric flowers are another trimming found only on costly gowns that is not difficult or expensive to do yourself. Flowers of organza, velvet, and such can be bought ready-made, and there are a number of different kinds of flowers you can make yourself. They vary in size from tiny satin buds to huge silk roses. Smaller flowers can be used to accent lace or in conjunction with embroidery; medium-size flowers are most often placed on the skirt or neckline; large flowers are attached individually around the hem or one is used with a bow at the waistline or shoulders (see *Figure 97*). Additional flowers can be made or purchased to trim a matching headpiece or hat.

Ready-made Flowers

These are sold in bunches or in strips. Bunches are usually wired together so they can be separated easily into individual flowers by unwrapping the wire. Most stems are made of wire and can be shortened with a wire cutter. Be sure to leave enough stem to sew onto the dress. If you want a continuous band of flowers around the neck or hem, a number of shorter strips of flowers can be wired together. Green-fabric-covered wire is available at hobby and craft stores. Fabric flowers may not be readily available in the usual trimming department. Other places to look are hat shops and departments, gift shops and departments, accessory departments, five-and-dime stores, and import bazaar shops. The flowers are sewn to the dress last, using hand stitches.

Organdy Flowers

Flowers are cut from organdy and outlined with machine satin stitch (see *Figure 98*). Various effects can be obtained by layering flowers of the same or graduated sizes so the flowers have many petals and are three-dimensional. If you are using layers, when you stack the flowers turn each so the petals are in different positions. The flowers can also be combined with flat appliqués and embroidery. Use real cotton organdy for best results. Spray the fabric with starch for extra crispness. You can use the appliqué patterns in *Figure 91*, or other patterns of your own.

1. Cut two squares of organdy 1 inch larger all around than the flower.
2. Using a sharp light blue pencil, trace the appliqué design onto one layer of organdy.

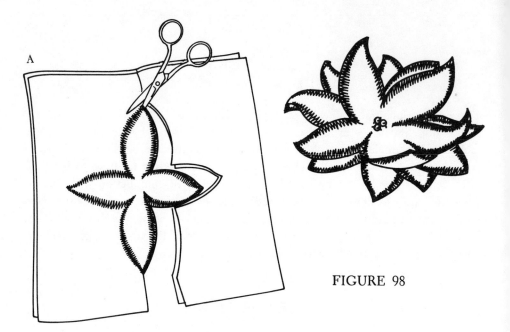

FIGURE 98

3. Pin two layers of organdy together with the design outline face up. Using a small machine stitch, follow the pencil outline on the organdy.

4. Readjust the machine for a narrow satin stitch. Stitch around the shape of the flower, following the straight stitch. You can also use satin stitch to add details, such as veins, to the flower. For an attractive effect, turn the stitch width dial slowly as you sew to vary the width of the satin stitch. This looks more interesting and realistic than using the same width.

5. Once the appliqué is stitched all around, use embroidery scissors to trim the excess fabric as close to the zigzag as possible (see *Figure 98A*). Be careful not to cut into the stitching. Lightly brush the edge of the appliqué with your finger and clip away any loose threads that come through.

Follow the same procedure for each layer. Stack the layers as shown in *Figure 98B*. Pin the layers together and machine-tack the flower centers. The flowers are attached to the garment at the center only, so the petals are free. You could embellish the centers by adding pearls or embroidered French knots. Roll the petals between your thumb and forefinger so they curl realistically.

Another pretty touch you can add to organdy flowers before they are stitched to the garment is to color the centers with water colors. First, dampen the center slightly with clear water. (Experiment on scraps first to make sure this works well on your fabric and the colors are right.) Place a small dab of color in the center of the flower. The color will blur outward into the damp part of the fabric. Once that dries, you can paint in some fine lines in a slightly darker shade if you like. The painting will not withstand washing or dry cleaning.

Satin Buds

These dainty buds can be made in white or pastel satin. Be sure the satin has enough body to hold its shape. For each bud, cut a square of satin measuring 2 to 3½ inches on each side, depending on the size of bud you want (see *Figure 99*). Fold the square in half into a triangle, as shown. The fold should be on the bias. Continue folding as illustrated. Turn under the raw edge at the bottom. Hand-stitch the bud on the wrong side. Satin buds are used to embellish lace and in combination with embroidery or appliqués. To attach, embroider the bottom of each bud onto the garment. You can also use a small leaf shape cut from a scrap of lace to cover the bottom of the bud when you stitch it to the fabric.

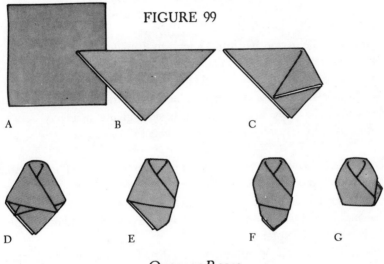

FIGURE 99

Organza Roses

These flowers are made by rolling up a bias ruffle. The size of the rose will depend on the length and width of the ruffle and also how much the ruffle is gathered in. Experiment to see what works best for your needs. Silk organza gives the best result, but other types will also work. Follow the directions on page 171 for making a bias fold ruffle, tapering the end of the ruffle (see *Figure 100*). Begin rolling up the ruffle fairly tightly. When making a large rose, you will have to pin and stitch as you go along—rolling a little bit and then stitching by hand to keep it in place. If you are making a small rose, you may be able to roll the whole thing

FIGURE 100

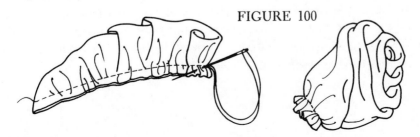

up and then stitch it together. Use a double thread and stitch by hand, being sure to go through all the layers to hold them securely. Trim the seam allowance of the ruffle rose and cover the bottom with a small patch for a neater appearance. Hand-stitch the flower to the garment, attaching the bottom of the flower to the garment fabric.

Ribbon Roses

You can also make roses by gathering satin or velvet ribbon into a ruffle and rolling it up, as for organza roses, above. This will make a smaller, budlike flower.

RIBBONS AND BRAIDS

Ribbons are available in widths from ¼ inch to 4 inches and are made in the following types: velvet, grosgrain, taffeta, moiré, satin, and picot-edge. Satin ribbon can be single-face or double-face. Single-face satin is fine for stitched-down trimming. For ties or sashes, use double-face because it doesn't have a wrong side. Picot-edge ribbon has tiny loops along each side, giving it a very dainty, pretty look. Taffeta ribbon is available in plaids, checks, stripes, and dots, as well as solids.

Braids are ribbonlike bands with floral or geometric designs. They are sometimes referred to as embroidered ribbons, although they are actually woven. Some have delicate patterns that could be used on the bride's gown, as well as for the maids'. The finest braids of this type are made in France and Switzerland. Embroidered bands are covered in Chapter 6.

Ribbons and braids can be applied by hand or by machine. They are not flexible, although narrow ones can be eased around curves. Baste, then whip-stitch by hand (*Figure 153*) for the nicest finish. By machine, use a medium-length stitch and a loose tension to prevent puckering. If you find that puckering occurs with sheer fabrics, place a piece of tissue paper underneath the fabric as you stitch and then tear it away when you have finished. It is sometimes better to stitch the trim at the top edge only, to prevent puckering. Be sure you do not pull or stretch the trim as you stitch it.

Ribbons and braids are often used in combination with each other and with lace edges and ruffles. One attractive treatment used on wedding gowns is alternating rows of several different trims around the hem. For example, you might have a row of gathered lace, a row of braid trim or ribbon, a row of flat lace, another row of ribbon, and so on (see *Figure 101*). The contrast of satin ribbon stitched to sheer organza looks very pretty. Grosgrain or satin ribbon goes well with velvet. If your presser foot flattens velvet ribbon, use a zipper foot.

FIGURE 101

FIGURE 102

FEATHERS AND FUR

FEATHERS Most feather trims are made of individual feathers bound together and sold by the yard. The most popular are marabou and ostrich. Marabou is delicate, fluffy, and furry-looking; ostrich is longer and shaggier. Feather trimming is used around necklines, cuffs, and hems, and on headpieces (see *Figure 102*). Several rows may be needed for a full effect. The trimming is applied by hand after the garment is completed. Stitch through the fabric and over the cordlike base where the feathers are attached. The stitches should be fairly loose and not too close together. After you've finished stitching, use a blunt tapestry needle to pull out any feathers caught in the stitches. This will conceal the stitches completely and fluff up the feathers. For removable feather trim, make thread loops (see *Figure 145*) at the edge of your garment, several inches apart, and pull the feather band through the thread loops as you would pull a belt through loops (see *Figure 103*). Use a tapestry needle to work the feathers out over the loops.

FUR Fur trims, both real and fake, can be bought by the yard in straight bands, usually about 2 inches wide. You could also have a furrier make fur parts, such as collar or cuffs, possibly with matching headband or muff. Choose a fabric substantial enough to support the weight of fur. These trims are attached after the garment is completed. Fur parts or trim are backed with a lining fabric. Stitch by hand from the garment through to the lining of the fur. Wider trims will probably need two or more rows of stitches. For removable fur trim, you can attach snaps to the lining of the trim and to the garment, as you see in *Figure 104*. Fur trims can be used again on another dress.

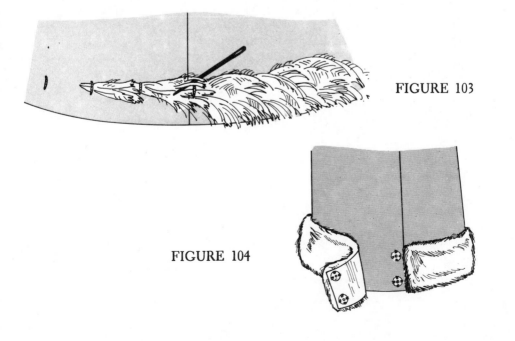

FIGURE 103

FIGURE 104

FIGURE 105

SHIRRING

Shirring consists of a number of rows of gathers that are used decoratively at waistlines, yokes, sleeves, and so on (see *Figure* 105). The fabric you choose should be soft and drape nicely. Sheers, crepes, and jerseys work well.

If your pattern does not call for shirring, when you're shirring a large area, such as a bodice, the shirring should be done before the pattern piece is cut. Cut a piece of fabric two to three times wider than the pattern piece. Shirr as explained below. Trace the outline of the pattern piece onto the shirred fabric. Using a very small zigzag stitch, stay-stitch just inside the outline. Cut the fabric on the outline, handling it very carefully to avoid pulling out the threads. Secure the side seams with a pin tuck (*Figure* 106). For a small area, such as the end of the sleeve, do the shirring after you cut your garment.

Shirring should be done on the crosswise grain or bias to fall softly. The bobbin thread will be the one that you pull to draw up the gathers, so it should be sturdy. For a sheer fabric, use clear nylon thread; for other fabrics, use heavy-duty thread. Use about 8 stitches per inch and loosen the upper thread tension. Test stitch length and tension on a scrap first to make sure that the thread pulls easily but is not too loose. Shirring rows are usually stitched ½ to 1 inch apart. Stitch the rows neatly and evenly, parallel to one another. Knot the thread for each row separately. Holding the bobbin threads, draw up the shirring to the width you want and work the gathers so that they are even. Secure the ends by making a tiny pin tuck, as you see in *Figure* 106. Never press shirring, as pressing would flatten it. Slide the point of the iron into the gathers below the shirring.

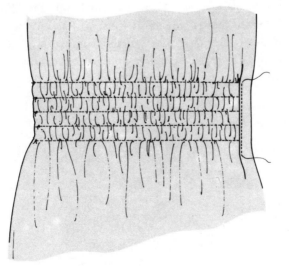

FIGURE 106

Elastic Shirring

This shirring will stretch because elastic thread is used in the bobbin. Usually the elastic thread will have to be wound onto the bobbin by hand. Use regular thread for the upper thread and a long stitch, about 7 per inch. Test first on a scrap. Stitch your shirring rows with the right side of your fabric facing up and holding the fabric taut. Stretch the fabric as you stitch each row so that the shirring will be even from row to row.

SASHES AND BOWS

SASHES Waistline sashes can be made of the same fabric as the dress, contrasting fabric, or ribbon or braid trim. If you are using a braid or embroidered trim that has an unattractive wrong side, stitch lightweight ribbon of the same width to the wrong side of the trim to cover the back. A wide fabric sash cut on the bias will fall into softly crushed folds at the waistline, which looks very pretty. A bias sash should be folded double, stitched on the wrong side, and turned, since bias will ripple if hemmed. To determine the length of fabric or ribbon you need for your sash, tie seam binding or a strip of fabric around your waist, then measure it. For a luxurious look, the streamers should be quite long. If you are making a straight-grain fabric sash, hem the edge, using the hemmer foot, for a neat finish. To prevent the bow drooping, make a thread loop (see *Figure 145*) at the waistline where the bow will be tied and pull the sash through the thread loop before you tie the bow.

BOWS Bows can be made from ribbon, lace, or braid. Tiny bows made of satin ribbon can be scattered around the skirt or used to accent lace appliqués. Larger bows are used at sleeve ends, neckline, waistline, and so on. For a pretty appliqué trim, make bows of satin or velvet ribbon and fasten a dainty lace flower motif at the center of each bow.

8

Designer Finishing Techniques

For a professional look, it is important to select the most appropriate finishing techniques for your fabric and style. A basic hem or seam is not always the best choice; when dealing with special fabrics such as laces, sheers, knits, and velvets, other methods will give you better results. Designer touches such as lining or lingerie strap guards help make your dress expensive-looking and a pleasure to wear.

SEAMS AND SEAM FINISHES

Seams should be straight and smooth, not puckered or wavy, and should have no ravelly edges. See Chapter 5 for information on making a test seam and the correct method of pressing seams.

Grading

When a seam is pressed to one side, or is made up of several layers such as the garment fabric plus underlining and interfacing, the seam should be graded to press flat and avoid forming a thick ridge. Grading is simply trimming the seam al-

FIGURE 107

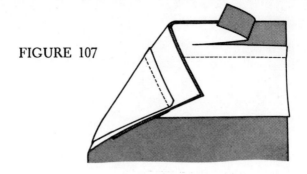

lowances to different widths. For example, in *Figure 107* the seam allowance of the garment fabric is left the full width, the underlining is trimmed to ½ inch, and the facing is trimmed to ⅜ inch. If your seam is pressed to one side, the underlayer of the seam allowance is left the original width and the upper layer is trimmed to ⅜ or ½ inch, depending upon the weight of the fabric.

Seams for Lighter-weight Fabrics

FRENCH SEAMS (*Figure 108*). This is the finest and neatest seam for sheers and laces. It can be made only on a straight seam, not on a curve. First, pin the garment wrong sides together and stitch ⅜ inch from the edge. You now have a seam on the right side of your garment. Press the seam flat and trim to about ⅛ inch from the stitching line. Press the seam to one side. Turn your garment wrong side out. Crease along the stitched seam and press again so that the stitched seam is at the edge of the garment. Stitch again ¼ inch from the edge, encasing the raw edges of the first seam. Be sure that none of the raw edge from the first seam protrudes beyond the second line of stitching.

FIGURE 108

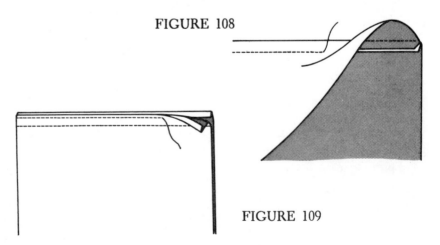

FIGURE 109

SIMULATED FRENCH SEAM (*Figure 109*). First, make a plain seam and press the seam flat. Turn the seam allowances ¼ inch under toward each other and edgestitch the folded edges together. This does not work on curves.

DOUBLE-STITCHED SEAM (*Figure 110*). This seam is used on curves where you can't use a French seam, or as a quicker seam than the French seam. Stitch a plain seam and press flat. Make a second row of straight stitching ¼ inch from the first row. Trim the seam allowance up to the second row of stitching. Press the seam to one side.

FIGURE 110

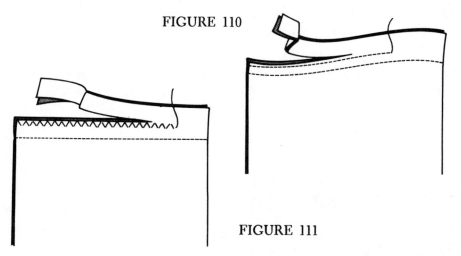

FIGURE 111

MERROW SEAM (*Figure 111*). Stitch a plain seam and press the seam flat. Using a close medium-width zigzag stitch, run a second row of stitching ¼ inch from the first row. Trim the seam allowance up to the zigzag stitch.

SELF-BOUND SEAM (*Figure 112*). Sew a plain seam and press flat. Trim one layer of the seam allowance to ¼ inch. Turn the edge of the other seam allowance under, encasing the trimmed seam allowance. Whip-stitch by hand, or machine-stitch.

FIGURE 112

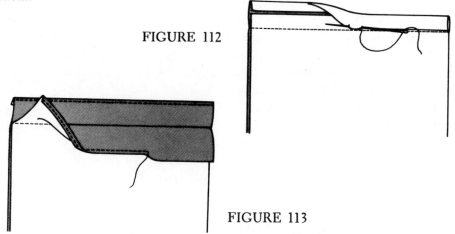

FIGURE 113

CLEAN-FINISHED SEAM (*Figure 113*). Stitch a plain seam and press it open. Turn under the raw edge of each side of the seam allowance and stitch close to the edge.

Seam Finishes

Each of the following finishes begins with a plain seam pressed open. They are used to keep fabric edges from fraying or raveling and to give a neat, finished appearance. Some are suitable only for a particular weight of fabric, as noted.

HAND-OVERCAST FINISH (*Figure 114*). After the seam is pressed open, machine-stitch ¼ inch from each raw edge. Trim to within ⅛ inch of the machine stitching. Overcast the edges by hand, following the line of the machine stitching. This finish is suitable for any weight of fabric.

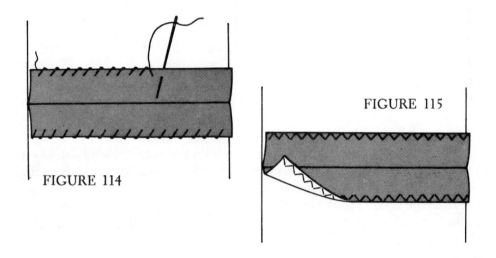

FIGURE 115

FIGURE 114

ZIGZAG FINISH (*Figure 115*). This finish can be used on most fabrics. It is frequently used on knits to keep the edges from raveling. For lightweight fabrics, use a smaller, closer zigzag stitch; for heavier fabrics, use a wider stitch. Zigzag along each side of the seam allowance ⅛ inch from the raw edge, as shown. Trim away the ⅛ inch, up to the line of stitching.

STRAIGHT STITCH FINISH (*Figure 116*). The simplest finish is a straight stitch, about ⅛ inch from each edge. You can also stitch ¼ inch from each edge and then pink the edge with pinking shears or scallop shears.

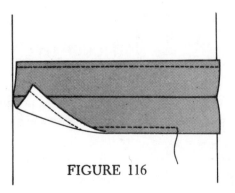

FIGURE 116

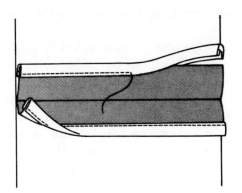

FIGURE 117

BOUND EDGE FINISH (*Figure 117*). This is used primarily on bulky fabrics, especially those that ravel easily. Using a bias binder attachment if you have one, encase each raw edge in purchased double-fold bias tape. If you don't have a bias binder attachment, place the slightly narrower side of the tape face up and edgestitch.

HONG KONG FINISH (*Figure 118*). This looks similar to the bound edge finish and is also used with bulky fabrics. You'll probably find this one easier to do than the bound edge finish if you don't have a bias binder attachment. Cut bias strips 1 inch wide from lining fabric, or use double-fold bias tape pressed open. Place the edge of the bias along the edge of the upper side of the seam allowance and stitch ¼ inch from the edge. Turn the bias to the underside of the seam allowance so it encloses the raw edge. Stitch again on the right side, just at the seam where the bias joins the garment seam allowance.

FIGURE 118

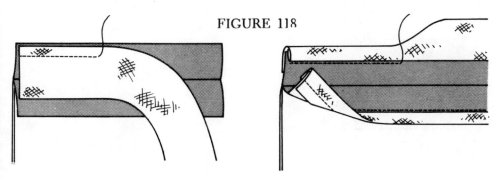

HEMS

The hem is a very important part of your dress and should be done with great care. Nothing makes a garment look homemade more than a thick, lumpy hem. There are different types of hems suitable for specific styles and fabrics; one hem does not suit all purposes. Strive to make your hem as inconspicuous as possible.

Hem depth usually ranges from 3 inches for a skirt with a straight hem to 1 inch for a skirt with a very curved hem. An exception to this is sheer fabrics, which are hemmed with a very wide hem (as much as 8 or 10 inches for a straight hem) or a very narrow hem, such as a hand-rolled. If your fabric is stretchy or cut on the bias, allow your dress to hang for a minimum of twenty-four hours so it will settle into its final shape before you mark the hem. A week is recommended for chiffon. Mark the hem by measuring up from the floor with a hem marker and while wearing the correct foundations and shoes. After the hem is stitched, it should be pressed carefully so no ridge is formed. The hem should be the very last thing you do, after all final fittings and adjustments have been made.

Hem Edge Finishes

Before you stitch the hem itself, the raw edge of the hem should be finished in some way. How you do this depends on the type of fabric you are using.

A TURN-BACK EDGE (*Figure 119*) should be used only on lightweight or sheer fabrics, as otherwise it would form a ridge. Turn back the edge ⅜ inch and edge-stitch. If you are using a sheer fabric, press the turned edge back and eliminate the edgestitch.

FIGURE 119

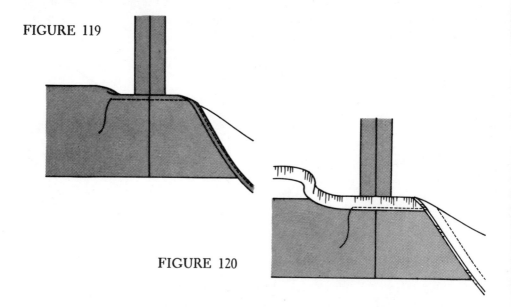

FIGURE 120

SEAM BINDING (*Figure 120*) is a good choice for bulky or ravelly nonstretchy fabrics and other medium- to heavyweight fabrics.

LACE (*Figure 121*). Half-inch wide, lightweight lace can be used instead of seam binding. This is a luxurious touch found on expensive garments and is especially appropriate for wedding gowns and formal dresses.

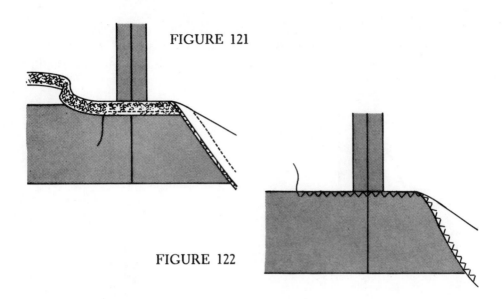

FIGURE 121

FIGURE 122

A ZIGZAG FINISH (*Figure 122*) is also used for bulky and ravelly fabrics. For a neater appearance, apply seam binding or lace after you zigzag-stitch.

HAND OVERCASTING (*Figure 114*) is also appropriate for thick or ravelly fabrics.

A STRAIGHT STITCH (*Figure 116*) is used for some fabrics that do not ravel but are too thick to turn under. Machine-stitch ¼ inch from the raw edge. A straight stitch with a pinked edge is sometimes suggested as an edge finish, but since this is used only on low-priced garments I don't recommend it.

HONG KONG EDGE See Hong Kong Finish (*Figure 118*). Apply the same finish to the edge of your hem.

Hemming Stitches

Hemming should be done using a single thread and a needle size appropriate to your fabric. The stitches should be evenly spaced and extremely tiny, picking up only 1 or 2 threads from your fabric with each stitch. Never pull the thread tight, because this will result in the hem showing on the right side. To minimize tangling and make your thread stronger, run the thread through beeswax (which you can buy at notions departments) before you begin stitching. Don't cut your thread too long, as this will only increase the chance of tangling and will not really save any time. Make a small, neat knot and try to end your stitching at a seam so you can knot into the seam allowance. You can lock hemming stitches every 6 inches or so by taking a couple of backstitches into the hem allowance only. This is a good idea for a wedding gown, since the hem or train can easily be stepped on and the stitches pulled out. If your sewing machine can do blind stitching, try it out on a scrap first. Machine hemstitches may not be fine enough for your delicate or special fabrics.

HEMMING STITCH (*Figure 123*) is appropriate for many fabrics of sheer to medium weight. It is generally used with a turn-back edge or seam binding. Pick up one thread of the garment and bring the needle diagonally through the edge of the seam binding or hem edge, as shown.

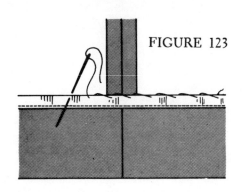

FIGURE 123

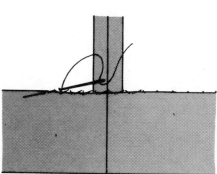

FIGURE 124

A BLIND HEM (*Figure 124*) is also used on sheer to medium-weight fabrics. Since it is almost invisible on both the wrong and right side, it is a better choice for sheer fabrics. Take a tiny stitch in the garment, then swing the needle down about ⅜ inch away from the first stitch, picking up a stitch in the edge of the hem. Pull the thread through. Make your next stitch in the garment directly above the last stitch in the hem.

A CATCH-STITCH HEM (*Figure 125*) is used for hemming knits because it stretches. Depending on the weight of your fabric, it can be made as a regular hem or an inside-stitched hem (see below). The stitches are made the same way for

FIGURE 125

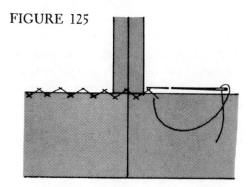

both. (Note that the stitches are worked from left to right.) Make a very tiny stitch on the inside of the fabric. Take up only 1 or 2 threads with each stitch or the fabric will show a dimple on the right side. Then, in the hem, make another stitch on a diagonal from the first stitch. Continue to stitch in a zigzag fashion, keeping the thread quite loose.

Inside-stitched Hem

The inside-stitched hem is a very important hemming method (see *Figure 126*). For some reason, it is unfamiliar to a great many home sewers, although it is frequently used in the garment industry. This hem should be used on most fabrics of medium to heavy weight. The stitches are taken in between the hem and the garment fabric. This is the secret for making a hem that does not show on the right side of your garment. The raw edge of the hem can be finished using any of the above finishes except the turn-back edge. If you use seam binding or lace to finish the hem edge, the hemming stitches should still be taken into the fabric of the hem, not into the seam binding or lace. Baste the hem ½ inch from the hem edge. Fold back the garment along the basting line so the edge of the hem projects ¼ to ⅜ inch. Take a tiny stitch, catching one thread at the edge of the fold. Then, about ¼ inch away, take another tiny stitch into the fabric of the hem. Continue stitching back and forth, taking a stitch in the fold of the garment and in the hem. It is very important that you do not pull the stitches tight. With fabrics such as brocade or wool, it is best to pick up a thread or two just from the back, so the stitch does not go through to the right side of the garment. If your dress has an underlining, make the stitch catching the underlining only. Press the hem carefully. The edge should not be a sharp crease but form a soft roll. With heavy fabrics, use the steam of the iron as much as possible. Do not set the iron itself down on the fabric or the hem will make a ridge.

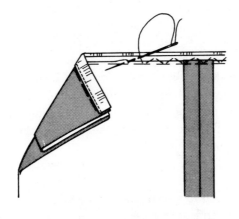

FIGURE 126

Couture Hems

Beautifully finished seams and hems are the mark of a finely made dress. Many wedding gowns and formal dresses need a special kind of hem designed for a particular fabric or style. Each of the hems below requires a little extra time and care, but the professional results will be worth the effort.

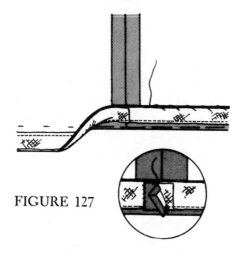

FIGURE 127

HORSEHAIR BRAID HEM (*Figure 127*). Horsehair braid is actually a stiff, transparent nylon mesh. It is available in ½-inch and 1-inch widths. The narrow width is used on sheer and lace dresses with gathered or flared skirts to give body to the hem and make the skirt stand out. For A-line styles in heavy fabrics such as brocade, velvet, and satin, the wider width is used to give the hem shape and body. After the hemline has been carefully marked, trim the hem allowance to ¼ inch for sheer fabrics or ⅝ inch for heavy fabrics. Press the braid to remove creases. Working with the garment right side up, align one edge of the braid with the finished edge of the hemline. Topstitch along the hemline edge of the braid. Overlap the ends of the braid by ½ inch. The ends of the braid are quite wiry and should be finished to avoid snagging your stockings or dress lining. Enclose the ends of the braid with a strip of lining fabric or seam binding, as shown. Press the hem up and hand-stitch using blind hemming or hemming stitch. If the garment is underlined, catch the hemming stitches to the underlining only. If you are applying wide horsehair braid to a curved hem, the braid should have a thread at the top that can be pulled to make it curve.

INTERFACED AND PADDED HEMS (*Figure 128*). Fine dresses do not have a knife-sharp hem edge but, rather, a soft roll at the hem. Interfacing is used in the hem to give this soft roll, and also to give the hem body when using a heavy fabric. An interfaced hem is not as stiff as a horsehair braid hem. Interfaced and padded hems are generally applied to dresses that have an underlining. (However, these hems can be used in a dress without an underlining if you can make stitches catching only the back threads of the fabric so none show on the right side of the garment. Test on a scrap.) Mark the hemline with thread tracing (*Figure 38*). For an interfaced hem, cut a bias strip of soft woven interfacing the same width as the hem itself. If you have to piece the bias, do not make a regular seam, but lap one piece over the other and topstitch. If you are applying the interfacing to a curved hem, preshape the interfacing by pressing first. Place the strip along the hemline so the bottom edge of the interfacing extends ⅝ inch below the thread tracing. Stitch the interfacing to the underlining, using long running stitches along the hemline and long catch-stitches along the upper edge. Turn the hem up and baste. Finish, using an inside-stitched hem.

The padded hem is made in the same way as the interfaced hem except that the bias strip is cut from softer fabric, such as cotton flannel or lightweight wool, instead of interfacing. It is used for medium-weight fabrics such as taffeta, linen, and lighter-weight satins.

FIGURE 128

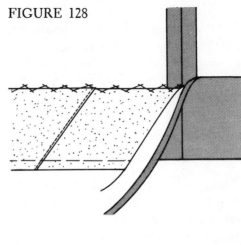

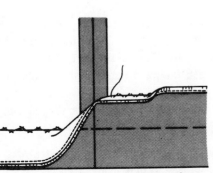

FIGURE 129

A DOUBLE-STITCHED HEM (*Figure 129*) is used on medium-weight or heavy fabrics where the weight of the hem would tend to pull or stretch and cause the hemming stitches to show. It is also used when the fabric is bulky and would not form a flat hem without excessive pressing. This hem is used on fabrics such as double knits, brocades, and velvets. First, baste along the center of the hem. Fold the hem back on the basting line and make the first row of stitching in this location. For an underlined dress, use a catch-stitch, catching only the underlining. Otherwise use an inside hemming stitch, picking up the tiniest stitch possible. Finish, using an inside hemming stitch for the second row.

HAND-ROLLED HEM This is the finest and most elegant finish to use on sheer fabrics. There are two different methods for making a hand-rolled hem. For either method, mark the hem, then trim the hem allowance to ½ inch. Machine-stitch ¼ inch from the raw edge and trim close to the stitching.

Method 1 (Figure 130A). Roll ⅛ inch of the edge between your thumb and forefinger. The rolling will be easier if you keep your thumb and forefinger slightly moistened. Stitch, picking up a single thread of the fabric with each stitch.

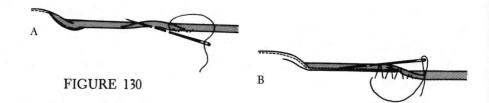

A

FIGURE 130   B

Method 2 (Figure 130B). Turn the edge under about ⅛ inch and crease sharply. Pick up a stitch at the crease and bring the thread diagonally over the raw edge and pick up a thread along the side of the raw edge. Work back and forth in a zigzag fashion, making stitches about ¼ inch apart, for a distance of 1 inch. After you have made an inch of stitches, pull on the thread, which will tighten the stitches and form the roll.

Curved Hems

Because the hem of a flared or circular skirt is curved, it requires more attention than a straight hem. The hem edge is the widest part of the skirt, so the extra fullness must be eliminated by easing or notching. The more curved the hem, the narrower the hem should be, ranging from 2½ inches wide for a slight curve to 1 inch for a pronounced curve.

The other method of finishing a curved hem is by using a bias or shaped facing. To make a pattern for a shaped hem facing, refer to *Figure 21*.

EASED HEM If you are adding seam binding or a lace finish to the edge of your hem, ease the hem first and then add the finish. When using a zigzag or other stitched finish, stitch first and then ease your hem. On a hem with a turned-back edge, the stitching used to turn back the raw edge can also be the easing stitch. Mark the hemline with pins or thread tracing (*Figure 38*). Machine-stitch ¼ inch from the edge, using about 10 to 12 stitches per inch. Place the dress on a table or flat surface. Turn the hem up along the marked line and baste the hem near the hemline (see *Figure 131*). Using a pin, pull the easing stitch and ease in the extra hem fullness just as you would ease the cap of a sleeve. If you are working with a fabric that can be steamed, hold the iron above the hem (do not place the iron down on the hem) and let the steam ease some of the gathers. To prevent an

FIGURE 131

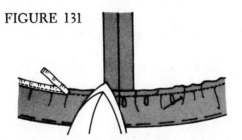

impression of the hem from forming on the right side of your dress, insert a strip of brown paper under the hem between the hem allowance and the dress. Pat the hem lightly with your fingers or the heel of your hand as you steam.

NOTCHED HEM (*Figure 132*). For fabric that does not ease well and cannot be steamed, use a notched hem. Mark the hemline, turn up the hem, and baste near the hemline. Cut out wedges about ½ inch wide from the hem allowance at evenly spaced intervals. The point of the wedge should be no closer than ⅜ inch from the hemline. Bring the cut edges together and join with hand stitching. You will see where to cut the wedges by the way the ripples form in the hem. Apply the hem edge finish after notching.

FIGURE 132

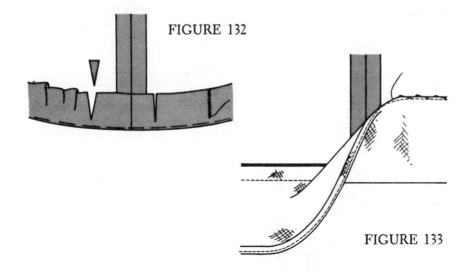

FIGURE 133

BIAS-FACING HEM (*Figure 133*). A bias facing can be made using a bias strip cut from lining fabric, or you can use commercial bias facing if the color matches. Before you apply the facing, trim the hem allowance to ⅝ inch. Cut your bias 2½ inches wide for a very curved hem and 3½ inches wide for a less curved hem. Preshape the bias into a curve by pressing. Turn back the upper edge of the bias ⅜ inch and press. Edgestitch by machine. Apply the bias facing to the skirt as you would apply an ordinary facing. Clean-finish the bias by overlapping the ends. Hand-stitch the upper edge of the facing to the skirt using a hemming stitch (*Figure 123*) or blind hem (*Figure 124*).

Narrow Hems and Edgings

Unlike traditional hems, these are decorative as well as functional. They are not suited to heavy fabrics, and some are meant for specific fabrics, such as sheers or knits. These hems require a zigzag machine and some make use of machine embroidery stitches. There are several things to keep in mind while doing these stitches. When working on a single layer of fabric, you may have trouble with the stitches not being even or the fabric not feeding smoothly. If you have either of these problems, do your stitching with a strip of tissue paper under the fabric. The finished side of the garment should be face up as you stitch. Since the stitching will show, the choice of thread is important. Machine embroidery stitches done with ordinary sewing thread look coarse and unattractive. Try to use either silk thread or a thread made specifically for machine embroidery.

A NARROW ZIGZAG HEM (*Figure* 134) can be used on straight edges with woven fabric and straight or curved edges with knits. Fold the raw edge back ⅜ inch and zigzag-stitch ⅛ to ¼ inch from the edge. Trim away excess fabric close to the stitching. Experiment by varying the width and length of your zigzag stitch and by using matching or contrasting thread.

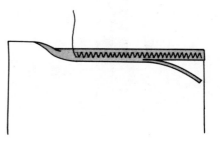

FIGURE 134

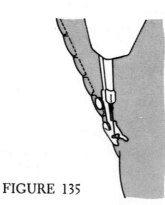

FIGURE 135

A SHELL EDGING (*Figure* 135) is used on sheer fabrics and lightweight knits. For this stitch, your machine must do blind hemming. Turn the raw edge under about ⅜ inch, but do not press. Because of the way the blind hemming operates, you will have to hold your fabric in the sewing machine to the right of the needle instead of to the left side as you usually do. Use a wide stitch setting and a short stitch length. You'll have to experiment on a scrap to get the right length and width stitch, and to see just how to feed the fabric into the machine. The result should be that when the needle swings over to the left it actually swings off the folded edge of the fabric and the stitch gathers in the fabric, forming a little shell.

SCALLOPED EDGING (*Figure 136*). Set your machine to make a scalloped embroidery stitch. Do not turn the raw edge under. Stitch ⅝ inch from the cut edge. After you've made a row of scalloping, with small embroidery scissors very carefully trim away excess fabric beyond the scallop so the scallop forms the garment edge. This edging can be used on knits or wovens of light to medium weight. To keep knits from stretching, stitch with tissue paper underneath. For a ripply edge like a lettuce edge, stretch the knit as you stitch and do not use tissue paper. When making an unstretched scalloped edge, if using tissue paper still does not give a neat result, cut a strip of organza and place it under the knit fabric as you stitch. Trim away the organza after you have stitched. This edging can be used almost anywhere: around collars and cuffs, along a front opening, neckline, armholes, or sleeve edges, and so on.

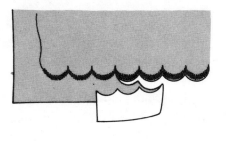

FIGURE 136

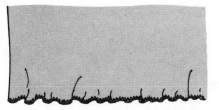

FIGURE 137

A LETTUCE EDGING (*Figure 137*) is used on knit fabrics only. Try each of the methods listed below on a scrap to see which works best for your fabric. The quickest method is simply to turn back the raw edge ¼ inch or less and machine-zigzag, stretching as you stitch. To make any lettuce edging, you must grasp the fabric firmly in front and back of the presser foot and stretch very hard. On many fabrics, turning back the edge will not form an attractive lettuce edge but simply an odd-looking ripple. If this is the case, you will have to use a satin stitch and not turn the edge under. To do this, set your machine for a narrow satin stitch and stitch ¼ inch from the raw edge. Trim up to the satin stitch, being careful not to cut into the stitches. For a very ripply edge, use a cording of pearl cotton under the satin stitch. Follow the directions below for corded satin stitch hem, stretching the fabric as you stitch.

A CORDED SATIN STITCH HEM (*Figure 138*) is used for chiffon or other sheers. A lightweight cord gives body to the skirt edge. You will need pearl cotton, No. 5 (a type of embroidery thread), in a color that matches your fabric. Experiment on a scrap first to get your machine adjusted properly. Use a satin stitch just wide enough to encase the cord. Stitch ⅝ inch from the raw edge, positioning the cord so that the zigzag goes back and forth over it. Once you have finished stitching, with embroidery scissors trim away the excess fabric right up to the stitching. The corded satin stitch forms the edge of your garment. Rub your finger along the trimmed edge so that any loose threads will pop up and you can trim them away.

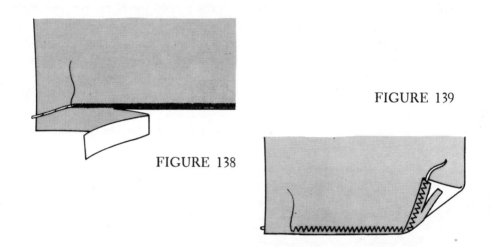

FIGURE 139

FIGURE 138

A CORDED ZIGZAG HEM (*Figure 139*) is used with chiffon or other sheers. To make this hem, you will also need No. 5 pearl cotton in a color to match your fabric. The pearl cotton is used to give the hem body and to keep it from puckering during the stitching. Fold back the raw edge ⅝ of an inch, positioning the pearl cotton in the fold. Set your machine to make a zigzag just slightly wider than the pearl cotton. Stitch carefully so that the right swing of the zigzag is at the edge of the fold and the left swing encases the pearl cotton. Trim away the hem allowance close to the stitching line.

A WIRE HEM (*Figure 140*) is used on chiffon and other sheers for a swingy hem with extra body. For this you will need a fine, flexible fabric-covered wire, which can be found in hobby shops. Follow the directions for a corded zigzag hem,

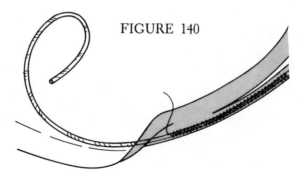

FIGURE 140

above, using wire instead of pearl cotton. Another method is to zigzag-stitch the wire ¼ inch from the edge of the hem and trim to ⅛ inch. Make a hand-rolled hem by rolling the fabric around the wire. Be sure you roll the fabric enough so that the zigzag stitch is on the wrong side of the hem.

MACHINE-EMBROIDERED HEMS (*Figure 141*). You can achieve a number of different effects by using one of your machine embroidery stitches to stitch a hem. Don't get carried away with using a lot of different stitches and thread colors, as this will get to look very homemade. A thread that matches the fabric looks attractive, especially if the fabric is sheer so that the texture of the embroidery contrasts. Turn back the raw edge ½ to 1 inch and stitch. Trim away excess hem allowance up to the stitching. This hem can be used on straight edges for wovens or on curved or straight edges for knits.

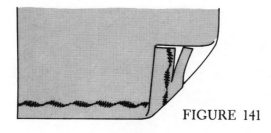

FIGURE 141

Hemming Lined and Underlined Dresses

The hem of a lining should be free and separate from the hem of the dress. First mark and hem the dress hem, then mark and hem the lining ½ to ¾ inch shorter than the dress. Unless the dress fabric is sheer, the hem of the lining is turned toward the dress, as you see in *Figure 158*. The lining should be anchored to the dress with French tacks (*Figure 158*).

When you are hemming an underlined dress, the underlining and dress fabric should be treated as one. Do not cut the underlining from the hem allowance. Your hem edge finish should be applied to both the dress fabric and the underlining fabric together. Use an inside-stitched hem and catch only the underlining.

Facing Edges

Except when using lightweight fabrics, the raw edge of a facing should not be turned under because a ridge would show on the right side of the garment. The facing edge can be finished in a number of the ways used to finish the edge of a hem, such as stretch lace, zigzag stitch, hand overcasting, or straight stitch. Follow the directions given near the beginning of this chapter for hem edge finishes.

ZIPPERS

A finely applied zipper is one of the marks of a well-made dress—many dresses look homemade because the zipper is put in poorly. Often the zipper is stitched too far from the opening edge so that the zipper lap is too wide. The lap should be just wide enough to allow the zipper pull to slide easily, about ¼ inch from the opening edge on a centered zipper, and about ⅜ inch on a lapped zipper on light-to medium-weight fabrics (see *Figure 142*).

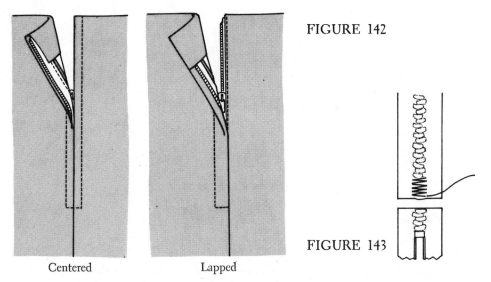

FIGURE 142

FIGURE 143

Centered   Lapped

Patterns specify the length of the zipper for persons of average height, about 5′5″. If you are short, you may do better with a zipper that is shorter than called for; if you are tall, you may need a zipper that is longer. When an odd-length zipper is needed (for example, a zipper on a fitted sleeve is 4 to 5 inches long), you can shorten the zipper yourself. Select a zipper with non-metal teeth. Using a very close zigzag, stitch just below where you want the zipper to end. Cut off the extra zipper, leaving a tail of about ¾ inch (see *Figure 143*). If you don't have a zigzag-stitch machine, you can use a small stitch (about 20 to the inch) and sew back and forth, six or eight times, to make a bar tack.

Inserting a Zipper

You will need a minimum of ⅝ inch seam allowance on each side to insert the zipper. If your seam allowance is less than that, you can attach a strip of seam binding to increase the width. Press your zipper first. When you pin the zipper, start at the top and work down. Be sure that the right and left neckline and waistline seams meet. To avoid shiny spots on your fabric, do not place the iron down on the fabric covering the zipper after it has been inserted. If you are putting in the zipper by machine, be sure to use a zipper foot. (An invisible zipper requires a special foot. Follow the directions included with the foot. Test an invisible zipper with a scrap to be sure that it works with your fabric.)

Hand-applied Zipper

For a fine dress in a costly fabric, a hand-applied zipper is best. It looks much more attractive and is found only on the most expensive ready-made dresses. It is also easier and less risky because you have more control and are not likely to make a mistake. Use a single strand of thread for lightweight fabrics or a double strand for some heavier fabrics. A hand application can be used for a centered or a lapped zipper. If a lap is used, you can machine-stitch the underlap if you prefer. The zipper is applied with a prick stitch, which is a variation of the half backstitch. Although you'll see only a tiny stitch on the top, it is strong because the stitch is reinforced underneath. Pin and baste the zipper in place. Refer to *Figure 144*. Working with the right side up, draw the needle through the fabric from the wrong side. Stitch back a few threads (about $\frac{1}{16}$ inch) and bring the needle out again ¼ inch in front of the first stitch. Stitch back a few threads again and continue in the same manner. Do not pull the thread tight.

If you are using bulky fabrics or a number of layers, sewing through all the layers would be difficult and cause puckering. To avoid this, use a combination of hand and machine stitching. First, baste the zipper in place. Then, using the zipper foot, machine-stitch the zipper tape to the seam allowance only. (No stitches will show on the right side of the garment.) With the garment right side up, hand-stitch the zipper, catching the top layer of the fabric and the first layer of seam allowance only. Do not stitch through all the layers.

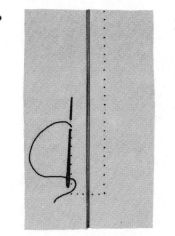

FIGURE 144

BUTTONS AND LOOP CLOSINGS

A row of tiny buttons with delicate loops is the finest closing for a wedding gown. This is admittedly time-consuming, but it looks beautiful and is used on the most expensive gowns. Remember that during the ceremony the guests will be looking at the back of your gown. Button and loop closings can also be used at the center front, at the wrist of a long fitted sleeve, or at the cuff of a full sleeve.

When you are using button loops, there is not the same overlap as with regular buttonholes. You can use either a pattern with a zipper or a button opening. In either case, you will need to make an adjustment in the pattern seam allowance at the opening (see page 44 for how to do this). If you have already cut your garment and it does not have the extra seam allowance at the opening, the opening can be extended by stitching woven seam binding to the seam allowance. A simulated button closing can be made by applying a lapped zipper, then stitching a row of covered or pearl buttons very close together along the zipper lap. Ready-made button loops can be ordered by mail (see Shopping Guide).

Thread Loops

See *Figure 145*. Use a single strand of silk buttonhole twist, size D. Take two or three foundation stitches the length of your loop and secure the ends with small backstitches. These foundation stitches are the actual size of your loop, so they must be correct. Slip one of your buttons through the foundation to make sure that it is large enough. Then, using the same thread that you used to make the foundation stitches, begin at the top of the loop and work buttonhole stitches very close together along the length of the foundation thread, as shown.

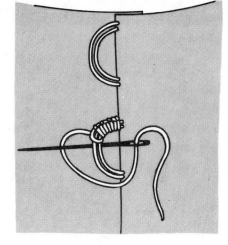

FIGURE 145

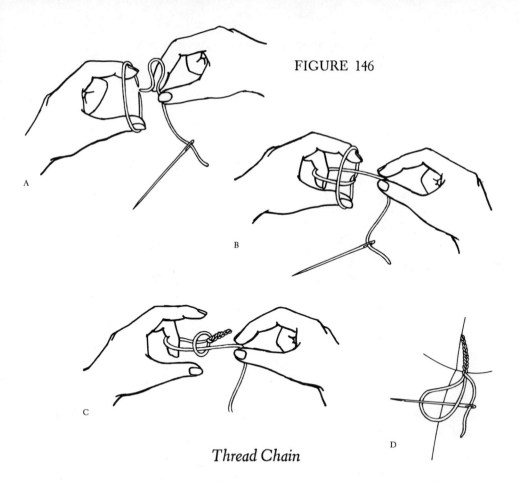

FIGURE 146

Thread Chain

This is another way of making thread loops. Thread chain is not quite as fine-looking as the thread loops above, but once you get the knack of it, the loops can be made quickly. Use a single or double strand of silk buttonhole twist. Refer to *Figure 146*.

1. Bring the needle through from the wrong side and take a tiny stitch at the same spot to form a loop, as you see in *Figure 146A*.

2. Insert your index finger and thumb of your left hand into the loop and spread the loop open.

3. Form a second loop with your right hand, and insert through the first loop, as shown in *Figure 146B*.

4. Hold the second loop with your left hand and pull on the thread to tighten the first loop (*Figure 146C*).

5. Insert a third loop into the second loop and pull to tighten in the same way.

In order to get a neat-looking chain, keep the tension even in your left and right hand and pull evenly on each loop. Coninue making loops until your chain is the necessary length.

6. Insert the needle through the last loop to finish the chain (*Figure 146D*).

7. With the needle, sew the end of the chain to the dress.

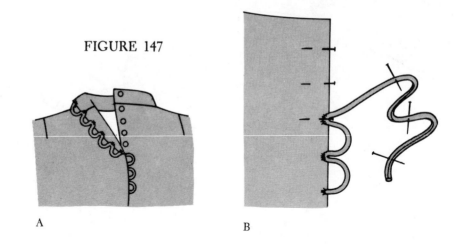

FIGURE 147

A   B

Fabric Loops

Fabric loops can be made from purchased satin cord or other thin tubing such as spaghetti (see *Figure 147*A).

BUTTON LOOPS ON GARMENT EDGE If the tubing is flexible enough and not too bulky, it can be stitched to the edge of the finished garment as in *Figure 147*B. Determine the size of the loop that will be needed to accommodate your button. On the edge of the garment, measure and mark the width of the loops with pins or tailor's tacks, as shown. Measure and mark the size of the loops in the same manner. Allow ⅜ inch extra tubing at the beginning and end of the cord to fasten to the wrong side of the garment. Beginning at the first mark and matching the marks, attach the cord to the edge of the garment with small hand stitches. You can slide the needle to the next mark through the fold of the garment. If the cord has a seam, be sure that the seam is not turned to the right side.

BUTTON LOOPS ON FACED EDGE Loops can be placed in a continuous row, as you see in *Figure 148*A. For larger buttons, individual loops are used, as shown in *Figure 148*B. For continuous loops, you can figure the amount of the tubing you need by multiplying the length of the opening times 5. For example, if your opening is 12 inches, 5×12 equals 60 inches of tubing needed. For individual loops, figure 2 times the diameter of the button plus 1¼ inches for each loop. For example, for a ½-inch diameter button, you would need 2¼ inches for each loop. Allow more if the cord is bulky. Fabric loops are first stitched to a paper guide so that the loops will be uniform in size and spacing. Before you make your paper guide, you must determine the length and width of loop needed to accommodate your button. Make an actual test loop on a scrap and check by slipping a button through, then measure the length of the opening and width of the loop (see *Figure 148*C).

FIGURE 148

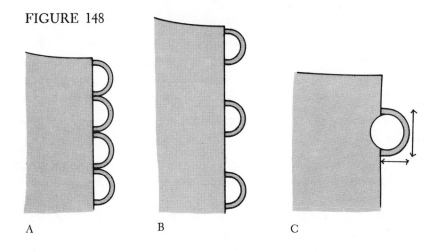

A   B   C

PAPER GUIDE FOR CONTINUOUS LOOPS Cut a strip of sturdy paper, such as type-writer bond, about 2 inches wide and the length of the opening (see *Figure 149*).

1. Draw a line ⅝ inch from the edge of the paper (line A). This indicates the stitching line. The ⅝ inch distance from line A to the edge of the paper is the seam allowance.
2. Draw line B parallel to line A. The distance between line A and line B is the width of the loop.
3. Draw parallel lines crosswise (line C). The distance between each line is the length of the loop.
4. Once the paper is marked, position the loops as shown. Hold the loops in place with Scotch tape or masking tape in the seam allowance. If the cord has a seam, keep the seam face up (it will be face down on the finished garment).

If the tubing bends easily, you can form loops from a continuous piece. If that doesn't work well, cut the tubing into pieces and make the loops individually.

PAPER GUIDE FOR SPACED LOOPS Follow steps 1 and 2 above; see *Figure 150*.

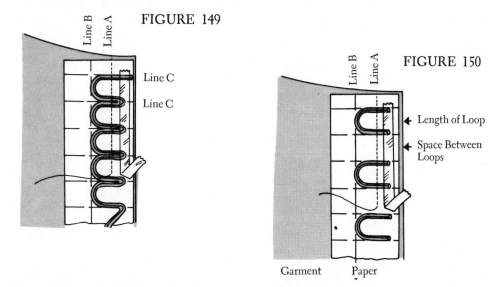

FIGURE 149

Line B Line A

Line C
Line C

FIGURE 150

Line B Line A

◄ Length of Loop

◄ Space Between Loops

Garment   Paper

3. Draw a crosswise line at the top of the paper.

4. Draw the next crosswise line parallel to the first line. The distance between the first and second line is the length of the loop.

5. Draw the next parallel line crosswise. The distance between lines 2 and 3 is the space between the loops.

Continue marking the paper as shown. Hold the loops in place with tape in the seam allowance.

ATTACHING THE LOOPS Machine-stitch the loops to the paper guide just to the right of the seam allowance line. Remove the tape. A strip of interfacing should be stitched to the wrong side of the garment (not to the facing) before the loops are attached, to keep the edge smooth and crisp and to minimize bumps from the ends of the loops. Pin the paper guide to the garment as shown. Be sure the loops face away from the garment edge and that the first loop is positioned ⅝ inch down from the top to leave seam allowance at the neckline. Stitch the paper guide and loops to the garment opening, just to the right of the seam allowance line (the same line as the first row of stitches). Tear away the paper. The ends of the loops can be trimmed to ¼ inch if they do not fray. Pin the facing on top of the loops, and turn the garment over so the wrong side faces up. Stitch the facing just inside the stitching line that holds the loops. Trim the seam allowance of the facing to ⅜ inch and press.

Shank or ball buttons must be used with loops, not the regular sew-through type. If the shank is small, the buttons may require a thread shank for adequate stand.

HAND-FINISHING STITCHES

These stitches are used for inside finishing details and to attach laces and trimmings.

CATCH-STITCH (*Figure 151*) is used to attach interfacing and facings to linings. It is made the same way as the catch-stitch hem (see *Figure 125*).

FIGURE 151

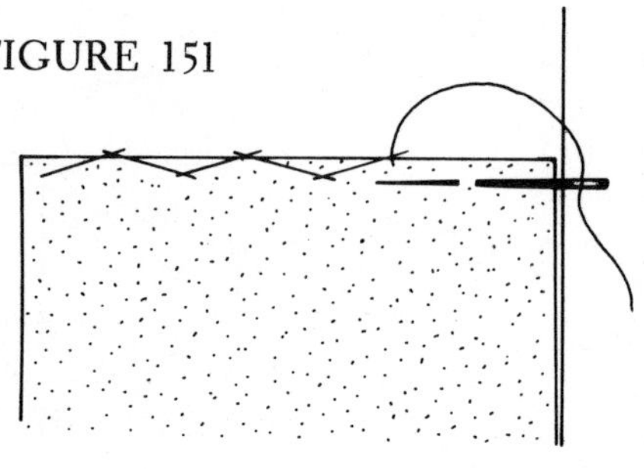

FIGURE 152

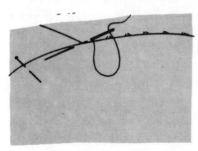

SLIP STITCH (*Figure 152*) is a tiny, almost invisible stitch used to attach linings and some trimmings. For a slip stitch to be invisible, the stitch must be taken inside the fold of the fabric. Begin by inserting the needle through the fold so the knot is inside the fold. Pick up one or two threads of the garment fabric very close to the folded edge. Insert the needle into the fold right alongside the stitch you just took. Slide the needle along the fold about ¼ inch and bring it out again. Take a tiny stitch in the garment fabric, then insert the needle back into the fold, next to the stitch you just took.

FIGURE 153

WHIP STITCH (*Figure 153*) is used to attach lace appliqués and other trimmings and to join lace. Insert the needle as shown, taking very tiny stitches.

HOW TO ADD A LINING

If your dress pattern does not include a lining, you can still add one yourself. A lining is a very fine couture touch. Fabrics that are scratchy, rough, or very ravelly may require one. If your dress has a gathered skirt, you can cut down bulk by using an A-line skirt pattern for the lining, or by reducing the amount of fullness in the gathered skirt pattern. You will need pattern pieces for the front and back bodice and skirt. Gathered sleeves are not lined. Short fitted sleeves are generally lined, and long fitted sleeves may or may not be lined, as you prefer. You do not need the small pattern pieces, such as facings, collars, and cuffs. To figure the amount of yardage you'll need for a lining, see pages 47–48.

When sewing a dress with a lining, you may have to change the order of the construction steps given in the pattern directions. Construction of the dress itself should be completed except for facings and the skirt hem. The zipper, if any, should be inserted and sleeves should be hemmed.

Lay out and cut your lining. Stay-stitch the armholes and neckline. Construct the lining in the same way as the dress. If the dress has a waistline seam, do not join the lining at the waistline. If the sleeves are lined, make the lining sleeves but do not attach them. Press the darts of the lining in the opposite direction from the darts of the dress to reduce bulk.

A dress form is very helpful when attaching the lining. Or try to have someone wear the dress while you pin the lining. The dress does not have to fit the person or the form perfectly. It is just much easier to have the dress on a three-dimensional figure rather than hanging limply from a hanger. If you can't get a dress form or a live body, then use a padded, shaped hanger.

Attaching Lining to Dress with Waist Seam

1. Place the dress on the form or hanger wrong side out.
2. Place the skirt lining over the dress right side out (see *Figure 154A*). Pin the seam allowance of the lining to the seam allowance of the skirt at the waistline, matching the side seams, darts, and other pattern marks on the lining and the dress. Be sure not to catch the bodice fabric. The pins should be through only the seam allowance.
3. If the garment opening has a zipper, turn the seam allowance of the lining under along the zipper opening, so that the folded edge of the lining is ¼ inch from the teeth of the zipper. Pin the lining along the zipper. If the skirt opening has a facing, pin the lining to the opening, matching the raw edge of the lining and the garment fabric.
4. Using small hand stitches, attach the skirt lining to the dress along the waistline seam, stitching only into the seam allowance of the lining and the dress. Do not stitch through to the bodice.
5. If there is a zipper, slip-stitch the lining edge to the zipper tape. If there will be a facing, baste the lining to the opening.

If you're using a dress form, you will probably find it easier to do all your hand stitching with your dress on the form. If you're using a hanger, pin the lining to the dress with the dress on the hanger, then remove it for hand-stitching.

6. With the dress on the hanger or the form wrong side out, place the bodice

A   FIGURE 154

B

lining over the dress right side out (see *Figure 154B*). Pin the lining to the
dress at the neckline, matching the shoulder seams and other pattern marks.

7. Pin the lining at the armholes, matching the raw edge of the lining with
   the raw edge of the garment armhole. (If you are using a hanger, this will
   be easier if you push the sleeves to the inside of the bodice.)

8. If the dress has a zipper opening, fold the lining under along the zipper
   opening so the folded edge of the lining is ¼ inch from the teeth of the zipper, and pin.

9. If the garment opening has a facing, match the raw edge of the lining with
   the raw edge of the garment opening, and pin.

10. At the neckline, baste the lining to the garment ½ inch from the raw edge.

11. Baste the lining to the garment at the armhole ¼ inch from the edge. If
    dress has lined sleeves, see sleeve lining instructions below, once the dress
    lining is completed. If sleeves are not lined, hand- or machine-stitch the lin-
    ing armhole to the seam allowance of the bodice armhole. Overcast or zig-
    zag-stitch the raw edges of the seam allowances together.

12. Slip-stitch the lining to the zipper tape, if you are using a zipper. Baste the
    lining to the opening ½ inch from the edge if you are using a facing.

As you pin or stitch, the lining must never be pulled or stretched to fit the dress,
even if this means pattern markings or side seams are not perfectly aligned. If the
lining is pulled or distorted, it will cause the fabric on the right side of your dress
to ripple and pull, which will look very unattractive.

13. At the waistline, fold under the bottom edge of the bodice lining and pin so that the folded edge of the lining meets the waistline seam and encloses the seam allowance. For wearing ease, do not pull the lining down snugly but allow the lining to blouse up slightly as you pin.

14. Slip-stitch the bodice lining to the skirt lining at the waistline.

If you are using a sleeve lining, see below to finish the lining. Otherwise, continue following your pattern instructions. Facings should be catch-stitched (*Figure 151*) to the lining only. The lining is not hemmed until the dress is completed (see page 227.

Attaching Lining to Dress with No Waistline Seam

Place the dress on the form or hanger wrong side out. Pull the lining over the dress right side out. Follow the directions given above from step 6 to step 12, to attach the lining at the neck, armholes, and openings. Disregard directions referring to the waistline.

Attaching Sleeve Lining

1. Put the dress on your form or hanger lining side out. Be sure you use the right sleeve lining on the right side of your garment and the left sleeve on the left side. Pull the sleeve lining over the sleeve of the dress.

2. Turn the seam allowance of the lining at the sleeve cap and pin the sleeve lining to the garment at the armhole seam line (see *Figure 154C*). Match the sleeve cap at the shoulder seam and other notches.

FIGURE 154

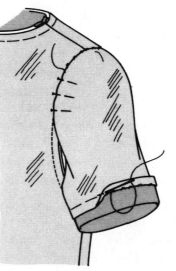

C

3. Slip-stitch the sleeve lining to the bodice lining, using very small stitches. Attach the lining to the other sleeve.

4. Put the dress on your hanger or dress form right side out.

5. If your sleeve will have a facing to finish the end, pin the lining to the garment at the end of the sleeve. Do not pull the lining. With a long sleeve, push the lining up a bit to allow wearing ease. Baste the lining to the garment at the end of the sleeve.

6. If your sleeve is finished with a hem, pin the lining to the sleeve about 2 inches from the end of the sleeve. Do not turn the lining under. Allow the lining to extend below the finished edge of the sleeve. Mark the lining so that it extends ½ inch below the finished edge of the sleeve and trim the lining to the ½ inch mark. Mark the other sleeve the same way.

7. Remove the garment from the hanger or dress form and remove the pins.

8. Turn the lining under 1 inch and press. (The lining will be ½ inch shorter than the sleeve.) Baste the lining to the sleeve 1 inch from the end of the sleeve.

9. Inside-stitch the lining to the hem of the sleeve as you see in *Figure 154C*.

FINISHING TOUCHES

Wrist Loop

A loop of ribbon attached to the underside of the train will enable you to hold up the train while walking into the church and at the reception (see *Figure 155*). You will need a piece of white grosgrain ribbon, ½ inch wide and 13 inches long. Fold the ribbon in half, crosswise, and stitch the ends together. Pin the loop at the center back seam so that the bottom of the loop is ½ inch above the lower edge of the dress, as shown. Securely hand-stitch the upper edge of the ribbon loop to the seam allowance. Slip the loop over your wrist to carry your train.

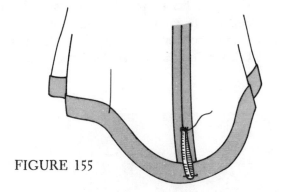

FIGURE 155

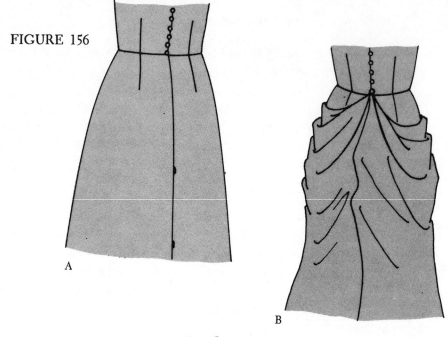

FIGURE 156

A

B

Bustling

For some dresses, bustling is another way to hold up the train. The dress must have buttons down the back, and an extended train rather than a panel train. One or more thread loops are made at the center back seam (*Figure 156A*). To bustle the train, these loops are buttoned onto one of the back buttons at the waistline (*Figure 156B*). You will have to experiment with your finished dress to see where to place the loops so the dress will bustle attractively. The loops should be flat against the seam to be as inconspicuous as possible.

Lingerie Strap Guards

Strap guards are attached at the inside shoulder seams of the dress to anchor bra and slip straps. This prevents straps from showing at the neckline of a scoop neck dress or at the shoulder of a sleeveless dress. They can be made from thread chain, as you see in *Figure 157*, or seam binding. Try on your dress with the bra that you will be wearing and mark where the bra straps fall on the shoulder seam. Use about 1½ inches of chain or seam binding. Anchor the seam binding or the thread chain to the shoulder seam toward the armhole of the dress. Attach the snaps toward the neckline with the ball snap on the free end and the socket snap on the garment.

FIGURE 157

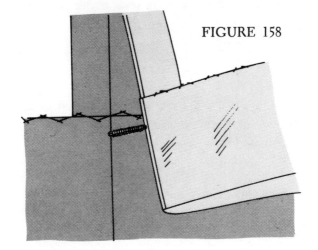

FIGURE 158

French Tacks

Figure 158. These tacks are used to anchor a lining loosely to the dress. They are made in the same way as thread loops and are usually about 1 to 1½ inches long. The tacks are stitched joining the seam allowance of the lining to the seam allowance of the dress at the side seams and other vertical seams such as center back and princess seams. Follow the directions for making thread loops (see *Figure 145*), taking the foundation stitches between the lining and the dress, as shown.

Inside Waistline Stay

A waistline stay is used when the fit and appearance of the dress would be improved by anchoring the waistline. Styles that would benefit from a waistline stay include those with fitted princess seams and those made of stretchy fabrics. If a dress has a bodice of lightweight fabric and a skirt of heavy fabric, a stay would be used to prevent the weight of the skirt from pulling on the bodice (see *Figure 159*). A waistline stay is made of grosgrain ribbon about ½ or ¾ inch wide. Cut the grosgrain to the same measurement as the waistline of the dress plus 2 inches for finishing the ends. On a princess dress, hand-stitch the ribbon to the seam allowance of the princess seams. On other styles, hand-stitch ribbon to the seam allowance and darts. Sew two hooks and eyes at the ends of the ribbon to fasten the stay. Do not attach ribbon to the seam allowance at the zipper.

FIGURE 159

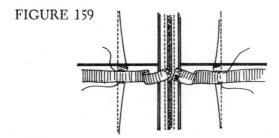

Inside Peplum Ruffle

Figure 160. This is a ruffle attached inside the waistline of a gathered skirt to make the skirt stand out. You can use lace, tulle, or a crisp fabric such as organdy or organza. The finished width of the ruffle should be 2 to 3 inches. To make a lace ruffle, follow the directions on page 144. To make a bias organdy or net ruffle, follow the directions on page 171. Pin and stitch the ruffle to the waistline seam allowance. Turn back the ends of the ruffle and slip-stitch the ends to the center back seam allowance. After you attach the ruffle, stitch seam binding to the waistline seam allowance for a neat finish.

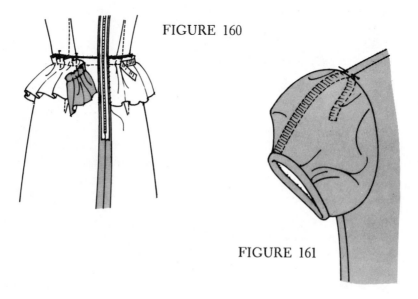

FIGURE 160

FIGURE 161

Puffed Sleeve Stay

Figure 161. A strip of ribbon is used to keep a puffed sleeve puffed. (It should not be used on sheer fabrics.) You will need two pieces of grosgrain or other ribbon, ½ inch wide, in a color to match your dress. When you attach your cuff or other finish to the bottom of the sleeve, also attach one end of the ribbon in the cuff at the center of the sleeve. After your sleeves are set in, try on the dress. Reach through the neckline and pull up the ribbons at the shoulders until your sleeves puff up the amount that you want. Pin each ribbon to the sleeve seam allowance at the shoulder. Take off the dress and stitch the ribbon stays at the shoulders. Cut off excess ribbon. Be sure that the stays of both sleeves are the same length.

9

Bridal Headwear

When it comes to selecting headwear, you have a wide choice of types and styles. There are hats of various shapes and sizes that are used with and without veils. Headpieces range from elaborate crowns to simple bands. Veils can be shoulder length to train length, long and sleek or short and fluffy. There are mantillas, hoods, and even wreaths of real flowers.

Things to consider in choosing your headwear are the style of your gown and the formality of the wedding, as well as your size, facial features, and hair style. Headwear should be in proportion, not so elaborate as to overwhelm a tiny bride or so dainty as to look lost on a tall or large girl. The shape of the hat or headpiece should be flattering. Add height to a round face with a crown, tiara, or hat with a high crown. Add width to a thin face with a brimmed hat, or a headpiece with flowers all around, not piled on top. When you try on a hat or headpiece, it is important to wear your hair the same way you will at your wedding.

For a very formal wedding, an elaborate headpiece trimmed with lace, pearls, and beads to match the gown is worn with a chapel- or cathedral-length veil or a very full fingertip veil. The veil usually includes a face covering called a blusher. A long mantilla could also be worn. For a formal wedding, you can wear a long, fingertip, or bouffant elbow-length veil with a simple or elaborate headpiece. A blusher is optional. A beautifully trimmed hat with a veil attached could also be worn. Another possibility is a long or fingertip mantilla. For a semiformal wedding, the veil is usually elbow- or shoulder-length, with a simpler headpiece. A hat draped in tulle or chiffon, or a picture hat trimmed with lace appliqués or flowers can be worn. A shorter mantilla is another option. More unusual would be a hood, made of lace for a spring wedding or of gown fabric trimmed with fur or feathers for a winter wedding. At an informal wedding, a simple cap or band trimmed in lace or flowers is worn with a shoulder-length veil or a pouf of tulle or maline. A more elaborate cap or band can be worn without a veil. You might wear a picture hat trimmed with ribbons, flowers, or a small veil. For a semiformal or informal wedding, some other possibilities are a kerchief of lace or sheer fabric to match the dress, a wreath of real or fabric flowers, or a few real flowers pinned in the hair.

Bridesmaids

The suggestions given above for an informal wedding would also be appropriate headwear for bridesmaids for more formal weddings. Stores that sell picture hats will sometimes have them dyed to match the color of the dress. A bow or hat can be made of dress fabric and trimmed with net in a color to match the dress.

Flower Girl

The flower girl can wear any of the headwear styles appropriate for bridesmaids except a sophisticated hat. Her hat or headpiece should be scaled down to child size. A bonnet made of fabric to match the dress and trimmed in lace and ribbon can be charming on a little girl. For hats and bonnets, look in the children's wear and the costume sections of the pattern catalogues.

MILLINERY SUPPLIES AND FABRICS

You can either make the headwear from scratch or buy components and assemble and trim them in your own way. Plain hats and headpieces, as well as pregathered veils, can be purchased. Hats, headpieces, veils, and mantillas are decorated with the same trimmings used on gowns. Most popular are lace, beads and pearls, flowers, and ribbons.

A wig stand is helpful when you are trimming or decorating your hat or headpiece. White glue such as Sobo or Elmer's is sometimes used to apply trimming. Small combs are stitched to the inside of the headpiece, hat, or mantilla to hold it in place. These can be purchased in a five-and-dime store.

If you have trouble finding what you need, there are a number of sources for millinery supplies by mail (see the Shopping Guide).

Millinery Fabrics

Millinery fabrics are used to make veils and mantillas and to drape hats and decorate bridesmaids' headpieces. Most are of net construction.

ILLUSION is a very fine, delicate net. The best illusion is silk and is by far the prettiest fabric for bridal veils. It has a soft, gossamer quality, yet has body and drapes beautifully. Nylon illusion is stiffer and does not drape nearly as well. Illusion is sold in white and ivory in widths of 72, 108, and sometimes 144 inches.

TULLE is not as fine as illusion. The holes are larger and the thread is usually a little heavier. It comes in 54-inch width.

NET is more open than tulle and is usually the least expensive. English net, a fine-quality cotton net, is used as a gown fabric and to make mantillas. Net is usually 72 inches wide. You can use very inexpensive nylon net to make a test model veil.

MALINE is used to trim hats and bridesmaids' headwear. It comes in narrow, 27-inch width in a great many colors. It has diamond-shaped holes that may vary in size from tiny to large.

CHIFFON is used in bridal headwear to drape and wrap hats.

BUCKRAM is an extremely stiff interfacing used in making hats and headpieces.

HORSEHAIR is actually a stiff nylon mesh used for hats and headpieces.

Silk illusion and cotton tulle or net can be dyed to match bridesmaids' gowns, but nylon does not take dye well.

HEADPIECES

A headpiece is a cap, band, crown, or tiara that the veil is attached to (see *Figure* 162). Crowns and tiaras are made of pearls or a combination of various beads and are considered quite formal. Some are also made of lace appliqués held into a crown shape by wire. They are usually purchased ready-made. To attach the veil to a crown, see veils, below.

Where bridal fabrics are sold plain buckram caps or bands can be purchased ready to decorate. Caps are larger and cover more of the head than bands. For a narrow band, you can buy a plastic headband at a five-and-dime store and "slip-cover" it with dress or lining fabric before trimming it. To do this, measure the length and width of the band and add 1¼ inches to each measurement for seam allowance. Cut two fabric strips of that measurement. Stitch and turn the strips, leaving an opening at one end. Insert the band and slip-stitch the end. You can also glue ribbon to the band. Patterns for bridal veils sometimes include a pattern

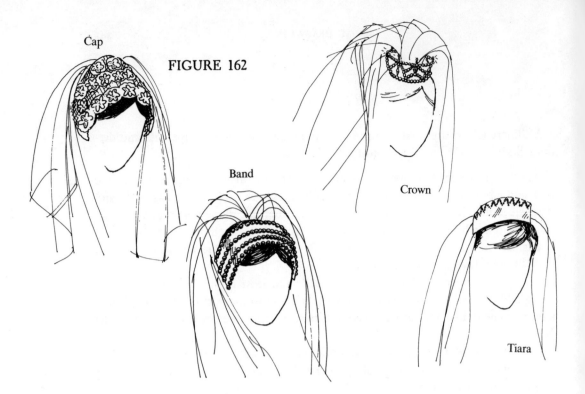

Cap

FIGURE 162

Band

Crown

Tiara

for a band or cap that you can make. They can also be purchased already trimmed with lace, flowers, or whatever, so that all you have to do is attach the veil.

Trimming the Headpiece

Usually the headpiece is trimmed first and then the veil is attached. However, if the trimming used on the headpiece will extend onto the veil, you will have to attach the veil first, then trim the headpiece. Setting the headpiece on a wig stand while you apply the trimming makes the job easier. Most often the same trimming is used on the gown and headpiece. It should be applied very closely, in overlapping layers, if necessary, to be sure that the foundation is completely covered. Lace appliqués should be small and simple. If your dress has large appliqués with big leaves and long stems, cut the appliqués into small parts, as you see in *Plate 18*, so that only the main flower motifs are used for the headpiece.

Venise daisy chain trim can be cut into individual small appliqués and sewn very close together, overlapping the petals. Chantilly or re-embroidered lace motifs can be cut and applied the same way as Venise. Lace motifs are best attached by hand, using a whip stitch (see *Figure 153*). Some Venise trims can be applied with white glue. Flower appliqués may be stitched in the centers only, so the free petals give a three-dimensional effect. In addition to appliqués, you can embellish the headpiece with pearls or beads. See "Jewel Trims" in Chapter 7. If sewing is difficult, the beads or pearls can be glued. Beads are usually applied more heavily to the headpiece than to the dress.

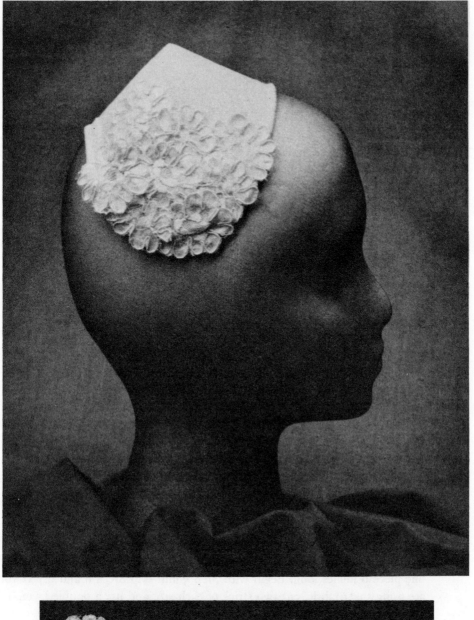

PLATE 18
Buckram Cap Foundation with Clipped Lace Appliqués

The headpiece can be trimmed with lace bands, flat or gathered, which can also be used to trim the edge of the veil. If appliqués are used on the headpiece, you might scatter a few on the veil, too. The band or cap can also be trimmed with rows of plain or embroidered ribbon to match the gown. Fabric flowers are another possibility. A strip of flowers can be applied to a headband. For a larger cap, remove the flowers from the strip or bunch and sew each one individually, placing the flowers very close together. A cap can be made of, or covered with, fabric to match the dress and embellished with scattered appliqués, pearls, beaded embroidery, ribbon bows, or a few fabric flowers. A strip of fur or feathers can be attached to a headband with hand stitches. These trimmings are covered in Chapter 7. For more information on lace trimmings, refer to Chapter 6.

To hold the cap or band securely on your head, stitch a small comb on each side, as you see in *Figure 163*.

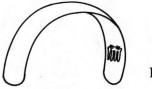

FIGURE 163

Tailored Bow

Figure 164A. A tailored bow made of ribbon, embroidered ribbon, or dress fabric makes a pretty headpiece for an informal bride or for bridesmaids. To make a tailored bow, first slip-cover a plastic headband, as explained above.

1. Cut one strip of fabric 28 inches long by 8 inches wide, and one square of fabric 6 inches by 6 inches. (For ribbon, cut one piece 28 inches long and one piece 6 inches long. Begin with Step 5 and skip Steps 8 and 9.) If you are using sheer fabric, cut two strips of each size and use a double layer. To give body to soft fabric, iron lightweight fusible interfacing to the wrong side.

2. Fold the strip in half, lengthwise, wrong side out. Stitch on the long side (*Figure 164B*). Press the seam open and turn right side out.

3. Place the strip on the ironing board so the seam runs along the center, and press, as you see in *Figure 164C*.

4. Tuck in the raw edge at each end of the strip and slip-stitch.

5. Fold the strip in half crosswise. Measure 5½ inches from the finished ends and stitch across (see *Figure 164D*).

6. Crease along the fold lightly with your fingernail. Bring the crease to meet the stitching line, forming a bow (*Figure 164E*).

FIGURE 164

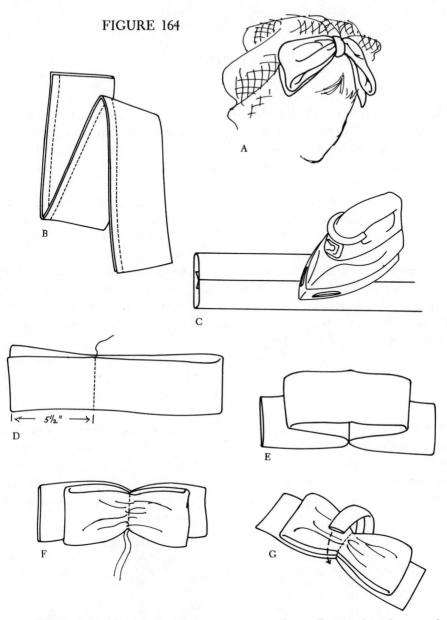

A

B

C

D |← 5½" →|

E

F

G

7. Stitch along the crease, using a long stitch. Pull the thread to gather slightly, as shown in *Figure 164F*.

8. Fold the square of fabric in half, wrong side out, and stitch on the long side.

9. Turn the small strip right side out and press.

10. Wrap the small strip around the center of the bow and hand-stitch on the wrong side (*Figure 164G*).

11. Hand-stitch the bow to the headband.

12. Stitch combs to the inside of the headband.

VEILS

The most popular lengths for veils are cathedral, chapel, fingertip, elbow, and shoulder. Generally, the longer the veil, the more formal it is considered. More tiers and fullness also add to the formality of the veil. Many veils consist of several tiers, often of varying lengths. For example, a chapel-length veil may have a second tier of fingertip length. With a long veil, usually only one tier is floor-length. In addition, many veils have a separate shoulder- or elbow-length face covering called a blusher. The blusher is worn over the face before and during the ceremony. When it comes time for the groom to kiss the bride, the maid of honor helps the bride throw back the blusher, revealing the headpiece.

A cathedral veil is about four yards long, measured along the center back of the veil. A chapel veil measures about three yards, and a fingertip veil is 45 inches long. An elbow-length veil measures 30 inches, and shoulder-length is 18 inches. These measurements are guidelines for standard veils, but there is no reason why you can't change length or width.

Designing Your Veil

The options of length, shape, number of tiers, and kind of trimmings give you many possibilities in designing your veil. Give some thought to how the veil and headpiece will look together, as well as with the dress. Of the three, at least one should remain fairly simple for the best design effect. If you have an elaborate headpiece and gown, leave the veil untrimmed or use only a small amount of trim.

FIGURE 165

When the gown is simple, you could use an elaborately trimmed veil and head-piece. Veil trimming, if any, matches the headpiece or the gown. Usually the blusher is left plain. The edge of the veil can be finished with a hand-rolled hem or lace trim, such as an edge, galloon, flower chain, or scalloped border, that has been used on the gown. The lace can be applied to only one or to all the layers. Lace appliqués to match the gown or the headpiece are another trimming idea. You could use tiny flowers scattered about the veil or a few large appliqués placed at the sides or the bottom of the veil. For applying lace edge trimmings or borders, follow the directions in Chapter 6. If you use pearls or beads on the gown or head-piece, you can scatter individual pearls about the veil.

Trimming is usually applied before the veil is gathered. However, if you are using trimming that covers the headpiece and extends onto the veil, then you must gather the veil and attach it to the headpiece before applying the trim. Each veil shown in *Figure 165* is stitched to a band; then the lace is stitched along the edge of the veil and over the band in one continuous piece. The lace must be stitched to the band by hand.

Separate patterns are available for veils and are also sometimes included with the gown pattern. The pattern envelopes usually suggest tulle for making a veil, but bridal illusion is a much better choice. It is not hard to make a veil without a pattern, since it does not have to fit the body the way a dress does. Instructions are given below.

The entire width of the illusion is gathered into a veil. There should not be any seams. A 72-inch width will make a veil of average fullness, 108-inch will make a full veil, and 144-inch will make an extremely full bouffant veil. If your pattern is designed for 72-inch-width illusion and you would like to use 108-inch or more for a fuller veil, that is no problem (see *Figure 166*). Fold the illusion in half length-wise, and place the pattern edge on the fabric edge. Pin the pattern to the illusion. The fold line of the pattern will be 18 inches or more from the fold of the fabric. Mark the rest of the outline of the veil, using pencil, to continue the line of the pattern to the fold of the fabric, as shown.

FIGURE 166

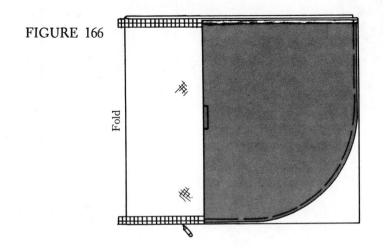

FIGURE 167

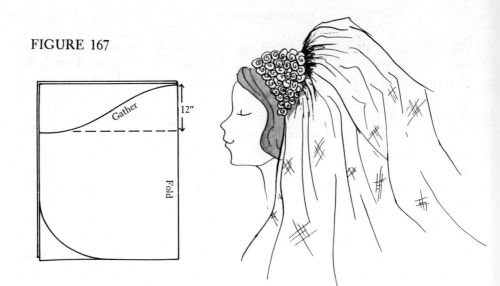

Veil Patterns

PUFFED CROWN VEIL This veil will puff up at the top of the head, as you see in *Figure 167*. It should be attached to either a band or a tiara headpiece, not a cap. The drawing gives the shape of the pattern. You can adapt the length and width for the look you want. Notice that the top of the pattern curves upward toward the center back fold on the gathering line. It is this shape that makes the puffiness at the top of the veil. For a highly puffed veil, raise the line 12 inches. For a medium amount of puff, raise the line about 6 inches.

CASCADE VEIL (*Figure 168*). This veil can be attached to any headpiece. Because the gathering line is straight rather than curved, the veil does not puff much on top and will fall in a smoother line.

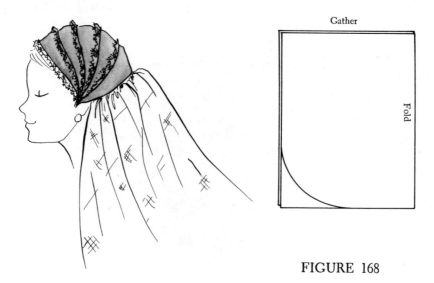

FIGURE 168

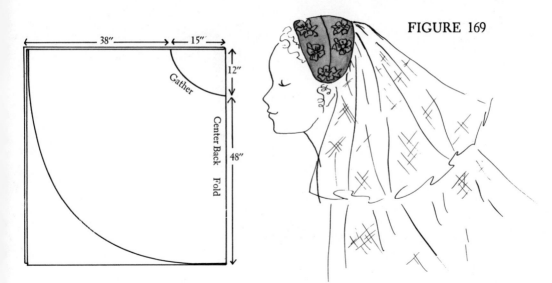

FIGURE 169

CIRCULAR FLARED VEIL (*Figure* 169). This veil has a slight amount of gathers and flares out toward the bottom. It is more modern-looking and is suitable for sleeker-style knit gowns. The diagram shows a fingertip length. It could be shorter or longer. Notice that the back is longer than the sides.

CIRCULAR VEIL (*Figure* 170). This veil is made from a circle and has no gathers at all. The circle is folded in half and the folded edge is attached to a narrow band or small headpiece. For fingertip length, use 2 yards of 72-inch illusion. Fold the illusion in half lengthwise. Fold again into quarters, and pin. Tie a piece of string to a pencil and mark the string 36 inches from the pencil. Using a thumb tack, attach the end of the string with the 36-inch mark at the corner of the illusion, as shown. Holding the pencil so the string is taut, mark a quarter circle on the illusion. The taut string will act like a compass and you will be able to make a perfectly shaped circle. Cut the illusion along the line.

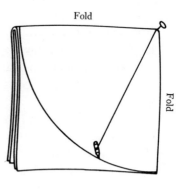

FIGURE 170

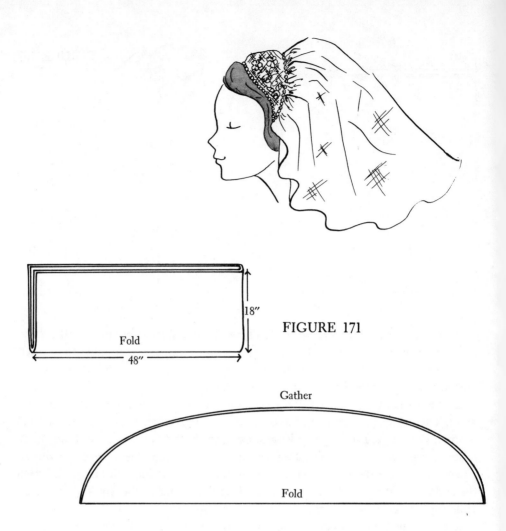

FIGURE 171

POUF VEIL (*Figure 171*). This is a very pretty short veil. It can be made shoulder-length for informal or semiformal weddings. It can also be worn by maids in shoulder length for a very formal wedding or shorter for a less formal wedding. Notice that the bottom edge of the veil is on the fold and the gathers are made on the curve. Fold the illusion in half lengthwise, and then fold it in half again crosswise, and pin carefully. Mark the shape as shown. After the veil is gathered, do not iron a crease at the edge but pull the layers apart to separate them and make the veil puff up.

BLUSHER (*Figure 172*). A face-covering blusher can be added to most veils unless the headpiece is very large or elaborate. The drawing shows the shape to cut the blusher. The width of blusher varies from 36 inches to 54 inches, depending on how full your veil is. The length of the blusher ranges from 18 to 30 inches. It can be shorter than the length of your veil but should not be longer. Notice that the gathering line curves upward somewhat toward the fold. This amount can vary from 4 to 12 inches. Four inches will give just a slight puff at the crown for the blusher to cover a low headpiece. Twelve inches will give quite a high puff, needed to go over a crown or tiara.

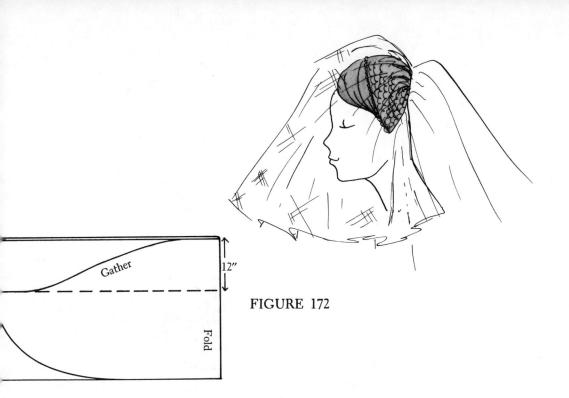

Gather

12"

Fold

FIGURE 172

Sewing the Veil

Because illusion is a net construction, it has no grain and does not need to be straightened. The edges will not fray and require no finish. Since the cut edge is the finished edge of the veil, it must be cut smoothly and carefully with sharp scissors so there will be no jagged edges. Cover your work table with felt or a sheet to keep the fabric from slipping. Fold and pin the illusion carefully to prevent shifting.

For gathering, use silk or polyester thread and about 8 to 10 stitches to the inch. If you use a very large stitch, the illusion will not gather nicely. To prevent the thread from tangling, place strips of tissue paper under the illusion as you sew. Rip the tissue paper away when you finish stitching. If you have several layers, gather each one individually. For best results, use two rows of gathering stitches. When you have a long distance to gather, stop every yard or yard and a half, pull the fabric out of the machine, and cut the thread. Then begin stitching again ½ inch back from where you stopped. By doing this, you will divide the gathers into sections that are much easier to handle and there is less chance of the gathering thread breaking. Once the veil is gathered to fit the headpiece, tie the ends securely. Run a row of zigzag or straight stitch along the seam allowance ⅜ inch from the gathering stitch and trim close to the zigzag stitching line to flatten out the bulk in the seam allowance. If the raw edge of the gathers will show on the inside of the headpiece, use a bound edge finish (see *Figure* 117) to neaten it. Baste the veil to the headpiece and try it on. Hand-stitch the veil to the headpiece. You can also make the veil so that it snaps onto the headpiece. That way the veil can be removed from the headpiece for the reception.

FIGURE 173

Pressing

Use a very low heat and a pressing cloth or tissue paper over the illusion. Test iron temperature on a scrap first. For the final pressing to refresh and crisp the veil, press between wax paper as follows. Place a sheet of tissue paper on the ironing board, then a sheet of wax paper over the tissue. Place the veil on the wax paper, cover with another sheet each of wax paper and tissue, and press with a low heat. You must use the tissue paper to protect the iron and the ironing board from the wax paper.

MANTILLAS

A mantilla is a flat circular veil made entirely of lace or of lace-trimmed net or illusion. It has no gathers or headpiece (see *Figure 173*). A 72-inch circle will be train-length, a 54-inch circle about knee-length, and a 36-inch circle slightly longer than waist-length. Smaller than 36 inches is apt to look too skimpy. Cut your circle following the directions given above for a circular veil (*Figure 170*). Remember that since the fabric is cut on the fold, the string should be only one half the length of the finished veil. You can cut the circle first from inexpensive nylon net to check size.

To make a lace mantilla, use sheer Chantilly or Alençon. Cut the circle from lace, and finish the edge with a hand-rolled hem (see *Figure 130*) or a matching lace trim. Select a lace with an allover tossed design, not one that is arranged in bands or strips. Follow the directions given in Chapter 6 for cutting the lace and applying the lace border. The other possibility, which is more economical than using solid lace, is to use English net or silk illusion trimmed with lace. Do not use nylon net or illusion because it is too stiff and does not drape well. You can use lace trim around the edge with scattered lace appliqués to match your gown. The edge could also be finished with a hand-rolled hem (*Figure 130*) or a narrow satin piping. Follow the directions in Chapter 6 for applying lace appliqués and trims.

The mantilla is held in place by a comb, band, or small cap. A comb is hand-sewn to the top of the mantilla 3 or 4 inches from the edge (see *Figure 174A*). The mantilla covers the cap or band and extends beyond it by several inches (see *Figure 174B*). To position the mantilla, try on the cap or band and drape the mantilla over it until it falls nicely. Be sure you have the center of the mantilla placed at the center of the cap. Pin the mantilla to the cap, then attach it with small hand stitches. Sew combs at each side of the inside of the cap or band, as you see in *Figure 174C*.

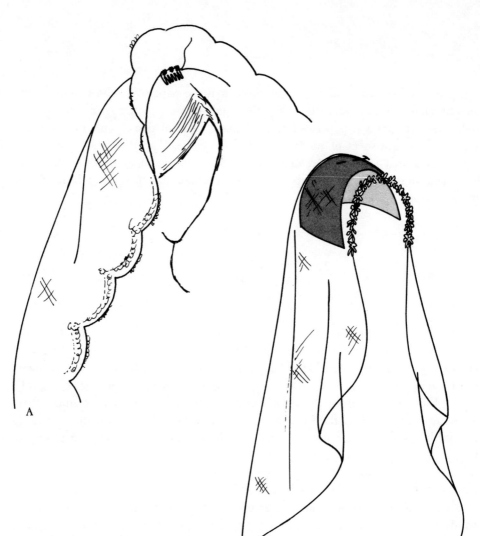

FIGURE 174

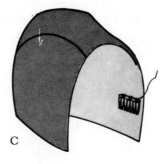

HATS

Hats are popular headwear for both the bride and the bridesmaids. Often the same hat style is worn by both, trimmed elaborately for the bride and more simply for the maids. There are many types of hats available—wide-brimmed picture or garden party hats, smaller-brimmed hats with a flat or rolled brim, or brimless hats, such as a pillbox or toque. Bridal hats that are custom made in bridal salons are very expensive. The salon must order the trimmings to match the gown from the gown manufacturer and then have the hat made in the store. In making the hat, the salon would use a plain, basic hat body and add the trimmings. Since you can buy the same hat body at a low cost and already have matching trim from making your gown, you can create your own hat for a tiny fraction of the cost of one purchased in a bridal salon. Decorating a hat is surprisingly easy, and fun to do. It is so much freer than regular sewing because there is no fitting and there is really no right or wrong. It is almost impossible to make a mistake, because if your trim is pretty, almost anything that you do with it will look attractive.

In addition to purchasing a basic hat to decorate, you can also make the hat yourself. Hat patterns are available in the accessories section of the pattern catalogues. These hats are often shown in sporty materials, but try to visualize the style made up in your fabric. For a softer look you might try using a fusible interfacing instead of buckram. A hat can be made of organdy, lace, or the same fabric as the bride's dress, if it's appropriate. The edge of the hat can be trimmed in a scalloped lace. For bridesmaids, the hat can be made of fabric to match the dress. You can decorate and trim the hat as you would a purchased hat.

HATS WITH VEILS A veil can be attached to a hat as it would be to a headpiece. The cascade or flared gathered veil would be good choices to use with a hat. The veil can be stitched under the brim, or over the brim attached to a band.

The circular drape veil is explained below. You can also attach a blusher to the front band of the hat.

Draping

Draping refers to swirling and wrapping a lightweight fabric or net around a hat to give a soft, romantic effect. This is much easier than you might think and is a good way to create your own style. A drape can be used in addition to or instead of a veil. Hats with a veil usually have small drapes. Most hat types, either with or without a brim, are suitable for draping. Use a light gossamer illusion, tulle, net, or maline, point d'esprit, a sheer lace, chiffon, or organza. The drape can be held in place with trimming such as flowers, ribbon, or appliqués. You will need a wig stand to park the hat while you work on it. If you don't have a wig stand, you can improvise by using a small lamp and padding around the shade with tissue paper. (Don't turn the lamp on while you work.) Below are some ways of draping a hat. The measurements given are only meant as a guide—you can change them as you wish. If you experiment, you can also invent your own ways of draping a hat.

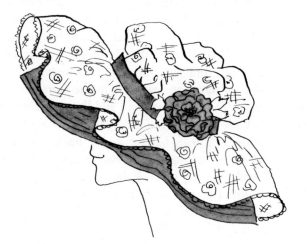

FIGURE 175

CIRCULAR DRAPE (*Figure* 175). This one is really easy and quick. Cut two circles about 36 inches in diameter of tulle or illusion, or one circle of sheer lace. Finish the edge of the lace with a narrow hem or lace trim. Place the circle on top of the hat so that the center of the circle is in the center of the hat. Pin the fabric to the crown of the hat. Wrap a band of ribbon or trim around the crown of the hat to hold the drape in place. Pin the band to itself but not through to the drape fabric. Unpin the fabric and gently pull it up from under the band so it puffs and drapes nicely over the crown, as you see in the drawing. Arrange the fabric around the brim so it forms an attractive ruffle. Baste the trim band to the hat to hold the drape. Hand-stitch the band through the drape, attaching it to the hat. You can add a bow or streamers to match the band, flowers, or other trimming.

DRAPE WITH BOW AND STREAMERS The crown is wrapped separately and then the bow with streamers is added. Use 27-inch-wide maline or 108-inch illusion. Cut a square of net 27 by 27 inches. Wrap the net around the crown, crushing it into soft folds (see *Figure* 176A). Tuck in the raw edges and hand-stitch to the hat at the center back. To make the bow, cut a piece of net 27 inches wide by at least 108 inches long. Cut a second piece 12 inches square. Crush and fold the illusion,

FIGURE 176

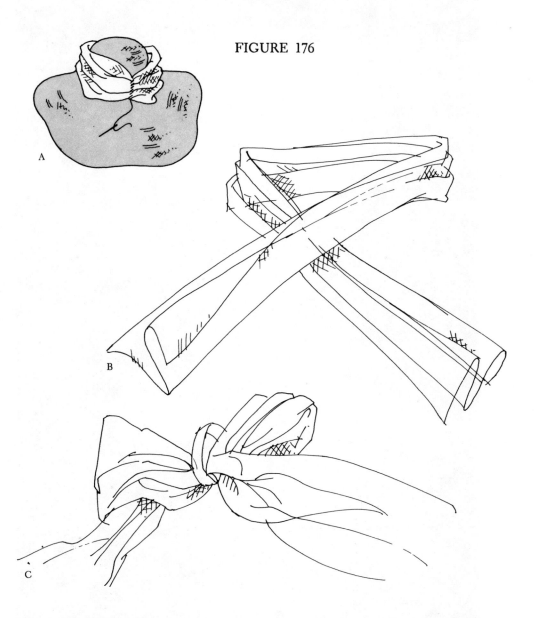

overlapping into a bow shape, as shown in *Figure 176B*. Pin and baste. Compress the small square into a strip and wrap the strip around the middle of the illusion, forming a bow (*Figure 176C*). Pin securely. Hand-stitch through all layers and then hand-stitch the bow to the center back of the hat. You can also make this drape using chiffon. In that case, the edges of the streamers must be finished with a narrow hem. A maline or illusion drape will look fluffy and crisp; a chiffon drape will look soft and floaty. *Plate 19* shows a horsehair picture hat with a maline bow and streamers. Maline is also draped around the brim, where it is held in place with several Venise appliqués.

GATHERED DRAPE (*Figure* 177A). A ruffle of net, illusion, or organza is used for this drape. It can be made of one or several layers, with full or minimal gathers. Measure the width of the hat brim and multiply the width by 3. Cut a strip of net or fabric measuring three times the brim width by a minimum of about 3 yards for each tier. Tiers can be made by wrapping one long strip around the brim several times. Woven fabric is best cut on the bias. Fold the strip in half lengthwise, and gather along the cut edges. See "Sewing the Veil," above, for gathering directions for net. Pin the ruffle to the hat crown and tighten or loosen the gathers to achieve the look you want. Baste the ruffle to the crown along the stitching line. Turn under the raw edge at the end of the ruffle and slip-stitch to the adjoining layer (*Figure* 177B). Hand-stitch the ruffle to the crown of the hat. Cover the raw edge of the ruffle with a band of ribbon or other trimming (*Figure* 177C). You can add matching bow or flowers to the band. Pull the layers apart for a fluffy look.

FIGURE 177

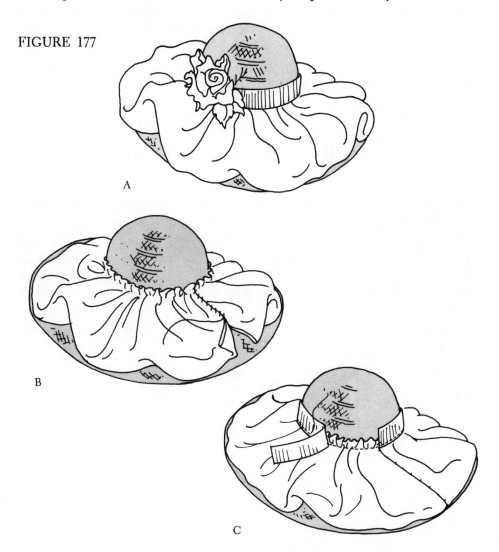

A

B

C

PLATE 19
Picture Hat with Maline Drape

Trimming the Hat

In addition to draping your hat, ribbons and other band trims, flowers, lace appliqués, pearls, and beads can be used for decoration. Many hats use a combination of different trimmings. Lace appliqués stitched to an organdy or sheer horsehair hat look very pretty. Chantilly or Alençon appliqués can be applied very close together, overlapping each other so that the hat looks as if it's made entirely of lace. You can place appliqués on the crown or the brim only, or scatter individual appliqués or organdy flowers here and there around the hat. The centers of the flowers could be embellished with pearls or beads. Flower appliqués can be stitched at the centers only so the petals curl up for a three-dimensional effect. You can use ruffles of lace around the crown or brim. Streamers of maline or ribbon can be attached above the ears to tie softly under the chin. A galloon band can be stitched around the crown of the hat, or small lace appliqués can be stitched to a band of ribbon. A group of fabric flowers can be attached at one side of the crown or even under the brim.

STORING YOUR HEADWEAR

Headwear can be a problem to store because it gets crushed easily. If at all possible, keep a hat or veil on a head form. Sometimes the veil can be pinned to a hanger. Avoid covering with a plastic bag because that attracts dirt. Just before the wedding, have your veil ironed with wax paper (see above, under "Pressing"). If you have to store your hat or veil flat, use a drawer or box and stuff it, as well as the hat or veil, with tissue paper to fill out the shape.

10

Sewing the Attendants' Outfits
and Bridal Accessories

By selecting your own patterns, fabrics, colors, and trimmings, you can co-ordinate a beautifully styled wedding. Sewing for the wedding party will also save a substantial amount of money, since the cost of ready-made bridesmaids' and flower girl's dresses can be quite high. Even those who purchase their wedding gown often have the outfits for the rest of the wedding party sewn.

The type of wedding and the formality of the bride's outfit determine the styles appropriate for the groom and attendants. See Chapter 2 for an explanation of different types of weddings and suggestions for wedding themes. The styles and colors of the attendants' outfits should form a beautiful background for the bride, never overwhelm her. The final decision as to what the attendants wear is up to the bride. Each attendant is responsible for his or her own outfit (or the parents, in the case of flower girl and page boy), so the bride should discuss cost with them beforehand. If each attendant will be sewing her own outfit, be sure that they can all sew well enough to do a nice job.

BRIDESMAIDS

Generally, each bridesmaid wears the same style dress although the dresses may differ in color. For the prettiest effect, the design of the bridesmaids' dresses should relate to the bride's gown by design feature, silhouette, trim, or mood. Most patterns for bridal gowns also show variations of the dress made for bridesmaids. Using the same or a similar pattern can be an effective way to relate the styles. If your gown has a design feature that you especially like, you can switch pattern pieces (explained in Chapter 3) so that the neckline shape or sleeve style are used on the maids' dresses as well as the bride's. Trimming used on the maids' dresses could be a simpler or smaller-scale version of the trim used on the bride's gown. With a bride's dress trimmed in lace and pearls, the maids' dresses might have a narrow band of pearl trim at the neckline, sleeves, or waist. If the bride's gown has silk flowers as trim, the maids' dresses might have one flower attached at the waist with a sash. With a gown made of allover lace, a narrow lace of the same type or a few lace appliqués on the bodice or sleeves could be used to trim the maids' dresses.

There is a wide range of styles suitable for bridesmaids. Usually, very bare dresses are not considered acceptable unless covered by some sort of shawl, capelet, or jacket during the ceremony. Lengths are floor-length for formal weddings, floor-length or current fashion-length for less formal weddings. Do give some thought to the back of the dresses, because this is what your guests will see during the ceremony. A soft sash with long streamers, gathers, a panel, or a row of pretty buttons instead of a zipper will add back interest. The test muslin that you made before making your final gown (explained in Chapter 4) would also be a good idea for maids' dresses, especially for ones with fitting problems. If the maids don't want to go to the trouble of making a muslin, you might suggest they make the dress first in an inexpensive fabric to try out the pattern before cutting the dress in good fabric. For suggestions for bridesmaids' headwear, see Chapter 9.

Maid of Honor

The maid of honor's outfit can be the same as the other bridesmaids' or vary slightly. The choice is up to the bride. In a small wedding, the maid of honor usually dresses the same as the bridesmaids. Her position in the processional and during the ceremony will distinguish her, even if she is wearing the same outfit. If you prefer to have her wear something different, the distinction should be subtle. The maid of honor can wear the same dress as the bridesmaids but in a different color or a different shade of the same color. She might also wear the same dress with a slight change in the fabric or trim. For instance, if the maids wear velvet dresses with narrow lace edge trim, the maid of honor could wear the same style dress with a velvet skirt and a lace bodice. The maid of honor could wear the same dress as the bridesmaids but with different headwear. Her headpiece could have a small veil attached, or her hat could have somewhat more elaborate or different color trim. She might also carry a larger bouquet, a basket of flowers, or different flowers from the rest of the maids.

Fabric Suggestions

Here are some fabric suggestions for bridesmaids. Most are also suitable for flower girls.

SPRING AND SUMMER WEDDINGS The most popular fabrics for this time of year are sheers, either plain or fancy. The soft sheers, chiffon and georgette, are more sophisticated and are usually available in a wide range of colors. A procession of maids looks beautiful walking down the aisle in dresses of chiffon because of the way the fabric drapes and floats. The crisp sheers, organdy, organza, and voile, are available in solid colors, flocked, printed, and embroidered. Since embroidered fabrics are expensive, you can use embroidery for parts of the dress and make the rest of matching plain fabric. The cotton classics, plain or embroidered, always look crisp and cool for a summer wedding. These include dimity, gingham, leno, eyelet, and piqué with its many variations, including ribbed, bird's-eye, or waffle.

White leno or eyelet over a colored backing looks very pretty because the color peeks through the openwork. Also consider linen in sherbet pastels, lightweight crepes such as crepe de chine, or floral patterns such as water colors, wallpaper prints, or delicate Victorians. Sheer fabric can be used over a flower print for a soft, muted look. Jerseys in delicate tints or bright colors are also worn for spring and summer.

FALL AND WINTER WEDDINGS Velvets and velveteens in almost any color are good choices for fall and winter. Richly colored velvets are often trimmed with white or ivory to match the bride's gown. Knits such as jersey, maracaine, and soft, fluffy sweater knits can be worn at this time of year. Light- or heavyweight crepes, as well as moiré and taffeta, are additional possibilities. Woven taffeta plaid is often combined with Cluny lace or eyelet. Chintz in bright or dark country prints looks attractive in fall or winter. Chiffon is also worn, usually in deeper tones rather than pastels.

Also read about trimmings in Chapter 7. Many of the ideas are suitable for bridesmaids' gowns.

FLOWER GIRL

A flower girl can be a charming addition to the wedding party. The girl is usually between three and a half and seven or eight years old; after that she becomes a junior bridesmaid. (Be sure that the little girl has enough poise to carry out her role. I've seen a number of weddings spoiled by young children who screamed for their mothers during the ceremony or refused to walk down the aisle.)

The flower girl's dress can be a scaled-down or simplified version of the brides-maids' dresses or a totally different style, depending on your preference and the ap-propriateness of the maids' attire. If the style or fabric of the maids' dresses is not too sophisticated and the color not too harsh for a child, then it can probably be adapted for the flower girl.

It is important to keep the flower girl's dress in proportion for the size and the age of the child. The best silhouette for little girls is a raised waistline with a gathered or flared skirt and puffed, shirt, butterfly, Juliette, or leg-of-mutton sleeves. The skirt can be long or short. If you can't find a pattern for the style you want, you can modify or combine parts of children's patterns, as with adult pat-terns, as explained in Chapter 3. If the bridesmaids' dresses have complicated de-tails, they should be omitted or simplified for the flower girl. Bust-line shirring or intricate bodice seaming would look silly on a little girl and should be changed to a plain or princess-seam bodice. One of the sleeves mentioned above can be substi-tuted for large elaborate sleeves on the bridesmaids' dresses. Where wide lace is used on the maids' dress, choose a similar, narrow lace for the flower girl's. Do the same for width and amount with ribbons, ruffles, appliqués, or other trims.

If the maids' style is not suitable for a flower girl (a red jersey dress trimmed in marabou would be dreadful on a four-year-old), you can make a different style just for her. Her dress could be made of white or a lighter shade of the maids' color, and trimmed with the color of the maids' dresses. For instance, the dress could be white or pastel organza, voile, taffeta, or velvet with a ribbon sash or smocking in the bridesmaids' color. White can be used for the bodice and sleeves and the maids' color used just for the skirt. The flower girl's dress could also be the same color as the maids' with a fluffy white lace or organdy pinafore over the deep color to soften it.

The flower girl usually carries her flowers in a basket. You might want to save some trimming from the dress for the florist to use in decorating her basket. On her head she could wear a ribbon bow with long streamers, or a bonnet or kerchief to match her dress. If the maids are wearing one of the smaller headpieces, a scaled-down version could be made for the flower girl.

PAGE BOY

The page boy is usually about three and a half to five or six years old. He either holds the bride's train as she walks down the aisle or carries the wedding ring (ac-tually a fake ring) on a pillow. Although there are tuxedos made for little boys, I think they are rather inappropriate for children of that age. Traditional children's wear such as an Eton suit or bobby suit looks far better on young boys. An Eton suit has short pants and a three-button jacket with no lapels. It is usually worn with a white round-collared shirt and no tie. For a winter wedding, the Eton suit could be made of velveteen in a color to match the bridemaids', flower girl's, or men's outfits, or of white flannel. At a summer wedding, the suit could be made of linen in a pastel to match the bridesmaids' or flower girl's dress. White linen or piqué can also be worn in summer. A bobby suit consists of short pants buttoned onto a blouse. The blouse is usually white and is often trimmed with tucks or rows of lace. The pants can be white or colored, and of the same fabrics mentioned for the Eton suit. Another variation of the bobby suit is made with knickers instead of short pants.

GROOM AND MEN ATTENDANTS

Men's formal wear is generally rented. However, if you have the time and inclination, making a part of your groom's outfit or something for each man in the wedding party would be a nice personal touch. Patterns are available for mens' formal wear, including dinner jacket and pants, as well as formal accessories: ascot, bow tie, cummerbund, and waistcoat (a waist-length vest). The groom and all men attendants do not dress exactly alike. The groom and best man can wear the same outfit, the groom being differentiated by his boutonniere, which is taken from the bride's bouquet. (The other men generally wear carnations.) The difference between the groom's outfit and those of the rest of the men is usually subtle—perhaps a different shirt or pattern to the waistcoat, or a different tie and cummerbund.

You might want to make a formal shirt for your groom, possibly trimmed with some of the same lace used on your gown. If appropriate, you could make his shirt of the same fabric as your dress, or make him a bow tie and matching cummerbund or waistcoat. Matching accessories could be made for the men if the maids' dresses are of a medium- to heavyweight fabric. Velveteen, taffeta, satin, brocade, and tapestry fabrics are suitable.

Fathers wear outfits similar to the men attendants'. A set of formal accessories that you made yourself would be a good thank-you gift for your father.

MOTHERS OF THE BRIDE AND GROOM

Mothers wear long dresses to formal weddings, long or daytime-length for less formal weddings. Dress and jacket combinations are popular. For a winter wedding, a dressy suit is another possibility. With the flurry of wedding preparations, don't let your dress be thrown together at the last minute. Try to set aside enough time so that you can make a really lovely outfit for yourself. If you are using very expensive fabric or a new, complicated pattern, a test muslin dress is a good investment. Follow the fitting directions given in Chapter 4.

Fabrics for the mothers of the bride and groom for fall and winter include velvet, velveteen, satin, moiré, jersey, satin-back crepe, crepe, brocade, and metallic or beaded fabrics. For spring and summer you might select chiffon or georgette (either printed or plain), jersey, crepe, satin-back crepe, silk, or linen. Consider a luxurious, sophisticated trimming such as marabou or ostrich feathers, beaded embroidery, silk flowers, or real fur.

BRIDAL ACCESSORIES

Slips and Petticoats

Most gowns that are not fully lined look better worn with a slip or petticoat. It can range from a simple taffeta A-line slip for a clingy knit dress to a multilayered gathered petticoat for a gown with a full skirt. When you are making a slip or petticoat, a dress or skirt pattern may work better than the usual lingerie pattern. Most lingerie patterns for petticoats are gathered onto elastic, and slips fit loosely. For wearing under a wedding gown, a slip or petticoat with a zipper will allow a closer fit. A gown with a gathered skirt would be worn with a petticoat made of one or two layers of net over taffeta. For a fuller petticoat, it is better to use a pattern with a hip yoke and the skirt gathered into the hipline seam so there will not be too much bulk at the waistline. The yoke and underlayer of the petticoat should be made of taffeta and the overlayers (as many as four or five) of net. Since net does not ravel, an edge finish is not necessary. For a pretty touch, the edge of the net petticoat could be finished with an inexpensive narrow lace or with a net ruffle.

Bridal Garter

The traditional bridal garter (see *Figure* 178A) provides the "something blue" for the bride to wear.

MATERIALS 15 inches of ½-inch elastic (for thinner or heavier than average leg, cut elastic 1 or more inches shorter or longer); 1½ yards of blue satin ribbon, size 5 (⅞ inch wide); ¼ yard of blue satin ribbon, size 1 (¼ inch wide); ¾ yard Val lace edge, 1¼ inches wide; ¼ yard Val edge, ½ inch wide.

1. Cut the wide ribbon in half so you have two pieces 27 inches long.

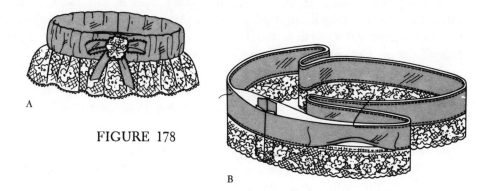

FIGURE 178

2. With one piece of the wide ribbon right side up, and the wide lace wrong side up, stitch the edge of the lace to the edge of the ribbon.

3. Seam the ends of each piece of wide ribbon so you have two ribbon rings.

4. Pin the ribbon rings together, right sides out. Topstitch the ribbon rings together along the upper and lower edges, leaving a 2-inch opening at one edge (see *Figure 178B*). Insert the elastic through the opening. Overlap the ends of the elastic and stitch together to join into a ring. Stitch the opening.

5. Gather the narrow lace into a ruffle and roll up the ruffle to form a rosette. Hand-stitch the rosette on the wrong side.

6. Make a bow of the narrow ribbon. Stitch the bow to the garter, and stitch the rosette in the center of the bow.

Ring Bearer's Pillow

Figure 179A. The best man carries the real ring, and a fake ring is attached to the ring bearer's pillow. The pillow can be square, round, oval, or heart-shaped, usually 10 to 12 inches across. You can make a pattern on tracing paper for the

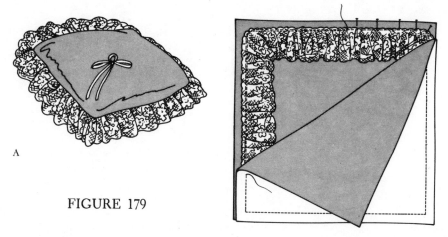

FIGURE 179

shape you prefer. For a heart shape, fold the tracing paper in half and draw free-hand. To make a circle pattern, trace around a plate. For a square pattern, use a ruler or L square. After you draw the shape, use a ruler to add ⅝ inch seam allowance all around. Cut out the heart pattern on the fold.

MATERIALS ⅜ yard of white satin, or fabric scraps from the bride's dress, if appropriate; 2 to 3 yards of lace edging about 2 inches wide; muslin for the pillow cover; polyester stuffing; fake wedding band. Optional trim: pearls, ribbons, and so on.

1. Using your pattern, cut two pieces each in muslin and satin.
2. Stitch and turn the muslin pillow, leaving an opening of about 5 inches. Stuff with polyester batting and stitch opening.
3. Gather the lace. Pin the lace ruffle wrong side up to the right side of one of the satin pieces. Have the ruffle facing inward, as shown in *Figure 179B*. Stitch the ruffle to the satin.
4. Pin the second layer of satin wrong side up (so the right sides of the satin are together). Turn pillow cover over and stitch the two layers together, following the stitching line of the ruffle. Leave an opening to insert the pillow.
5. Slip-stitch the opening after the pillow has been inserted.

The pillow can be decorated with rows of pearls, scattered pearls, ribbon streamers, or other trim. The fake ring is hand-tacked to the center of the pillow.

SHOPPING GUIDE

You can send to the firms listed below for catalogues to order things by mail.

Supreme Novelty Fabrics Company
325 West Jackson Boulevard
Chicago, Illinois 60606

CATALOGUE COST: $2.00
This catalogue has almost anything you would need to make your wedding gown and accessories, including five imported laces, and bridal fabrics such as satin, satapeau, velvet, and chiffon. The catalogue includes swatches. The company also carries hats, headpieces, and hard-to-find items such as real silk illusion, ready-made thread loops, and wide horsehair braid.

California Formal and Bridal Fabrics
763 South Los Angeles Street
Los Angeles, California 90014

CATALOGUE COST: $3.00
This company carries merchandise similar to Supreme's. Its catalogue is also swatched.

The two places above also sell retail.

House of Kahaner
55 West Thirty-eighth Street
New York, New York 10018

CATALOGUE FREE
This company makes and imports beautiful trimmings, many of which are used by the finest dress manufacturers. It specializes in beaded trimmings, but also carries beautiful Swiss embroidered trimmings and many other items.

Evelyn Forsythe Creations, Inc.
2 Penn Plaza
Suite 1500
New York, New York 10001

LEAFLET FREE
This company is a manufacturer of bridal headwear, including picture hats, ready-made crowns, caps, and decorated headpieces.

Lee Wards
1200 St. Charles Road
Elgin, Illinois 60120

CATALOGUE FREE
All sorts of trimming supplies, including a large selection of beads, sequins, and pearls; embroidery threads and supplies; instructions and materials for making flowers, crochet lace, tatting, and so on.

If you write to the manufacturers listed below, they will send you the name of a store in your area that carries their products.

Emil Katz & Company, Inc.
21 West 38th Street
New York, New York 10018

This company makes beautiful fine laces: Chantilly, Alençon, and Cluny, both imported and domestic, that are used by the best bridal manufacturers. Write to Doris Katz.

Stern & Stern Textiles, Inc.
1359 Broadway
New York, New York 10018

This company carries a large selection of fine imported laces, as well as domestic, that you have seen used on gowns in bridal magazines. They also carry Heirloom Bridal Patterns, which are wedding gown patterns designed specifically for a particular lace. The pattern includes diagrams for cutting the lace and positioning motifs, borders, and so on. Write to William Price.

Roth Import Company
13 West 38th Street
New York, New York 10008

This company imports silk flowers, Venise laces, feathers, bridal hats and frames, and all sorts of delicious trimmings, as well as bridal and embroidered fabrics. Write to Thomas Roth.

House of Kahaner
(See address and information above)

Write to George Germer.

   If you live or plan to visit in the New York area, it is definitely worth making a trip to the garment center to buy fabrics, laces, and trimmings. Here you can find many things not available elsewhere, because some companies that sell wholesale to manufacturers also sell retail. There are also a number of fabric places that get sample cuts from designers' work rooms. The prices here are often considerably better. It's best to have some idea of what you want before you go, since things are piled to the ceiling in most of these places. For fabrics, one block—Fortieth Street between Seventh and Eighth avenues—has a number of good stores. Shop and compare prices, because they can vary for the same merchandise and sometimes they are negotiable. In this block check out Art-Max at 250 West Fortieth; Felsen Fabrics Corp. at 264 West Fortieth; Broadway Lace & Fabrics, also at 264 West Fortieth; and B & J Fabrics, 263 West Fortieth. These places carry laces and fabrics. For trimmings, Thirty-eighth Street between Fifth and Sixth avenues is a must. House of Kahaner, mentioned above, has a retail outlet at the same address. Also be sure to visit Hyman Hendler at 67 West Thirty-eighth Street. They specialize in imported ribbons, and the entire store is devoted to the most beautiful ribbons you have ever seen. There are several places on this block that sell retail as well as wholesale and carry bridal headpieces, flowers, ribbons, and all kinds of beads and trimmings. Stop at Max Bridal Co. at 13 West Thirty-eighth Street. Just around the corner at 1014 Avenue of the Americas, between Thirty-seventh and Thirty-eighth streets, is Arden. It sells bridal accessories and millinery supplies, including hats, veils, crowns, illusions, and petticoats.

INDEX